Communication and Information Technology in Society

Communication and Information Technology in Society

Volume 3 Social Communication

Edited by

Anna Kuzio,

Jolanta Kowal

and Mirosława Wawrzak-Chodaczek

Cambridge
Scholars
Publishing

Communication and Information Technology in Society:
Volume 3 Social Communication

Edited by Anna Kuzio, Jolanta Kowal
and Mirosława Wawrzak-Chodaczek

Reviews
Ali Al-Badi
Mazen Ali
Alicja Keplinger
Jarosław Klebaniuk
Mieczysław K. Leniartek
Anna Mitręga
Janusz Sowiński
Krystyna Węgłowska-Rzepa

This book first published 2015

Cambridge Scholars Publishing

Lady Stephenson Library, Newcastle upon Tyne, NE6 2PA, UK

British Library Cataloguing in Publication Data
A catalogue record for this book is available from the British Library

ISBN (10): 1-4438-7540-6
ISBN (13): 978-1-4438-7540-0

As a three volume set:
ISBN (10): 1-4438-7625-9
ISBN (13): 978-1-4438-7625-4

TABLE OF CONTENTS

SOCIAL COMMUNICATION – OUTLINE OF ISSUES

The most important thing in communication
is hearing what isn't said.
(Peter Drucker)

"Communication is one of those human activities that everyone recognizes but few can define satisfactorily" (Fiske, 1982). Consequently, communication studies look at the process of communication in a different way and researchers define communication from different perspectives (Littlejohn, 2001). Shepherd (1992) divides studies about human communication into rhetorical and relational studies. Rhetorical communication studies concentrate on how to influence and persuade others while relational communication focuses on the transaction and coordination of communication among people to reach a shared cognition (Richmond & McCroskey, 2009). On the other hand, a classification, such as the one just mentioned, has not been valuable in guiding researchers to any integrated type of studies in communication. In the area of relational communication, several studies have focused on the way that communication works and shared cognition is shaped; yet, there are still difficulties in measuring and analyzing shared cognition.

People communicate to each other with different knowledge and backgrounds. In some cases, communication takes place between a person who has in depth knowledge about certain items and a person who has very broad knowledge (Węgłowska–Rzepa et al., 2008; Kowal et al. 2010a, 2010b). The question is, how is the shared meaning or shared cognition formed between them?

People employ categories to communicate; the language, which is exploited in communication, is categorical. Additionally, knowledge can be expressed in categories, and the categories are shaped based on the knowledge that the person possesses. If the person has superficial knowledge about a specific subject, he or she creates superficial categories; whereas, if they have in–depth knowledge they create detailed and technical categories.

The communication process between a person with technical categories of knowledge and a person with non–technical categories can be portrayed by how they match their categories. Shared cognition is shaped if a category exists or is formed that is entirely comprehensible for both parties. Literature on communication studies has paid little attention to how people with categorical knowledge communicate. There are not enough theories and studies to build this research on; therefore, this exploratory study is designed to understand the process of communication when people have categorical knowledge.

Katz and Kahn (1978), in *The Social Psychology of Organizations*, describe communication as "the exchange of information and the transmission of meaning which is the very essence of a social system". Human communication comprises different basic components that frame the communication process. In this process, the message is sent by a sender thorough a communication channel to a receiver. The sender of the message encodes the message. The message is conveyed through the channel, and the receiver decodes the message. This process can be completed by communicating feedback from the receiver to the sender that can guarantee the accuracy of the communication process. The message, sender, receiver, channel, encoding, decoding, transmitting and feedback are basic parts of the communication process (Krone et al., 1987).

Different research areas in communication have concentrated on different elements of the communication process in accordance with researchers' perspectives. For example, some researchers have paid attention to the communication channel and the transmission of a message, whereas some studies have focused on how the characteristics of the sender and receiver affect the communication process (Krone et al, 1987).

One of the topics, which has been analyzed expansively in communication, is the accuracy of the message in the process of communication (Powers & Lowry, 1984). When a sender sends a message through a communication channel, there is no assurance that the receiver understands the exact message. The message might be distorted as a consequence of the noise in the channel or problems in the encoding/decoding process. In communication literature, this problem is recognized as fidelity. Nevertheless, various researchers employ this term in a different way. Krone et al. (1978:34) affirm that "message fidelity refers to the extent to which a message is similar at two points on the channel", and they distinguish it from congruence, which denotes "consensus of meaning in interpreting events".

Many studies have indicated that people have a limited capacity for processing information (Macrae & Bodenhausen., 2001); therefore, people aspire to categorize it based on some features of the received information. One familiar example of this phenomenon is stereotyping, in that a person chooses a character (e.g., geographic location, race) and categorizes people based on it. One then bases his/her communication on specific stereotypes (Kunda, 1999). Gestalt laws explicate that people categorize items following specific rules, such as proximity and similarity of items (Rollinson, 2005).

People not only think categorically, but also talk in categorical ways. When people want to talk and transfer a message in mind, they put it into words (Searle, 1998). On the other hand, words are a category themselves. For example, the word "chair" can denote many different types of chairs. The sender of the message might have a concrete example of a chair in mind; however, by sending the message "chair", the receiver might not recognize the same item as the sender. This problem is a consequence of the "categorical relationship" (Duimering & Safayeni, 1998) between words and categories.

Bertrand Russell (1927) states that when a word is expressed it is considered to be a single entity; however, a word seems to be a set of more or less similar events. The meaning of the word is specified in accordance with its context. In this sense, "words are like categories" that are labeled for a set of similar entities (Duimering & Safayeni, 1998).

Moreover, people are apt to talk in general and put events into categories. The tendency of employing broad and general words for a specific item increases when the word is associated with "positive valence" (Lewin, 1935), which is shaped through social forces (Duimering & Safayeni, 1998). In their research on the role of language and formal structure, they discovered that, in the organization they investigated, a buzzword such as "team" is credited and legitimated by higher–level managers, and employees then try to put their tasks into this category (i.e. team) to legitimate what they are dealing with (Duimering and Safayeni 1998). Additionally, Rosch (1978) observed that when adults want to communicate about an item they employ the category that the item belongs to as a message.

Taking this into account, a new representation for the communication process between technical and non–technical communicators and the manner of shared cognition can be examined. Having all these backgrounds in mind, this shows that communication plays an important role in everyday life. This volume will give special attention to communication as a social aspect.

This volume begins with an article written by Zdenka Stránská and Eva Brídová, called "The Impact of Parenting Style on Self–Esteem and Classroom Social Status in Early Adolescents". One can notice that human individuals are born to the world as organisms possessing a variety of genetically predisposed limits, and yet endowed with a great potential in development. Undoubtedly, one of the key components of this process is child rearing. Child rearing, or parenting, is a complex, intricate matter, encompassing many different forms, means, methods, and practices. The parenting process involves interaction and communication of the parent and the child in which the personalities of both transform and develop. For this and other reasons, family–based parenting remains one of the most discussed issues in everyday and professional contexts. The chapter presented by Anna Pawiak, "Teachers' Opinions on Feedback in Communication as an Essential Part of the Educational Process", emphasizes the role of feedback as constructive criticism with an important role in education through positively influencing a student's development. The article describes and characterizes the basic rules and tools of creating effective feedback. Part of the research referring to the meaning of constructive criticism in working with students is also presented. Correctly given feedback is a great way of communicating between the teacher and the students. This skill, however, requires knowledge and practice that may help in building correct relationships at school that are effective in teacher's educational work. Bianka Lewandowska, in her chapter "The Non–Stereotypical Image of Gender in the Process of Education: The Issues, Objectives and Methodology of Training for Teachers and Parents", pays attention to the issue of education in the field of gender equality that is now a compulsory part of the school projects funded by the European Union. This subject, undertaken in the framework of training and workshops, is addressed to all participants of the project, i.e. teachers and, in many cases, parents. Knowledge of gender studies helps them implement the image of gender, free from stereotypes, into the process of teaching and upbringing. Training raises the awareness of the impact of verbal and nonverbal messages on the psychological and cultural attributes of gender, student's social roles, realizing personal goals and functioning in interpersonal relations. This chapter presents the problems and methods of training as well as insights and reflections gathered during its course, also describing the results of research on defining the traits of a child's gender by its parents–the participants of the training. "Mediation: a Method of Conflict Resolution in the School Environment by Bożena Matyjas considers the issue of the increasing number of different conflicts in modern schools that have been a challenge for educators. Different types and sources of conflicts are experienced at school, the most common being student–student and student–teacher disagreements. One of the problem–solving strategies is mediation, a technique of soft intervention. Mediators show impartiality, respect and empathy with the parties. Educators, teachers, head teachers and students with training in problem–solving skills can act as mediators. The purpose of mediation is to help two parties resolve their dispute with a mutually acceptable agreement. It should be emphasized that participation in mediation is typically voluntary. The purpose of this chapter is to distinguish and discuss school–based conflict as well as present mediation as a method to manage and resolve disputes.

Barbara Jezierska, in "Communication in a Rehabilitation Institution as a Condition of its Functionality in the Assessment of Educators in Youth Educational Centres", discusses the aspect of youth socio–therapy centers that deal with socially maladjusted children and teenagers with behavioral disorders to the degree that they hinder the realization of life tasks without special help and who, for emotional reasons, are unable to learn in a regular general education school. They were set up with the purpose of eliminating reasons and manifestations of behavioral disorders to prepare their inmates for life in accordance with the existing social and legal norms. The research aims at determining a real and postulated functionality of youth socio–therapy centers in its communication aspect in the opinions of 98 educators employed in these institutions. The research was carried out in Lower Silesia with the use of a specially designed questionnaire on ways of communication inside and outside the institutions. The educators of youth socio–therapy centers participating in the research indicated reasons for the difficulties they had while discharging their educational obligations and they put forth a number of postulates with regard to possible favorable changes in the functioning of rehabilitation institutions. The educators' opinions indicate that the form and quality of communication connections in their structure influence the adequacy of accomplishing their objectives.

Ivana Poledňová, Jindřiška Šmejkalová and Jana Borůvková, in "The Relation of Personality Factors to Classroom Sociometric Status in Secondary School Students", state that the relationship between personality characteristics of students and their sociometric statuses in the classes of secondary technical schools should accounted for while discussing communication. Its main aim is to reveal whether the personality characteristics of students in late adolescence affect their sociometric statuses from the point of view of influence and popularity. Also discussed are how school competency results and commends affect sociometric status in connection with personality dimensions, and how sociometric status (influence and popularity in the school class) is gained through the sociometric method SO–RA–D and individual personality dimensions measured by NEO–PI–R. The results of the research show that a higher degree of agreeableness affects the popularity of an individual in the class as well as the evaluation of the schoolmates. A higher degree of extraversion increases authority in the class, while a higher degree of conscientiousness decreases it. Individual components of neuroticism also influence the degree of authority in the class, and depression and self–consciousness decrease authority while impulsiveness increases it. School results do not affect the sociometric status in connection with personality characteristics, but commends decrease the popularity of introverted persons. Students in the period of late adolescence are able to reflect their personality characteristics and their development in time. They are also able to evaluate the positives and negatives of their personality in a school group.

Teresa Bogacz and Beata Konopska, in "A Map as an Instrument in the Educational Communication Process at School Level", see a map as a useful way of communication as it represents any objects or phenomena usin graphic symbols which users should be able to understand intuitively or through description. In this respect, maps are a form of visual communication and are subject to all the rules associated with it. The primary aim of every cartographic publication is to provide information about objects, phenomena and the area where they appear in a way that is legible and understandable to the user. However, the correct interpretation of map content is possible only after gaining basic knowledge in this field, mainly at school. In other words, a map is a form of visual communication and its correctness can be judged by the effectiveness with which it is able to convey its message. To prepare a correct map one must know the principles of map editing. Therefore, while preparing a map, one must firstly identify its intended use; that is, state the purpose of its preparation and characterize the traits of its user. In the case of maps used at school the user is a student who, depending on the teaching level, has different perceptive abilities related to their developmental stage. Once the purpose of the map and its target audience are defined, one can decide on the content, symbols and methods of data presentation appropriate and match the student's perceptive abilities. On the one hand, maps are ubiquitous in today's social communication system – from weather maps to political preference maps to car navigation maps. On the other hand, map–reading and map–using skills are still insufficient due, among other reasons, to limited access to topographic maps. If all this is taken into consideration, one can understand the particular importance of cartographic education at school. Therefore, the aim of this chapter is to address the important aspects of the topic, namely: how maps should be used as means of communication at various teaching levels; how technological advances affect the process of modernization of maps as a tool; how this translates into the potential effectiveness of education and how students can use their acquired skills outside of school. The authors of the chapter also point out that as the boundary between the humanities and the natural sciences becomes more blurred, it is important that in the near future the concept of a "common" map as a universal tool for teaching both geography and history is introduced at all school levels. To illustrate the abovementioned themes, the authors use the example of traditional (printed) maps as well as multimedia (interactive) ones, the latter being increasingly used and compatible with modern methods of teaching through demonstration. Particular attention is given to examples of combining historical and geographical data on maps.

The second part of the volume focuses on the role and meaning of the newest forms of communication, involving computer–mediated communication. Mirosława Wawrzak–Chodaczek and Małgorzata Biedroń, in "The Psychological and Social Consequences of Playing 'Aggressive' Computer Games for Children and Teenagers", outline that both games and play have always been essential instruments of adopting and training determined competences, generalized into real social situations. It is accepted that a game acts at a higher level because it requires strict rules and a uniform structure, thus limiting randomness with the player learning self–discipline and the conscious controlling of his/her own actions with reference to definite rules. Ludic behaviors can take different forms depending on individual preferences and the rules or community life. Agon will fulfill the will of fight and rivalry at different levels, mimicry will enable playing roles, impersonating various personalities, "trying" diverse identities, and ilinx and alea will give an exciting feeling of uncertainty, hazard and an additional dose of adrenalin. The still modernized "toys" will make the ways of satisfying the desires more and more attractive. Technical development and the common accessibility of the specialized devices have opened great possibilities in the range of multidirectional development support, improving social competences and fulfilling ludic needs. It turns out that, in spite of the multiplicity of the offers on the electronic media market and the accessibility of attractive educational programs adapted to each age, games are the most often type of software bought. It can be legitimately affirmed that they constitute a large part of computer use, and their attractiveness manifests itself at different levels of pleasure.

Zhechka Georgieva, in "Media and their Contribution to the Creation of the Global Culture and the Great, Universal Public", concentrates her attention on the issue of the most general characteristics of traditional and digital media and traces their influence in the process of forming a universal audience and global culture. Pointing out its purpose, she defines it as a heuristic attempt to identify diachronic and synchronic interactions, theoretical interpretations, and pragmatic results in media status and development. The main task of this work is to trace the media positioning and analyze their coordination in the context of today's globalized structures and systems.

One should be aware that communication is not free of stereotypes. Anna Kuzio, in "The Amelioration of Stereotypes in Computer–Mediated Communication Versus Vocal Communication: a Reproduction Involving Three Theoretical Models", argues that computer–mediated communication (CMC) inherently inhibits the reduction of stereotypes. The study challenges this assertion theoretically by offering rival hypotheses. Methodological issues concerning the limitation of interactive communication and the inappropriate operationalization of CMC are also addressed. The findings reveal that CMC is functionally equivalent to vocal communication in its ability to reduce negative stereotypes and that it can be superior in creating and/or retaining positive impressions

Magdalena Sirecka–Wołodko's chapter, "The Use of ICT for Terrorism", states that information and communication technologies are the accelerators of economic and social growth in the developing countries and constitute a very useful tool in the hands of terrorists who skillfully exploit all the latest technologies for their own use. At the turn of the 20th and 21st centuries, the operation of terrorist groups has undergone significant qualitative changes, being largely the result of the implementation of ICTs in the developing countries, from which these groups often come from. The widespread promotion of computers, mobile phones and the Internet has allowed terrorists to streamline the communication process within their organizations, expand the sources of funding for their activities and create of a network–based, transnational structure with global range. ICTs, especially the Internet, have also impacted the manner with which terrorist groups communicate with their audience – it has become more direct and tailored to the needs of potential recipients. Yet another result of the application of ICTs by terrorists refers to the increase of their operational capabilities to plan and coordinate attacks, and at the same time use new technologies as a means to attract and destruct (so–called "cyber terrorism"). The extensive application of ICTs in terrorist activities undoubtedly makes them more dangerous and unpredictable. They pose a major challenge both for the developed countries which are dependent on the smooth operation of information and communication systems, as well as for the developing countries which have increasingly based their development on investment in ICTs without resources for their effective protection and sufficient experience in this field.

Łukasz Kłuskiewicz discusses the interesting issue of scripted reality and its role in a series of reality shows in "The Phenomenon of Scripted Reality Programs Based on the Pamiętniki z wakacji ("Holiday diaries")". These views reflect the concept that people live in a culturally diverse society due to globalization. As the world grows, expands and become increasingly more interconnected, the need for effective interpersonal communication among differing cultures/groups has become evident. When people from various cultures interact with one another there is intercultural communication because different cultures create different interpretations and expectations about what is perceived as competent behavior, enabling the construction of shared meanings. Communication basically affects and influences communicating since culture and communication are interdependent. The way one acts and the things people say determine the culture that individuals belong to, while culture also determines how one acts and communicates. In particular, one needs to acquire the necessary knowledge to understand, communicate and cooperate with people who are different with the aim of benefiting from a diverse society. In these volumes we discuss the barriers to communication for interaction with the "Other" and how to overcome these barriers in different fields. There are issues surrounding the problem of communication and we have chosen to include culture, ethnocentrism, categorization, stereotyping, prejudice, pedagogy, marketing and the representation of the "Other" in our volumes.

The monograph appears to be an attempt to approach issues related to the development of communication and its media in psycho–social and pedagogical aspects. The authors of this volume may hope that this monograph is a contribution to the discussion on communication and the role of media in the contemporary world, perhaps filling the gap in social research regarding the theme.

Our book indicates some problems on various issues in the social, culture and education spheres and provides insight mostly from European countries in transition.

REFERENCES

Duimering, P. R. & Safayeni, F. (1998). The role of language and formal structure in the construction and maintenance of organizational image. International Studies of Management and Organization , 28, No.3, 57–85.

Fiske, J. (1982). Introduction to communication studies. New York: Methuen & Co.

Katz D & Kahn R. (1978). The social Psychology of Organizations. JOHN WILEY & SONS.

Kowal, J., K. Węgłowska-Rzepa (2010a). Social communication in management and its psychological and marketing aspects. In: Proceedings of the 6th European Conference on Management, Leadership and Governance : The College of Management "Edukacja" and the Professional Development Center Edukacja Wroclaw, ed. by Ewa Panka and Aleksandra Kwiatkowska. - Reading, UK : Academic Publishing Limited.

Kowal, J.A. Kwiatkowska, I. Patro (2010b). The prospects of graduates' career development in Poland: the example of the competence survey in Lower Silesia Region 2006–2010. In: Proceedings of the 6th European Conference on Management, Leadership and Governance: The College of Management "Edukacja" and the Professional Development Center Edukacja Wroclaw. Reading, UK : Academic Publishing Limited.

Krone et al. (1987). Communication Theory and Organizational Communication: Multiple Perspective. In F. Jablin, L. Putnam, K. Roberts, & P. L, Handbook of Organizational Communication (pp. 18–40). SAGE Publications, Inc.

Kunda, Z. (1999). Social cognition. Cambridge, MA: MIT Press.

Lewin, K. (1935). Dynamic theory of personality. New York: McGraw–Hill.

Littlejohn, S. W. (2001). Theories of Human communication. Belmont, California: South–Western Educational Publishing.

Macrae, C. N. & Bodenhausen G. V. (2001). Social cognitio: categorical person perception. British Journal of Psychology , 92, 239–255.

Powers, W. G. & Lowry, D. N. (1984). Basic communication fidelity: A fundamental approach. In B. R. L., Communication Competence (pp. 57–71). Beverly Hills: SAGE.

Richmond, V. P. & McCroskey, J. C. (2009). Human Communication theory and research. In D. W. Stacks, An integrated Approach to communication theory and research (second ed., pp. 223–231). New York: Taylor & Francis Group.

Rosch, E. (1978). Principles of Categorization. In E. &. Rosch, Cognition and categorization (pp. 27–48). Hiisdale, NJ: Lawrence Erlbaum Associates, Inc.

Roter D. et al. (1988). Patient–physician communication: A descriptive summary of the literature. Patient Education and Counseling, 12(2), 99–119.

Russell, B. (1961). Language. In R. E. Denonn, The basic writings of Bertrand Russell: 1903–1959. New York: Simon and Schuster.

Searle, J. R. (1998). Mind, language and society. New York: Basic Books.

Severin, W.J. & Tankard, J.W. (1979). Communication theories. New York: Hastings House. Węglowska–Rzepa, K., J. Kowal, H. Lee Park, K. Haeng Lee (2008) The presence of Spiritual archetypes among representatives of eastern and western cultures. Jung Journal. Vol. 2: 3, pp. 58–72.

Anna Kuzio
Univeristy of Zielona Gora

Jolanta Kowal
University of Wrocław

1. REAL COMMUNICATION

Zdenka Stránská
Eva Brídová
Masaryk University
Brno, Czech Republic

THE IMPACT OF PARENTING STYLE ON SELF–ESTEEM AND CLASSROOM SOCIAL STATUS IN EARLY ADOLESCENTS

ABSTRACT

Human individuals are born to the world as organisms possessing a variety of genetically predisposed limits, and yet are endowed with a great potential of development. Undoubtedly, one of the key components of this process is child rearing. Child rearing, or parenting, is a complex, intricate matter, encompassing many different forms, means, methods, and practices. The parenting process involves the interaction and communication of the parent and the child in which personalities both transform and develop. For this and other reasons, family–based parenting remains one of the most discussed issues in both everyday and professional contexts

KEYWORDS: parenting style, self–esteem, early adolescents, social status.

1. INTRODUCTION

Human individuals are born to the world as organisms possessing a variety of genetically predisposed limits, and yet endowed with a great potential of development. Undoubtedly, one of the key components of this process is child rearing. Child rearing, or parenting, is a complex, intricate matter, encompassing many different forms, means, methods, and practices. The parenting process involves the interaction and communication of the parent and the child in which the personalities of both transform and develop. For this and other reasons, family–based parenting remains one of the most discussed issues in both everyday and professional contexts.

There has been a long and rich tradition in psychology concerning the topic of parenting and its impact on personal development. Research outcomes by different authors converge and complement each other in the conclusion that family parenting practices have a strong influence on the child's behavior and experience, as well as the development of different aspects of personality (Čáp, 1996). The aim of this chapter, which provides a summary of a research study conducted in collaboration with E. Brídová (2007) (as a part of a Master's Thesis project), is to help understand the link between the perceived family parenting styles, self–esteem, and classroom social statuses of teenage primary school students in more detail. Although similar studies have generally demonstrated that parenting practices effect both of the variables mentioned, we believe that it is still possible to discover new connections concerning this issue. The concept of parenting in this study is based on the theoretical model by J. Čáp and P. Boschek (1994), which accentuates the complexity of the parenting process and especially the importance of the subjective perception of parenting for one's personal development. The authors emphasize two principal dimensions within the model: emotional quality of the relationship between parents and child, and parental control.

Our research focuses on primary school 8th and 9th grade students, covering the approximate period of early adolescence which is characterized by a whole range of fundamental changes. The connection between an individual and the individual's self is transformed and intensified, and the issue of self–esteem becomes a primary concern. In addition, adolescence is the time of essential development in the sphere of interpersonal relationships within the classroom peer groups, which are of key importance to teenagers.

One of the main objectives in our study is to help increase the understanding of the impact of parenting styles on children's self–esteem. M. Blatný (Blatný & Plháková, 2003) points out that the criteria foundations for self–evaluation are laid in childhood and are shaped by parents, significant others within the family context, or other people carrying out the parenting function. For example, S. Coopersmith (1968) argues that although the origins of individual self–esteem are complex, the two factors contributing most to its development are parenting style and personal goals. He claims that personal self–esteem is promoted by parenting practices which encompass the ingredients of respect, clear delineation of values and demands, and guidance towards an autonomous approach to problem solving. Research on the effect of parenting styles on self–esteem has been going on since the 1960s. At this time, a comprehensive study by the above mentioned author was published dealing with self–esteem in American boys. The results indicated that the parents of boys with high self–esteem were not particularly permissive, but reasonably strict and consistent. The boys came from families who provided them with substantial amounts of love and understanding (appreciation, respect and praise) through everyday expressions of affection and concern. They also showed true interest in their children's affairs and expected high standards from them. Conversely, the parents of children with low self–esteem were overly critical, treating their children as burdens, showing much less interest and had significantly lower expectations (Coopersmith, 1968). More recent studies support Coopersmith's findings and suggest additional factors associated with the development of low self–esteem in children. One indisputable factor producing low self–esteem is an authoritarian parenting style. Conversely, warmth and secure attachment in the early stages of development are associated with high self–esteem (Fontana, 1997). Other studies also support the idea that authoritative parenting involving warmth, perceptiveness, sensitivity, reasonable demands and expectations, and an autonomy–supporting approach has a much more positive influence on personal development than other parenting styles, especially with regard to self–esteem (Lamborn, Mounts, Steinberg & Dombusch, 1991). Similar results confirming the link between self–esteem and parenting approaches were also obtained in the study by Macek and Širůček (2005) who examined the level of self–esteem, perceived warmth, parent reliance and perceived parental control in children of 12 and 14 years of age. The strong relationship between self–esteem and parental support was documented by a number of developmental studies indicating that parental support belongs, up to early adolescence, to the strongest predictors of self–esteem (Quatman & Watson, 2001).

The second major objective in our study is to learn more about the effect of parenting styles on the child's social status within the classroom peer group. To a certain extent, parenting practices influence all aspects of personality, all traits and behaviors which, in turn, are projected onto the nature of one's integration within the system of interpersonal relationships. Past research has also shown that parenting seems to have an impact on children's classroom social status. The socio–metric status of a child in the class is determined by the mutual relationships between children based on whether they are liked or disliked by their peers. The source of these positive or negative evaluations lies in the child's behavior, which is a product of previous socialization processes and associated experience. According to Zaťková (2002), the greatest part in this process can be ascribed to one's family environment. The studies conducted by Dekovic & Janssens (1992) support the idea that popular and rejected children possess different kinds of family experience. Zaťková (2002) studied parents' personal characteristics, parenting styles and disciplinary practices, finding that all these variables do have an impact on the social status of children. The high degree of sociability in parents, the warm acceptance of children, a positive emotional relationship and reasonable disciplinary practices predicted the higher social status of children. On the other hand, parents of rejected children were characterized by poor sociability, authoritarian or neglectful parenting styles, and inadequate disciplinary practices, often involving physical violence and corporal punishment. Hart, Ladd and Burleson (1990) examined the link between the child's socio–metric status and the mother's parenting style in children attending school in the 1st to 4th grades. Their results indicate that children of autocratic mothers have greater difficulties being accepted by their classmates. Similarly, Dekovic and Janssens (1992) demonstrate that popular children have parents who employ a authoritative/democratic parenting style, and are both warmer and more supportive than the parents of unpopular children, whose parenting style is mostly authoritarian/restrictive. The research by Širůček and Širůčková (in Macek & Lacinová, 2006) shows that adolescents who benefit from "good" relations with their parents, involving positive emotional attachment and support, also enjoy more satisfying relationships with their friends within peer groups. These teenagers report greater mutual interest, understanding and trust, accompanied with fewer conflicts, less violence and less rejection. It can be therefore concluded that the opportunity for trust in and emotional congruence with one's parents in childhood and adolescence probably also results in a "better opportunity" to trust and be more forthcoming towards one's peers.

2. RESEARCH AIMS AND HYPOTHESES

The main objective of our study is to examine the interaction between different parenting styles in the family and the teenager's self–esteem, as well as their classroom social status.

Hence, the study had two **major research aims**:

1) To examine the link between the level of teenager's self–esteem and perceived parenting style of their parents.
2) To examine the link between the teenager's classroom social status (given by their popularity and influence) and perceived parenting style of their parents.

Based on the previous theoretical models and empirical findings, two **main hypotheses** were formulated following the research aims:

1) Perceived parenting styles are significantly correlated to self–esteem in teenagers.
2) Perceived parenting styles are significantly correlated to the classroom socio–metric status of teenagers.

3. PARTICIPANTS

The sample consisted of students attending the 8th and 9th grades of primary school. Altogether, 384 respondents participated in the study, 209 (54%) male and 175 (46%) female, ranging from 13 to 15 years old (M = 13.95). The distribution by age and gender is shown in Table 1 below.

Table 1. Distribution of respondents by age and gender

Age / Gender	13	14	15	Total
Boys	61	90	58	209
Girls	47	99	29	175
Total	108	189	87	384

4. METHOD

Three types of self–assessment measures were used in the study:

1) The Family Parenting Style Questionnaire (Dotazník pro zjišťování způsobu výchovy v rodině) by Čáp and Boschek (1994) is a frequently used Czech measure which has proven to be both valid and reliable.

The questionnaire is administered to children and adolescents who respond to items concerning their parents' behavior (mother and father separately) in common everyday situations. The measure consists of 40 items – 10 items for each of the four parenting components, including positive and negative, demands, and the laxity component. These are analogous to four parenting approaches (according to Schaefer; Schuldermann and Schuldermann; the Czech questionnaire ADOR, cited by Čáp, Boschek, 1994, p. 17): positive, hostile, controlling, and autonomous. There is a separate set of items for mother and father, and all items are answered using a three–point scale representing the answers "yes", "in part" and "no". The individual components in both mother and father can be viewed separately as parenting approaches. When combined, however, a more apt and accurate synthesis representing the true nature of parenting patterns within the family can be obtained. Such a combination yields more information about the quality of the emotional relationship of the parent to the child, the nature of parental control, and eventually the nature of parenting in the family as such, which is represented by one of the nine "fields". The emotional relationship in each parent combines the scores of positive and negative parenting components. Behavior control style, on the other hand, is in each parent a combination of the demands and laxity scales. The synthesis of the mother's and father's emotional relationship scores yields the score of general quality of emotional relationships in the family. Similarly, the combination of behavior control styles in both parents produces the general family parental control style score. Finally, the synthesis of general emotional relationship quality and general parental control scores yields the general parenting style in the family, represented by one of the nine fields (see Figure 1 below). However, the authors emphasize the fact that such synthesis is not purely quantitative in nature, but that the individual categories differ qualitatively from each other as well. Hence, the upper-level combinations of individual components cannot be explained by these individual components only, or by their arithmetic average (Čáp & Boschek, 1994).

<table>
<tr><th>Control
Emotional relationship</th><th>Strong</th><th>Moderate</th><th>Weak</th><th>Inconsistent</th></tr>
<tr><td>Negative</td><td colspan="2">1. Autocratic, traditional, patriarchal parenting style</td><td>2. Liberal, neglectful parenting style</td><td>3. Pessimal (malign) parenting style</td></tr>
<tr><td>Negative–Positive</td><td colspan="4">9. Emotionally ambivalent parenting behavior (one parent is rejecting, the other extremely positive; formation of parent–child coalitions)</td></tr>
<tr><td>Positive</td><td rowspan="2">4. Strict-but-benevolent parenting style</td><td rowspan="2">5. Optimal parenting style with mutual understanding and adequate control</td><td>6. Benevolent undemanding parenting style, lacking boundaries</td><td rowspan="2">7. Inconsistent control relatively compensated by positive emotional relationship</td></tr>
<tr><td>Extremely positive</td><td>8. Friend-like relationship, observing norms and rules optional</td></tr>
</table>

Figure 1. A nine-field model of parenting styles in the family according to Čáp (1999)

2) Coopersmith's Self-Esteem Inventory - CSEI was designed by Coopersmith (1981). The measure consists of 50 items divided into four subscales: Social Self – Peers, School-Academic, Home-Parents, and General Self. Apart from these, the inventory includes a Lie Scale. For each item, respondents can only choose from two dichotomized responses (e.g. like me/unlike me) and are therefore forced to make a clear decision for or against the statement. However, since the original version of the inventory was not applicable in the Czech environment, the version of CSEI used in our study was an adaptation developed for the ELSPAC project by Macek and Širůček (2005). For the purpose of this study only the General Self subscale was used (20 items; Alpha = 0.79).

3) Socio-metric Test

A socio-metric test of our own design was used to determine the classroom socio-metric status of teenagers. The test, developed on the basis of an analysis of literature and similar measures, consisted of 7 items. Its purpose was to capture the pattern of relationships within the class based on popularity and unpopularity. With regard to our research objectives we chose criteria related to socio-emotional bonds. Three selection criteria were chosen concerning the dimensions of friendship, trust and spending time together. Respondents could make both positive and negative nominations. Hence, the individual items can be divided into two groups according to whether participants are favored or rejected with respect to the criterion. The last item asked about the student's general opinion on the most and least influential individuals in the classroom. In this last choice, students could also nominate themselves.

The nominations were limited to the students of the respondent's class with a maximum of three people for each item. Petrusek (1969) argues that the validity of nominations declines significantly in the fourth and subsequent positions. A lower limit for the number of choices was not given; hence, every student could nominate three or less people.

Data from the socio–metric test were analyzed quantitatively using socio–metric indexes (adapted from Petrusek [1969]). Specifically, we were interested in indexes of passive socio–preferential behavior based on the sums of individual nominations. For each individual, four indexes were calculated:

- Socio–emotional Popularity Index (ISS_popularity) – a measure of positive socio–metric status of the individual in the system of socio–emotional relationships;
- Socio–emotional Unpopularity Index (INS_popularity) – a measure of the negative sociometric status of the individual in the system of socio–emotional relationships;
- Influence Index (ISS_Influence) – a measure of the positive socio–metric status
- a general estimate of the most influential individual;
- Non–Influence Index (INS_Influence) – a measure of negative socio–metric status – a general estimate of the least influential individual.

We focused on passive choices, i.e. the number of nominations the students received in each category from their classmates. The individual sums of choices in each category yielded 4 raw scores, which would however be difficult to interpret in a broader context due to the different numbers of students in each classroom. These raw scores were therefore transformed into standard scores (indexes) which allowed for both different numbers of students and different numbers of items in each category.

The obtained data were used in a K–means cluster analysis to arrange the research participants into clusters according to popularity and influence as represented by the above mentioned four indexes. Four and five cluster solutions were tested. Since the five–cluster solution was more easily interpretable, it was used in further analysis. Below, the five clusters are briefly described. Table 2 shows individual index means for each cluster, while Table 3 summarizes cluster frequencies. Figure 1 shows the mean plot of all clusters.

Cluster 1 (N = 30) – Students with greatest levels of both popularity and influence; yet, their strong social position also becomes a source of relatively high unpopularity.

Cluster 2 (N = 72) – Students who are both highly popular and influential, but not to the same extent as the previous group.

Cluster 3 (N = 194) – The "Grey mice" of the classroom, these students are undistinguished and just mildly popular; no one finds them annoying, and are not particularly interested in their company. They received minimum nominations in all categories.

Cluster 4 (N = 86) – Students who are both unpopular and non-influential, but not to the same extent as the last group.

Cluster 5 (N = 55) – Students with extremely high unpopularity and little influence, who received a great number of nominations in both negative categories.

Table 2. Four socio-metric index means in the five clusters

	Cluster 1	Cluster 2	Cluster 3	Cluster 4	Cluster 5
Popularity	0.21	0.18	0.11	0.08	0.07
Unpopularity	0.17	0.09	0.05	0.19	0.25
Influence	0.67	0.25	0.03	0.03	0.01
Non–Influence	0.01	0.02	0.03	0.17	0.51

Table 3. Cluster frequencies

Cluster	Absolute frequencies	Relative frequencies
Cluster 1	30	6.86 %
Cluster 2	72	16.48 %
Cluster 3	194	44.39 %
Cluster 4	86	19.68 %
Cluster 5	55	12.59 %

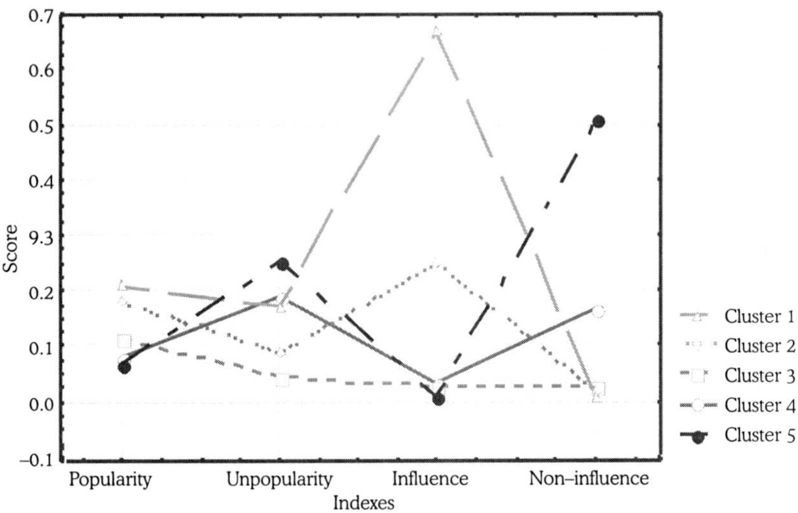

Figure 2. Plot of means for the four clusters

5. RESULTS

5.1. PERCEIVED PARENTING STYLE AND SELF–ESTEEM

The first examined aspect in our study was the association between the individual **parenting components** and the teenager's level of **self–esteem**. The data were analysed using a simple correlation analysis at the level of scores, and a simple analysis of variance at the level of categories of emotional relationship and parental control.

Table 4 below shows correlation coefficients for individual parenting components and self–esteem. Significant positive correlations were found between self–esteem and the positive parenting component in both mothers ($r = 0.32$, $p < 0.01$) and fathers ($r = 0.25$, $p < 0.01$). Conversely, significant negative correlations in both parents emerged between self–esteem and the negative parenting approach ($r = -0.30$ in fathers; $r = -0.37$ in mothers; $p < 0.01$). To put it simply, the warmer, more affectionate and more interested the approach to the child, the better the development of the child's self–esteem. In addition, high demands in both parents are correlated negatively to the teenager's self–esteem ($r = -0.21$ in fathers; $r = -0.31$ in mothers; $p < 0.01$). High levels of the demands component do not only entail assigning duties and having high expectations, but also exercising constant supervision and imposing restrictions on the behavior of the child who, as a consequence, lacks the opportunity to develop optimal self–esteem. Interestingly, the laxity component in our study had little or no effect on the student's self–esteem.

Table 4. Correlations between parenting components and the level of self–esteem in teenagers

Parenting component	Self–esteem
FATHER	
Positive	**0.25****
Negative	**–0.30****
Demands	**–0.21****
Laxity	0.02
MOTHER	
Positive	**0.32****
Negative	**–0.37****
Demands	**–0.31****
Laxity	0.06

$p < 0.01$

Our next point of interest is the impact of **emotional relationships** in the family on the teenager's level of **self-esteem**. As shown in Tables 5, 6 and 7 below, the association between emotional relationships in both parents as well as the family in general and self-esteem is statistically significant at the level of $p < 0.01$. Apparently, the most favorable condition for the development of high self-esteem is an extremely positive emotional family relationship. This connection has been confirmed not only on the part of both mother and father, but also regarding the general affective quality of relationships in the family. A negative emotional relationship between the mother, father and family in general results in the lower self-esteem of teenagers. This is in agreement with the claim that the basic prerequisite of optimal personal development is a loving relationship with a predominantly positive behavioral approach of the parent to the child, where both parents show a caring attitude, provide support, are generous in their praise, etc.

Table 5. Levels of self-esteem in teenagers in relation to the four types of emotional relationship with the father (ANOVA)

Emotional relationship with father		N	M	SD	F
Self-esteem	Extremely positive	62	**35.45**	3.02	**13.15****
	Positive	102	**35.45**	3.12	
	Neutral	54	35.19	3.49	
	Negative	137	33.03	3.83	
	Total	355	34.48	3.63	

**p < 0.01

Table 6. Levels of self-esteem in teenagers in relation to the four types of emotional relationship with the mother (ANOVA)

Emotional relationship with mother		N	M	SD	F
Self-esteem	Extremely positive	59	**36.22**	2.94	**19.69****
	Positive	152	**35.36**	3.10	
	Neutral	36	34.17	2.79	
	Negative	130	32.77	4.01	
	Total	377	34.49	3.64	

**p < 0.01

Table 7. Levels of self-esteem in teenagers in relation to the four types of general quality of emotional relationships in the family (ANOVA)

General quality of emotional relationships in the family		N	M	SD	F
Self-esteem	Extremely positive	67	**35.79**	2.75	**13.51****
	Positive	101	**35.97**	2.80	
	Neutral	14	35.00	4.63	
	Negative	168	33.16	3.81	
	Total	350	34.53	3.60	

**p < 0,01

Next, we observed the relationship between individual types of **parental control** and **self–esteem** in teenagers. The results are summarized in Tables 8, 9 and 10 below. Again, differences at the significance level of $p < 0.01$ were detected. The most favorable condition for the development of positive self–esteem is moderate to weak parental control from the father. A similar pattern can be observed in both the mother and general parental control in the family, where the best condition is weak control, followed by moderate control. As expected, the least favorable conditions include strong and inconsistent control. The detrimental effect of inconsistent control lies in the unpredictability, ambiguousness and obscurity. That is why, out of the four alternatives, this style is the least favorable for the child's development. The negative impact of the strong control style, on the other hand, could be explained by the fact that the child has little opportunity for autonomous decisions and action, which logically becomes reflected in the decreased levels of self–esteem.

Table 8. Levels of self–esteem in teenagers in relation to the four types of parental control in the father (ANOVA)

Parental control in the father		N	M	SD	F
Self–esteem	Strong	52	33.46	3.76	**7.17****
	Moderate	39	**35.13**	3.10	
	Weak	203	**35.05**	3.43	
	Inconsistent	61	33.02	3.93	
	Total	355	34.48	3.63	

** $p < 0.01$

Table 9. Levels of self–esteem in teenagers in relation to the four types of parental control in the mother (ANOVA)

Parental control in the mother		N	M	SD	F
Self–esteem	Strong	49	33.53	3.97	**8.14****
	Moderate	44	**34.73**	3.21	
	Weak	201	**35.22**	3.30	
	Inconsistent	83	33.14	3.98	
	Total	377	34.49	3.64	

** $p < 0.01$

Table 10. Levels of self–esteem in teenagers in relation to the four types of general quality of parental control in the family (ANOVA)

General quality of parental control in the family		N	M	SD	F
Self–esteem	Strong	32	33.84	3.94	**5.01****
	Moderate	13	34.85	2.94	
	Weak	168	**35.27**	3.22	
	Inconsistent	137	33.77	3.84	
	Total	350	34.53	3.60	

** $p < 0,01$

The relationship between the **general parenting style** in the family and students' **self–esteem** also proved statistically significant (see Table 11). It appears that the most optimal parenting style for the development of high self–esteem is represented by Field 6, characterized by positive emotional relationships and weak parental control, followed by Field 7, which involves positive or extremely positive emotional relationships and inconsistent control, and Field 8, a combination of extremely positive relationships and weak control. The least favorable condition for the adolescent's self–esteem proves to be Field 3, combining negative emotional relationships with inconsistent control (M = 32.88). Lower levels of self–esteem were also found in respondents who reported negative relationships and moderate/strong control (Filed 1; M = 33.83), or negative relationships and weak control (Field 2; M = 33.43). Looking closer at the results it becomes clear that within the model of parenting styles employed, those fields which involve positive emotional relationships of the parent with the child are normally associated with higher levels of self–esteem, whereas lower self–esteem can be expected in children in those fields where the general quality of emotional relationships is negative. Hence, our results support the claim about the key role of emotional relationships in the family in the development of the child's self–esteem, which might, as mentioned by Čáp and Boschek (1994), even have a moderating effect on the impact of unfavorable control styles. On the other hand, in participants within Field 5 (extremely positive or positive emotional relationship combined with moderate control), which is considered to be the most optimal parenting style, levels of self–esteem were merely average (M = 35.00). This might have been due to the fact that the field was represented by the lowest number of respondents (N = 8).

Table 11. Levels of self–esteem in early adolescents in relation to general parenting styles in the family (ANOVA)

Parenting model		N	M	SD	F
Self–esteem	Field 1	24	33.83	3.67	**7.12****
	Field 2	44	33.43	3.59	
	Field 3	97	**32.88**	3.96	
	Field 4	10	34.60	3.92	
	Field 5	8	35.00	3.59	
	Field 6	61	**36.13**	2.63	
	Field 7	31	**36.00**	2.34	
	Field 8	49	**35.96**	2.81	
	Field 9	11	35.00	4.63	
	Total	335	34.52	3.64	

**p < 0,01

Field 1: strong or moderate control / negative relationship; **Field 2:** weak control / negative relationship; **Field 3:** inconsistent control / negative relationship; **Field 4:** strong control / positive or extremely positive relationship; **Field 5:** moderate control / positive or extremely positive relationship; **Field 6:** weak control / positive relationship; **Field 7:** inconsistent control / positive relationship; **Field 8:** weak control / extremely positive relationship; **Field 9:** negative–positive ambivalent emotional relationship.

Hypothesis 1 about the statistically significant association between perceived parenting style in the family and level of self–esteem was hence supported. The statistically significant relationship between self–esteem and parenting style was confirmed at every level, starting with the level of individual parenting components. At this level, a significant positive association was found with the positive parenting component, and a negative association with the negative and demands component in both parents. Regarding emotional relationship, it was confirmed that a positive and extremely positive emotional relationship of the parent with the child, characterized by warmth, a caring attitude and emotional support, predicts higher levels of self–esteem in adolescence. Conversely, the negative emotional relationship of the parent, characterized by coldness and indifference, is a predictor of lower self–esteem. As far as parental control is concerned (setting demands and supervising their fulfilment), a significant association was found between higher self–esteem and moderate to weak control. According to our expectations, it was also evidenced that the least positive effect on self–esteem comes from inconsistent parental control, which is distinguished by strong ambivalence in parental control and guidance of the child. On the whole, the general parenting styles which seem to create the best conditions for the development of one's self–esteem are represented in the model by Field 6 – positive relationship and weak control, Field 7 – positive or extremely positive emotional relationship and inconsistent control, and Field 8 – extremely positive relationship and weak control. The least favorable combinations in this respect are represented by Field 3 – negative emotional relationship and inconsistent parental control, Field 1 – negative relationship and moderate to strong control, and Field 2 – negative relationship and weak control.

Another point of interest in this part of the study concerns the gender differences in relation to the above mentioned associations. At the level of individual components, significant differences were indeed detected. In girls, as opposed to boys, no significant negative relationship was found between the negative component and the demands component in the father. On the other hand, a significant positive correlation emerged between self–esteem and mother's laxity component in girls ($r = 0.21$, $p < 0.01$), but not in boys. Concerning the effect of the perceived emotional relationship of the father on the child's self–esteem, the association is much stronger in boys ($F = 10.583$, $p < 0.01$) than in girls ($F = 3.552$, $p < 0.05$). A similar pattern can be found regarding the general quality of emotional relationships in the family. The mother's emotional relationship with the child has a similar effect in both sexes ($p < 0.01$). Perceived parental control in the father was a significant predictor of self–esteem in boys only ($F = 9.583$, $p < 0.01$). In girls, this relationship was not significant. The same can be said about the general quality of parental control in the family. No such differences appeared in relation to the mother's control style. Finally, the association between general parenting style in the family and self–esteem in girls proved t be not significant. However, the relationship was indicated at a non–significant level, and the non–significance was most probably caused by a low and uneven representation of the individual fields in the overall sample of boys and girls.

5.2. PERCEIVED PARENTING STYLE AND THE CLASSROOM SOCIO–METRIC STATUS OF TEENAGERS

In the next part of the study, we turned our attention to the relationship between perceived parenting style and the classroom social status of the teenage participants. First, differences regarding individual parenting components between the clusters representing different types of socio–metric positions were assessed using a simple analysis of variance – ANOVA. At the higher levels of analysis, Pearson's chi–squared test was used.

Significant differences among the types of **classroom socio–metric status** were found regarding several **parenting components**. The results are summarized in Tables 12 (for fathers) and 13 (for mothers) below. The highest and lowest average scores of group difference are highlighted in the parenting components.

Table 12. The impact of individual parenting components in fathers on the teenager's classroom socio–metric status

FATHER								
Parenting component	Positive		Negative		Demands		Laxity	
Cluster	M	SD	M	SD	M	SD	M	SD
Cluster 1	**26.62**	3.81	13.59	3.48	16.76	3.50	20.83	3.70
Cluster 2	25.34	4.28	13.18	4.06	15.56	3.53	19.51	3.42
Cluster 3	25.57	4.11	13.20	3.58	16.11	3.50	19.58	3.34
Cluster 4	25.03	4.32	13.95	3.82	17.05	4.14	19.61	3.69
Cluster 5	**23.96**	4.94	13.81	3.94	15.73	3.77	19.83	3.70
Total	25.34	4.23	13.45	3.75	16.19	3.68	19.71	3.50
F	**2.48***		0.67		1.73		0.87	

$p < 0.05$

Cluster 1 – influential students who are highly popular, but also unpopular; **Cluster 2** – students who are both reasonably influential and popular, but not the most popular ones; **Cluster 3** – "ordinary students" who received only a few nominations in the popularity category and virtually none in other categories; **Cluster 4** – students who are relatively unpopular and non–influential; **Cluster 5** – highly unpopular and non–influential students.

As shown in Table 12, on the part of the **father**, differences at the significance level $p < 0.05$ emerged only within the dimension of the positive **parenting component**. The results indicate that students who enjoy a dominant and considerably advantageous social status, i.e. those who are both highly popular and unpopular and occupy a highly influential position (Cluster 1), reported the highest levels of the positive component on the part of the father (M = 26.62). In contrast, students with the least favorable classroom status, i.e. those who are considered both unpopular and non–influential (Cluster 5), scored lowest in this component (M = 23.96). This means that teenagers who perceive their fathers' approach to them as positive are more popular and influential than those who do not. Regarding other parenting components in the father, no further significant differences were found between individual clusters.

As far as **parenting components in mothers** are concerned, differences at the significance level $p < 0.05$ were found regarding the positive, negative and demands components (see Table 13 below). Again, students belonging to Cluster 1 (highly popular, unpopular and influential) reported the most positive parenting approach on the part of the mother (M = 27.79) as compared to the other socio–metric clusters. For most unpopular and non–influential students the average score in this component was the lowest (M = 25.58). This indicates that the teenager's classroom social status is affected by the positive parenting approach in both parents. Not surprisingly, the negative parenting component in the mother was the highest in Cluster 5 (M = 14.76) and lowest in Cluster 2 (M = 12.49), which consists of students with relatively (but not extremely) high popularity and influence. The demands component reached the highest values (M = 17.41) in moderately unpopular and non–influential students (Cluster 4) and the lowest values in moderately popular and influential teenagers (M = 15.34; Cluster 2). In the remaining three clusters, however, the levels of this component were relatively similar. Thus, if the demands component has any impact on the child's sociometric status at all, then fewer demands are associated with greater popularity and influence than higher demands.

Emotional relationship as a dimension of parenting style proved to be associated with the **classroom socio–metric status** only on the part of the father and the family as a whole. Interestingly enough, no such connection was found with regard to the emotional relationship with the mother.

As can be seen in Table 14 below, summarizing the distribution of different types of **emotional relationship in the father** among the five socio–metric clusters, there are obvious differences between the clusters. Putting aside the

Table 13. The impact of individual parenting components in the mother on the teenager's classroom socio-metric status

MOTHER								
Parenting component	Positive		Negative		Demands		Laxity	
Cluster	M	SD	M	SD	M	SD	M	SD
Cluster 1	**27.79**	2.69	13.86	3.95	16.14	3.21	21.38	3.53
Cluster 2	27.49	2.77	**12.49**	3.13	**15.34**	3.36	20.11	3.55
Cluster 3	27.16	2.72	13.19	3.30	16.65	3.61	19.85	3.46
Cluster 4	26.93	3.18	14.15	4.10	**17.41**	3.52	20.22	3.45
Cluster 5	**25.58**	4.88	**14.76**	5.31	16.96	4.21	19.94	3.64
Total	27.02	3.21	13.57	3.82	16.59	3.64	20.09	3.51
F	**3.36***		**2.53***		**3.06***		1.23	

$p < 0,05$
Cluster 1 – influential students who are highly popular, but also unpopular; **Cluster 2** – students who are both reasonably influential and popular, but not the most popular ones; **Cluster 3** – "ordinary students" who obtained only a few choices in the popularity category and virtually none in other categories; **Cluster 4** – students relatively unpopular and non–influential; **Cluster 5** – highly unpopular and non–influential students.

fact that the negative emotional relationship is quite prevalent in all clusters, which is consistent with our previous findings indicating a high degree of the negative emotional component in parenting in general, it is evident that the negative emotional relationship in the father is particularly frequent (54.08 %) in Cluster 5 of strongly unpopular and non–influential students. This type of emotional relationship also prevails in moderately unpopular and non–influential teenagers (Cluster 4; 47.97 %). The positive relationship is predominant in highly popular (but also unpopular) and influential students of Cluster 1 (41.38 %). An extremely positive relationship is most typical for Cluster 2 of mildly popular and influential students. In summary, it can be said that an emotional relationship with the father has a significant impact on the child's social status in the classroom peer group in the sense that a positive relationship probably predetermines a more favorable status among one's peer group regarding both popularity and influence, whereas a negative relationship will be more likely associated with a less advantageous position.

An emotional relationship with the mother showed only a marginally significant ($p = 0.06$) association with the social status of the respondent (see Table 15). However, certain trends are clearly observable in the presented results, and it can be assumed that significant relationships would have appeared had the sample been larger. Again, the negative relationship apparently predominates in Cluster 5 of highly unpopular and non–influential students (45.83 %)

Table 14. The impact of emotional relationship with the father on the student's classroom socio–metric status

Emotional relationship with father	Extremely positive		Positive		Neutral		Negative		Chi–Square
Cluster	N	%	N	%	N	%	N	%	
Cluster 1	4	13.79	11	**41.38**	2	6.90	11	37.93	19.40*
Cluster 2	14	**22.95**	20	32.79	8	13.11	19	31.15	
Cluster 3	24	15.79	47	30.92	31	**20.39**	50	32.89	
Cluster 4	12	18.70	15	22.73	7	10.61	31	**47.97**	
Cluster 5	7	15.67	8	17.75	6	12.50	25	**54.08**	
Total	63		102		54		137		

p < 0,05

Cluster 1 – influential students who are highly popular, but also unpopular; **Cluster 2** – students who are both reasonably influential and popular, but not the most popular ones; **Cluster 3** – "ordinary students" who obtained only a few choices in the popularity category and virtually none in other categories; **Cluster 4** – relatively unpopular and non–influential students; **Cluster 5** – highly unpopular and non–influential students

and Cluster 4 of moderately unpopular and non–influential students (43.24 %). A higher occurrence of the positive relationship is implied in Cluster 2 (moderately popular and influential students).

Table 15. The impact of emotional relationship with the mother on the student's classroom socio–metric status

Emotional relationship with mother	Extremely positive		Positive		Neutral		Negative		Chi–Square	p
Cluster	N	%	N	%	N	%	N	%		
Cluster 1	4	13.79	12	41.38	2	6.90	11	37.93	16.10	0.06
Cluster 2	14	**21.54**	30	**46.15**	4	6.15	17	26.15		
Cluster 3	24	14.81	68	41.98	22	**13.58**	48	29.63		
Cluster 4	8	10.81	28	37.84	6	8.11	32	**43.24**		
Cluster 5	9	18.75	15	31.25	2	4.17	22	**45.83**		
Total	59		153		36		130			

Cluster 1 – influential students who are highly popular, but also unpopular; **Cluster 2** – students who are both reasonably influential and popular, but not the most popular ones; **Cluster 3** – "ordinary students" who obtained only a few choices in the popularity category and virtually none in other categories; **Cluster 4** – relatively unpopular and non–influential students; **Cluster 5** – highly unpopular and non–influential students

Significant differences were found with regard to the **general quality of emotional relationships in the family**. Once again, Cluster 5, as well as Cluster 4 were characterized by the predomination of the negative emotional pattern (60.87% and 60.00% respectively). These two clusters were also distinguished by a relatively low prevalence of positive emotional relationships in the family, for which Cluster 1 was the most dominant group. An extremely positive relationship could be found mainly among Cluster 2 of the moderately popular and influential students. It must be remembered, however, that in all clusters the negative relationship occupied the leading position in relation to other emotional components, since it proved to be the most prevalent type of emotional pattern in the sample. The results are shown in Table 16 below.

Table 16. The impact of general quality of emotional relationships in the family on the classroom socio-metric status of students

Emotional relationship in the family	Extremely positive		Positive		Positive –negative		Negative		Chi–Square
Cluster	N	%	N	%	N	%	N	%	**23.57***
Cluster 1	5	15.79	11	**36.48**	2	6.90	11	41.83	
Cluster 2	14	**23.33**	19	31.67	2	3.33	24	40.00	
Cluster 3	26	17.22	48	31.79	4	2.65	61	40.40	
Cluster 4	11	16.46	12	18.46	2	3.54	39	**60.00**	
Cluster 5	7	15.39	7	15.22	3	6.35	28	**60.87**	
Total	63		97		13		163		

*$p < 0.05$
Cluster 1 – influential students who are highly popular, but also unpopular; **Cluster 2** – students who are both reasonably influential and popular, but not the most popular ones; **Cluster 3** – "ordinary students" who obtained only a few choices in the popularity category and virtually none in other categories; **Cluster 4** – relatively unpopular and non–influential students; **Cluster 5** – highly unpopular and non–influential students

Regarding the impact of **parenting control** on the **socio–metric status** of the student, it would be logical to assume a significant connection. Yet, no significant differences between individual clusters were detected in our study on the part of either the mother or father, or in the family in general. The results are summarized in Tables 17, 18 and 19 below.

Table 17. The impact of parental control from the father on the classroom socio–metric status of the student

Parental control from father	Strong		Moderate		Weak		Inconsistent		Chi–Square
Cluster	N	%	N	%	N	%	N	%	13.87
Cluster 1	15	22.73	5	7.58	30	45.45	16	24.24	
Cluster 2	21	13.82	18	11.84	89	58.55	24	15.79	
Cluster 3	6	9.84	9	14.75	39	63.93	7	11.48	
Cluster 4	2	6.90	2	6.90	18	62.07	7	24.14	
Cluster 5	8	16.67	5	10.42	28	58.33	7	14.58	
Total	52		39		204		61		

p = 0.31

Cluster 1 – influential students who are highly popular, but also unpopular; **Cluster 2** – students who are both reasonably influential and popular, but not the most popular ones; **Cluster 3** – "ordinary students" who obtained only a few choices in the popularity category and virtually none in other categories; **Cluster 4** – relatively unpopular and non–influential students; **Cluster 5** – highly unpopular and non–influential students.

Table 18. The impact of parental control from the mother on the classroom socio–metric status of the student

Parental control from mother	Strong		Moderate		Weak		Inconsistent		Chi–Square
Cluster	N	%	N	%	N	%	N	%	18.01
Cluster 1	10	13.51	9	12.16	33	44.59	22	29.73	
Cluster 2	25	15.43	20	12.35	78	48.15	39	24.07	
Cluster 3	4	6.15	10	15.38	43	66.15	8	12.31	
Cluster 4	2	6.90	1	3.45	20	68.97	6	20.69	
Cluster 5	8	16.67	4	8.33	27	56.25	9	18.75	
Total	49		44		201		84		

p = 0.12

Cluster 1 – influential students who are highly popular, but also unpopular; **Cluster 2** – students who are both reasonably influential and popular, but not the most popular ones; **Cluster 3** – "ordinary students" who obtained only a few choices in the popularity category and virtually none in other categories; **Cluster 4** – relatively unpopular and non–influential students; **Cluster 5** – highly unpopular and non–influential students

Table 19. The impact of general parental control in the family on the classroom socio-metric status of the student

Parental control in general	Strong		Moderate		Weak		Inconsistent		Chi-Square
Cluster	N	%	N	%	N	%	N	%	
Cluster 1	7	10.77	3	4.62	24	36.92	31	47.69	13.45
Cluster 2	18	11.92	5	3.31	69	45.70	59	39.07	
Cluster 3	3	5.00	3	5.00	38	63.33	16	26.67	
Cluster 4	1	3.45	1	3.45	15	51.72	12	41.38	
Cluster 5	3	6.52	1	2.17	22	47.83	20	43.48	
Total	32		13		168		138		

$p = 0.34$

Cluster 1 – influential students who are highly popular, but also unpopular; **Cluster 2** – students who are both reasonably influential and popular, but not the most popular ones; **Cluster 3** – "ordinary students" who obtained only a few choices in the popularity category and virtually none in other categories; **Cluster 4** – relatively unpopular and non-influential students; **Cluster 5** – highly unpopular and non-influential students

Our final intention was to test the potential associations between **general parenting styles** and the **classroom social status** of the teenagers. However, due to the fact that the contingency table was constituted by 5 clusters × 9 fields, it was impossible to provide enough respondents for each group in the model. Therefore, no significant relationship could be traced at this level. Yet, as we considered this aspect of the study to be of particular importance, we decided to combine the nine fields into three broader areas, representing parenting approaches which are favorable, neutral and unfavorable for the development of the individual. These three general categories were then analyzed in relation to the five socio-metric clusters. The results are summarized in Table 20 below. With reference to previous research we categorized Fields 4, 5 and 8 as the most favorable, Fields 1, 2 and 3 as the least favorable, and Fields 6, 7 and 9 as mildly favorable (neutral) for the personal development of the child (Čáp, 1996).

After such adjustment, associations between general parenting styles and individual socio-metric clusters were detected at the significance level of $p < 0.05$. As before, respondents reporting negative parenting styles outnumbered the other two groups. Compared to other clusters, in Cluster 2 (moderately popular and influential) a greater percentage of respondents fell into the positive parenting style group. Cluster 1 was the most numerous among the neutral parenting style. Finally, Clusters 4 and 5 (unpopular or extremely unpopular and non-influential students) were the most prevalent among the negative (i.e. least favorable) parenting style group.

Table 20. The impact of the general parenting style in the family on the classroom sociometric status of the student

Cluster / Parenting style		Cluster 1	Cluster 2	Cluster 3	Cluster 4	Cluster 5
Positive (most favorable)	N	4	16	27	13	7
	%	13.79	27.12	19.42	20.31	15.56
Neutral (mildly favorable)	N	12	19	51	12	10
	%	**41.38**	32.20	36,69	18.75	22.22
Negative (least favorable)	N	13	24	61	39	28
	%	44.83	40.68	43.88	**60.94**	**62.22**
Total		29	59	139	64	45
Chi–Square				**18.44***		

p < 0.05
Cluster 1 – influential students who are highly popular, but also unpopular; **Cluster 2** – students who are both reasonably influential and popular, but not the most popular ones; **Cluster 3** – "ordinary students" who obtained only a few choices in the popularity category and virtually none in other categories; **Cluster 4** – relatively unpopular and non–influential students; **Cluster 5** – highly unpopular and non–influential students

In summary, then, it can be concluded that Cluster 4 (unpopular and non–influential students) and Cluster 5 (extremely unpopular and non–influential students), occupying the least favorable positions in the classroom peer groups, often perceive the general parenting approach of their parents to be negative, with few expressions of positive emotion. In Cluster 3, which comprises particularly unexceptional individuals, no direction of influence of parenting styles on students' social status was detected, which can be ascribed to the very nature and indistinctiveness of this group of participants. Clusters 2 (popular and influential students) and 1 (extremely popular and influential, but also unpopular students) were demonstrably associated with a positive emotional approach from parents.

As far as parental control is concerned, no significant relationships could be affirmed. Regarding general parenting styles, Cluster 2 (popular and influential students) was represented by the greatest proportion of respondents among the positive parenting style group, Cluster 1 (highly popular and influential, but also unpopular students) was predominant in the neutral parenting style group, and Clusters 4 (mildly unpopular and non–influential) and 5 (highly unpopular and non–influential) prevailed in the unfavorable parenting style group, which is basically just a recapitulation of the previous section.

Reflecting on the fact that these results concerning family parenting styles only partially confirm our expectations and are generally not very robust, we have to conclude that **Hypothesis 2**, suggesting a significant relationship between perceived parenting style in the family and the classroom social status of the students, was not fully supported. It turns out that the link between the two variables is not that simple and straightforward, and the whole issue is much more complex, probably due to the effect of additional intervening personal, sociocultural, and other factors. On the other hand, it can also be assumed that had the research sample been larger and the representation of the individual categories stronger, the hypothesized associations would most probably reach the level of statistical significance.

6. CONCLUSION

The results of our study, which investigated possible associations between perceived parenting styles, self–esteem and classroom social status in teenagers, can be viewed as an expansion of previous research done in this area, but also as a contribution to the overall body of knowledge concerning the topic of parenting in relation to the two examined variables.

The main objective of the study was to test whether different parenting styles, as perceived by the teenagers themselves, have an impact on the teenagers' self–esteem and their social status among the classroom peer groups.

Out of the two formulated hypotheses, we may conclude that the hypothesis about the relationship between parenting style and self–esteem was fully supported. Significant associations were found between perceived parenting styles in the family and self–esteem at every level of analysis. An extremely positive emotional relationship and moderate and weak parental control predict higher self–esteem in teenagers. The analysis also detected significant gender differences, which might serve as a good basis for further examination.

On the other hand, the association between perceived parenting styles and classroom social status proved relatively weak in our study. An emotional relationship with the father and the family in general were identified as significant predictors of classroom social status. Whereas a positive emotional approach is apparently more likely to produce a more favorable status among the peer group, a negative approach seems to be associated with less favorable social positions. No connection was detected between classroom socio–metric status and the parental control aspect of the parenting style.

Different parenting approaches can work in various forms to either facilitate or inhibit the life and development of the child's personality, both in its individual aspects and as a whole. There are countless studies devoted to the topic of parenting styles and their effects; yet, the immense diversity of methodological procedures and conditions involved renders higher–order comparisons virtually impossible. Most researchers, however, agree that the basic condition for the optimal development in children is a positive emotional relationship in connection with appropriate parental control. These general findings and assumptions are therefore also in accordance with our own conclusions which emphasize the principal role of a positive emotional approach in optimal personality development, including the development of adequate self–esteem and a favorable social position. One has to bear in mind, though, that parenting style is just one of many factors participating in this process.

REFERENCES

Blatný M., Plháková A. (2003), Temperament, intelligence, sebepojetí: Nové pohledy na tradiční témata psychologického výzkumu, Tišnov: SCAN.

Brídová E. (2007), Některé souvislosti mezi percipovaným způsobem výchovy v rodině, sebehodnocením žáka a jeho postavením v třídním kolektivu [Unpublished Master's Thesis], Brno: Masaryk University.

Coopersmith S. (1968), Studies in self–esteem, "Scientific American", 218.

Coopersmith S. (1981), SEI: Self–esteem Inventories, Palo Alto, CA: Consulting Psychologists Press.

Čáp J., Boschek P. (1994), Dotazník pro zjišťování způsobu výchovy v rodině. Příručka, Brno: Psychodiagnostika.

Čáp J. (1996), Rozvíjení osobnosti a způsob výchovy, Praha: ISV.

Čáp J. (1999), Styly rodinné výchovy. Psychologie dnes, 5 (8).

Dekovic M., Janssens J.M.A.M. (1992), Parents' child–rearing style and child's sociometric status, "Developmental Psychology", 28 (5).

Fontana D. (1997), Psychologie ve školní praxi, Praha: Portál.

Hart C.H., Ladd G.W., Burleson B.R. (1990), Children's expectations of the outcomes of social strategies: Relations with socio–metric status and maternal disciplinary styles, "Child Development", 61.

Lamborn S.D., Mounts N.S., Steinberg L., Dombusch S.M. (1991), Patterns of competence and adjustment among adolescents from authoritative, authoritarian, indulgent, and neglected families, "Child Development", 62.

Macek P., Širůček J. (2005), Parenting style during childhood and perception of parents as predictors of adolescents' self–esteem, [in:] Book of Abstracts. 12th European Conference on Developmental Psychology, La Laguna: University La Laguna.

Petrusek M. (1969), Sociometrie. Teorie, metoda, techniky, Praha: Svoboda.

Quatman T., Watson C.M. (2001), Gender differences in adolescent self–esteem: An exploration of domains, "The Journal of Genetic Psychology", 162 (1).

Širůček J., Širůčková M. (2006), Vývoj a zkoumání vrstevnických vztahů, [in:] Macek P., Lacinová L. (eds.), "Vztahy v dospívání", Brno: Barrister & Principal.

Zaťková L. (2002), Zdroje sociálního odmietania u detí školského veku, "Psychológia a patopsychológia dieťaťa", 37 (4).

Anna Pawiak
Kazimierz Wielki University in Bydgoszcz

TEACHERS' OPINIONS ON FEEDBACK IN COMMUNICATION AS AN ESSENTIAL PART OF THE EDUCATIONAL PROCESS

ABSTRACT

Feedback as a form of constructive criticism plays an important role in the process of education. Its aim is to influence students' development positively. This chapter describes and characterizes the basic rules and tools of creating effective feedback. Research referring to the meaning of constructive criticism in work with students is also presented. A correctly given feedback is a great way of communicating between the teacher and the students. This skill, however, requires knowledge and practice that may help in building correct relationships at school and may be effective in teachers' educational work.

KEYWORDS: communication, education, educational process, teachers, students, feedback.

> I have just received a letter form a Young scientist, who dealt with an interesting maths problem. He drew a conclusion that is right and original; He also undertook a trial to prove it. However, in his counts I found two wrong assumptions, although the result is correct. He felt intuitively that his conclusion is correct but He could not give a reason for that. I corrected him, and wrote to him that the conclusion is right and that He can use my correction. I did not want to compete with that young man and wanted him to feel independent. This way he keeps the right to be the first as far as the idea is concerned, and he can search for the right solution himself without owing anything to me …
>
> Albert Einstein

An effective educational communication at school is the base for all educational processes. In contrast to other processes of interpersonal communication, educational communication is expressed in the intended and intentional teacher's influence on students, unconditional acceptance, and actions aiming at help, support and students' development.[1] The teacher's educational skills, which are based on the knowledge about the student, school, methods and ways of influencing the interpersonal and task oriented spheres, are essential in

[1] G. Koć–Seniuch, Nauczyciel i uczeń w sytuacjach szkolnych, Białystok, 1995, p. 127.

those processes. These skills include: effective communication, solving conflicts in student teams, active listening, decision making abilities, talking and, most of all, giving feedback in order to provide help and support for students' development.

Such skills thus have a decisive meaning for the quality and effectiveness of a teacher's work with a student. The teacher, as the person being in charge of the child's development in certain areas of knowledge, as well as having influence on the development of a young person's personality, is responsible for the creation of a student's positive image and the way of perceiving him/herself and the surrounding world. Thanks to certain skills and knowledge, the teacher should direct students' development in such a way as to create a positive image of the student themselves and other people. Due to many conditions resulting from the complexity of interpersonal relationships, it is very difficult and requires a huge amount of knowledge, competences and a teacher's true vocation.[2]

Teachers' skills in their relationship with students should be based on three important elements, i.e. the abilities to motivate, make contact and criticize. **Criticism** (lat. criticus "judging") is the analysis and evaluation of both good and bad qualities from the point of view of certain values (such as: practical, ethical, cognitive, scientific, esthetical and correct ones). It may concern many spheres like science (science criticism), formality correctness (logical criticism) and content–related correctness (content–related criticism or empirical criticism). In casual speech the word "criticism" is usually understood as being in opposition (in words or in writing) to a certain phenomenon, person, fact or way of solving problems, connected with a negative evaluation of such facts. Criticism may be of a constructive or destructive form. **Constructive criticism** is a type of criticism which is characterized by the fact that the person criticizing at the same time suggests a way of solving a problem. Constructive criticism is feedback information essential for following a correct path and implementing certain improvements. It requires effort and is at the same time a sign of honesty and treating the other person with respect.

Destructive criticism is usually expressed in a form of some general, subjective remarks concentrated on a person's characteristic features; it takes the form of a non–objective comments. A lack of criticism is also not good, as is its excess and unsuitable form.[3]

A constructive form of criticism in the literature of the subject is called feedback. Feedback in English means feed – to provide with food, and back – to give back. It is very often not translated into Polish, and the Polish equivalent and English version are used interchangeably.

[2] B. Strycharska–Gać, Za szkolnym progiem, Warszawa, 2005, p. 41.

[3] Wikipedia: wolna encyklopedia [online], modified: 31.12.2010 [access: 2.09.2012]. Krytyka, [in:] http://pl.wikipedia.org/wiki/Krytyka.

In the process of education, feedback as a constructive criticism plays an important role with the aim to positively influence students' development.

According to Bee and Bee, feedback is an essential part of a correct, two–sided communication. It is a fundamental part of the process of directing people to act and behave in a way most suitable in certain situations.[4] Feedback is constantly given by everyone in formal and informal ways. Feedback is also information from the environment when a person learns from experience about some facts and interdependences, and about their own and other people's abilities. An evaluating feedback is the base for human development, allowing for shaping of certain features and skills.

Feedback is also defined as 'information about acting or behaving, which leads to an action that is supposed to confirm or develop the action or behaviour', or 'awareness of the learners which of their actions reached a certain level, thanks to which, they will be able to perform the action, and explanation given to them on what was below a standard in order to agree on a plan allowing to avoid similar behaviour in the future, and to choose a way to a desired standard'.[5] Constructive feedback gives specific information, is concentrated on a task and is based on observation. It takes two forms:[6]

- **positive feedback** – respecting the needs of the other side, acting in order to make the contact better, striving to understand; the honest expressing one's opinions in such a way as not to hurt the other person,
- **negative/correcting feedback** – having own needs above the needs of the other person; acting in such a way leads to communication block, because the other side feels hurt, humiliated and in such conditions is unable to cooperate.

Both positive and negative feedback have benefits to teachers, students and parents.

The most important assumption in feedback is that the person receiving it can do something correctly or that there is a positive way of achieving certain results. In a school situation, such an approach to a student is mostly required. In the 1960s Rosenthal and Jacobson showed that if teachers assume that students will act wisely, they will probably do so. If, however, they assume that they will act stupidly, then this will happen.[7] It is important that feedback is of a constructive character, based on what is good and the best way to reach the aim. It should not be exclusively bad. The aim of the feedback given by the teacher is to provide students with information on their behavior and actions, which are evaluated on the basis of objective standards. It should be given in

[4] R. Bee and F. Bee, Feedback, Warszawa, 1998, p. 7.

[5] Ibidem, p. 10.

[6] O. Rzycka, Feedback w pigułce [online], modified: 11.04.2011, [access: 2.09.2012], [in:] http://manager.wieszjak.pl/zarzadzanie-zespolem/279636,2,Feedback-w-pigulce.html.

[7] A. Janowski, Uczeń w teatrze życia szkolnego, Warszawa, 1995, p. 72.

such a way that the receiver, in this case the student, can keep a positive attitude towards himself/herself and learning. Information given should encourage the student to implement their own plan of action in accordance with the standards of behavior and action implemented by the school. Feedback is an inseparable and essential part of the process of education as it helps in learning new skills, improving existing ones and changing behavior.

Feedback is necessary as a regular and constant part of interpersonal communication between parents and children, teachers and students and future husbands and wives, friends, employers and employees. It is therefore important to provide effective, well constructed feedback within such relationships, and to do so it must be based on some rules. It should be given at a certain time, and if possible immediately after the events it concerns. Giving feedback too late makes the information too old and lacking the required meaning. This is responsible for maintaining a negative feeling, which may lead to the outburst of aggression. The person giving constructive criticism at a given time should feel confident that they have enough time to pass the information on. The capabilities of the person receiving feedback should also be taken into account. Having in mind a person's readiness to receive criticism, three categories can be distinguished:

1) "buckets" – people who know their value, have confidence in their possibilities of development and change, are positive towards receiving a constructive criticism;
2) "mugs" – people who can receive a reasonable dose of criticism in the form of three pieces of information concerning them;
3) "thimbles"– people who require special carefulness and sensitivity due to their lack of belief in their own abilities and sensitivity due to former experiences connected with destructive criticism.

A specific group comprises those who wait for constructive criticism to improve the effects of their work, but who, after getting feedback, do not change a single thing about the way they act. Russell terms such people "buckets with a hole".[8] Students also have different levels of readiness for receiving feedback depending on their former experiences, their feeling of their own values, and their evaluations of the environment. The level of acceptance of feedback may be different every day, depending on the mood, difficult situations on a certain day, stress, etc. In such a case, it is difficult to provide feedback correctly.

Feedback is evaluated as a necessary part of cooperation and the effective functioning of groups working together in companies and organizations. A lot of theories concerning feedback can be implemented in school situations, and as feedback is not of an extorting form it allows for the avoidance of stressful remarks and punishments and at the same time encourages development, which

[8] R. Bee and F. Bee, op. cit., p. 33.

is essential in the process of education. Having the above in mind it can be stated that, as in the case of managing staff, in "managing" students at school feedback has some influential functions, for example:

- Sustaining and improving results. Feedback makes students realize which ways of behaving are effective and which are to be continued in the future. On the other hand, it allows for eliminating the behavior that negatively influences learning results.
- Getting new competences. Feedback is an essential part of the process of learning whereby the learner can observe their development and realize what should be improved.
- Development and unleashing potential. Constructive feedback at important stages in the process of learning may provide the right use of potential in students.
- Development of team work. The ability for students to provide feedback in a class is the basic element of their effective cooperation.
- Raising morale, motivation and involvement. The recognition of well performed tasks, the feeling of success, and the release of potential to grow and develop are key motivating factors.[9]

In order to achieve this, one the basic condition of proper feedback construction by the sender and the expression of constructive criticism should be fulfilled. Therefore, 10 tools for feedback creation have been formed:

1. Analysis of the situation.
2. Stating aims and results to be reached.
3. Adjusting the range of reception.
4. Creating a proper atmosphere.
5. Effective communication.
6. Description of the behavior to be changed.
7. Description of the desired behavior.
8. Collaborative search for solutions.
9. Focusing on what is good.
10. Reaching agreement.

The first step for the proper construction of feedback requires a deep analysis of the situation taking all its aspects into consideration. It should be stated where the problem is, what it results from, what needs to be changed and why. Using examples, the problem and its consequences should be made clear.

Another important step is stating the aims and results to be achieved. It is then essential to prepare the way to complete the stated aim, which should be positive and the emphasis should be on what is to be reached, not on what

[9] O. Rzycka, Feedback w pigułce [online], modified: 11.04.2011, [access: 2.09.2012], [in:] http://manager.wieszjak.pl/zarzadzanie-zespolem/279636,2,Feedback-w-pigulce.html.

should be corrected. Apart from this the aim should be clear and reachable, and should give the feeling of success. It should be supported by a strong vision of the success within reach. The aim has to be real, i.e. it should bring benefits and be set in time.

While giving feedback its reception should be adjusted. The different abilities of people receiving feedback should be taken into account, which also depend on a day and situation, as mentioned above.

The skills to create a proper atmosphere, providing the best possible conditions for understanding and accepting feedback, are also crucial. Feedback should be given in an atmosphere of trust, respect and openness, and one's experience has a decisive influence on this. For the feedback to be given successfully, people should create a contract in which they specify the rules. It is important to appoint a peaceful place in which the reception of information will not be interrupted. The most important aspects are honesty and empathy in the relations.[10]

While giving feedback it has to be remembered that the communicated information has to be efficient. It is crucial to realize that not only does verbal communication take place but so does non-verbal communication, used by the sender while giving the information, consisting of "body language" involving numerous elements, especially facial expressions and gestures.[11] Both forms usually appear simultaneously, complementing each other. However, as Argyle, Domachowski and Johson emphasize, in social functioning the non-verbal communication is as important, or even sometimes more important, than the verbal one. None of the authors responsible for the theories of communication has doubts as to the importance of non-verbal communication; the differences concern only the level of its importance. According to R. Briedwhistell, an American psychology professor, non-verbal communication is complementing, strengthening the direct, verbal communication which it is strongly connected with. It is important to bear in mind the fact that complementing verbal communication with the non-verbal cannot be avoided or ignored, as the oral component of direct communication is less than 35% and 65% of information given in a non-verbal way, which is as much as two thirds of the whole communication.[12] The effectiveness of giving constructive criticism (bearing in mind the level and the way of communication) depends on two forms: verbal and non-verbal communication. Other rules should also be remembered, such as full concentration (active listening is very difficult), having an open mind, avoiding speculation, keeping calm, showing interest by using eye-contact, nodding, making summaries and reflections, asking questions

[10] Ibidem, p. 30–34.

[11] W. Domachowaski, S. Kowalik, J. Miluska, Z zagadnień psychologii społecznej, Warszawa, 2004, p. 78.

[12] A. Pease, Język ciała, Kraków, 1997, p. 12.

to make sure that everything is understood, and helping the other side in solving the problem.

Feedback is a complex and difficult activity involving many skills. The behavior to be changed or corrected should be clearly described as the receiver of the feedback needs to understand the core of the issue, feel the importance of the problem, and be sure that it is necessary to change something. Everything should be said directly, avoiding speculation and judging statements such as "I don't like your attitude", etc. In explaining the negative influence of the wrong behavior people should stick to the facts and be ready to verify them according to feedback given by other people.

Behavior and attitude as the result of feedback should also be clearly described. The solution for a specific situation or problem should be sought together. However, the person receiving feedback should always be encouraged to search for solutions, and with help if needed.[13]

While giving feedback the focus should be placed on what is good. The technique of alternating good and bad news should be used. In order for the criticism to be constructive and have an expected effect the order of giving information should be as follows:

1) information of a positive character,
2) information of a correcting character,
3) information of a positive character.

Information of a positive character allows the receiver to open for the information.

At the next stage information of a correcting character can be given, showing the element in the behavior, skills or knowledge that the receiver should change or correct. Feedback should be closed by information of a positive character which will allow the action, enable the receiver to believe in his/her strength and the possibilities to reach the goal.

Another principle that allows for positive relations and building correct communication between the teacher and the student is the rule that the teacher should always judge the behavior, not the person. It is an important part of creative criticism, very often underestimated or not noticed by teachers.[14]

Finally, a positive result from feedback is possible if speakers reach an agreement. Nobody can be forced to any change. People can only be encouraged and helped in introducing changes, but these changes have to be made by people themselves. It is possible if the interested party accepts the introduction of objective standards. The person that is to change their behavior has to accept the necessity to undertake different actions that are crucial for the

[13] R. Bee and F. Bee, op. cit., p. 36–38.
[14] B. Strycharska-Gać, op. cit., p. 41.

changes to happen. It is helpful if there are deadlines to maintain time frames.[15]

The above described rules of feedback are included in the 10 basic rules that should be considered while giving feedback. By giving constructive criticism it is usually assumed that the person being its receiver is open to a dialogue. There are, however, some situations when giving feedback seems to be a huge challenge, for example when a person avoids contact or is difficult to reach an agreement with. Such situations happen when the receiver of the feedback:

- does not agree with being criticized,
- shows no interest or thinks it does not concern them,
- is shocked, worried or even cries,
- is furious,
- refuses the right to be criticized.

To be prepared for such situations their causes should be understood. These may result from:

- lack of self–confidence (one is afraid to get the results of the evaluation),
- acting out of stress,
- feeling of satisfaction of the state of things and the negative attitude towards taking new action,
- treating criticism as the threat to one's position, etc.

There are even more causes that depend on the specific characteristics of people, and their experience and emotions: '... understanding why people act in a certain way is valuable help in preparing to deal with them'.[16]

Using communicates of "I" and "You" types is also important.

A constructive and non constructive expression of feedback is completed by the two types of information. "I" information allows to give feedback in a constructive way, while "You" information does not create a chance for understanding and analysis of the problem that the sender would like to inform the other side about. It is therefore not a correct form. "I" information focuses on the sender's feelings which are difficult to discuss; these are the consequences of certain behaviors of the other person showing what aspects in the behavior of the other side makes the sender nervous or sad. It stops the problem from escalating and the aggression of the other person, and includes four elements:[17]

- **I feel ...** – a place for feelings,
- **When you ...** – a place for talking about a specific behavior that released the feelings,
- **Because ...** – explaining why the behaviur caused certain feelings,
- **I expect that ...**

[15] R. Bee and F. Bee, op. cit., p. 39–40.

[16] Ibidem, p. 43.

[17] Solution of Human Resources [online], [access: 2.09.2012], Feedback na bieżąco w rozwoju kompetencji, [in:] http://www.solution.pl/feedback-na-biezaco-w-rozwoju-kompetencji.html.

"You" information focuses on the other person, and is of a judgemental and accusing character. It includes generalizations, accusations, instructions and evaluation.

Sending "I" and "You" information, as H. Rylke states, also allows the teacher to recognize not only the student's but also teacher's psychical area. The teacher's ability to preserve an important balance and border between "I" and "You" does not mean not being involved in emotions and a relationship with a student. Sending "I" information is a responsibility for one's own words, actions and relationship with students. Overusing "You" information by the teachers does not solve cognitive and communication problems; on the contrary, it makes the problems grow and creates obstructions in the process of communication.[18]

A list of useful advice and recommendations that can be used in giving and receiving criticism in the teacher–student relation was created by H. Hamer.[19]

While giving critical information:

- express the accusation directly to the interested person and use eye contact,
- do not compare the criticized behavior to others, it causes humiliation,
- express the accusation right after the situation,
- when the receiver accepts the accusation, do not repeat it, it causes humiliation,
- criticize only behavior that can be changed,
- do not highlight dissatisfaction,
- express only one reservation at a time – any more makes the receiver nervous and stops them from listening! (this often happens when teenagers are "bombarded" with criticism),
- avoid being malicious and sarcastic,
- do not ask about the motives of the criticized behavior and do not try to guess,
- avoid the words "never" and "always", as they destroy creditability,
- if you do not praise a lot and often, do not expect openness to your criticism.

How to accept critical remarks?:

- stay calm and show that you are listening,
- maintain eye contact,
- try to understand the criticism, do not defend yourself,
- do not ascribe the sender hostile feelings towards yourself,
- do not change the subject,

[18] G. Koć–Seniuch, Teorie komunikacji a kształcenie nauczycieli, [in:] Z zagadnień pedeutologii i kształcenia nauczycieli, ed. H. Kwiatkowska, T. Lewowicki, Warszawa, 1995, p. 190.

[19] H. Hamer, Klucz do efektywności nauczania, Warszawa, 1994, p. 72–72.

- do not criticize the person that criticizes you,
- do not say to the critic that they are overreacting,
- do not joke,
- do not ascribe the sender with something that was not said,
- at the end of the conversation show that you have understood the accusation,
- give yourself time to be calm; order your thoughts before you further discuss the accusations.

The choice of place is also important while giving feedback. A student should not be criticized in front of their colleagues or other people as this multiplies the punishment by humiliation. Negative feedback should be given directly face–to–face. Similar to praising, students prefer to receive it in privacy, not in public, which may cause a hostile atmosphere and create an unpleasant reaction from the rest of the students.

Feedback should be descriptive information not evaluation, and should refer to the aspects of behavior that can be changed. For feedback to be proper it is necessary to emphasize that it is the opinion of the person forming it. It is also important that the person forming feedback has a positive attitude to the receiver and that the latter is prepared to accept feedback. It cannot be forced as it should take the form of an offer.

Correctly given feedback is a great form of communication between teacher and students. This skill requires knowledge and practice that help in building correct relationships at school, and can also be an effective way of the teacher's didactic and educational work. The teacher should not criticize a student if their knowledge or experience are beyond the area the criticism refers to. The issue we know nothing about cannot be criticized. The teacher is not an expert in every area of knowledge, is not someone who never makes mistakes as "there is no proof that God gave the tool of education and creation of everything to scientists".[20]

There is a sort of educational gap as far as giving feedback is concerned. Future teachers are very rarely taught how to correctly and constructively criticize students, and students therefore receive more destructive and constructive criticism at school. However, it is worth considering what can be changed in this sphere. Therefore, constructive information given to students should refer to certain ways of behavior in specific situations. Information given this way is to be a source of knowledge on how the actions undertaken by the student are seen by others and how they influence them. The student may thus compare their own intentions and approaches with their reception by others and the actual results. If there are discrepancies (and the student accepts the reservations), a correction can be made. This type of information is

[20] C. Banach, My i nasze sprawy, Kraków, 2000, p. 7.

not a sign of disrespect and does not negate the person itself, rather the behavior.

Non–constructive criticism referring to general features and behavior does not give the student a chance to draw conclusions concerning the aspects which are right in their behavior (to strengthen such behavior and improve it) and which are wrong. They have no chance to correct the action. This type of information is a source of uncertainty and makes people uneasy. These are especially negative generalizations that make communication difficult, enforce conflicts and tensions, and are often seen as an attack on and violation of dignity, causing negative emotions. Being aware of the existence of positive and negative feedback, the information given to students should not be one–sided, as each person is neither completely good nor bad. The knowledge about both good and bad behavior has its consequences, enabling the student to choose such behavior that will be approved. Constructive criticism in positive feedback concerns either negative or positive student behaviors, and does not provide objective knowledge about the student. It has a label form that is not easily changed. Unfortunately, as practice shows, labelling students happens very often. As A. Janowski states: 'together with a poor knowledge of children labelling happens, i.e. a situation when an opinion (especially negative) about a student becomes an opinion commonly adopted by other teachers who had no chance to have their own opinion about the student'.[21] Opinions are also adopted by colleagues and the student may be seen as weak and as having problems with learning. Giving only one–sided information on the student in a form of positive or negative feedback only sets the opinion become; the teacher closes their eyes to new experiences and maintains a stereotype about the student. This situation is considered very dangerous as it triggers a mechanism of self–fulfilling prophecy. As a result, the student who was often told that they are not clever and that little can be expected from them will actually start to behave this way, seeing no sense in changing the opinion.[22] It is also dishonest to label good students who, in teachers' opinions, are always nice, prepared for classes, clever and well behaved. This can cause situations in which such a student will discover that they don't need to try to be accepted, which has negative effects on cooperation and building relationships with teachers. Thus, it is important for teachers to use both positive and negative feedback in their work with students. Praise given to the student in class is motivating and of a great value, and is especially important for weaker students. Thanks to that, the student may change their motivation towards learning, set themmselves more difficult goals, understand the relationship between effort, its effects and the praise received from the teacher. A typical sign of such a change

[21] A. Janowski, Uczeń w teatrze życia szkolnego, op. cit., p. 72.
[22] Ibidem, p. 72.

will definitely be an increase in self–esteem and confidence. In a situation when a student gets a lower grade for their work, words of destructive criticism will make people expect only poor results from them. Teachers', parents' and friends' expectations will stay at a low level, not always in response to a student's actual abilities.[23] To avoid such situations, while giving feedback the teacher should:

- act quickly by giving criticism as fast as possible when everyone knows what the matter is.
- stay calm to have a conversation focusing on the facts.
- never criticize in writing; criticism should be given directly, in person.
- talk about what is seen, without analyzing what the student could possibly think or feel. The teacher should not look for hidden intensions. S/he should talk about the situation as if it was unexpected.
- present facts by giving examples of the behavior evaluated.
- focus on the problem, not the person.
- show the effects by talking about the consequences of the student's behavior.
- set action for the future together with the student and at the same time explain what the situation taught both of you, and what conclusions can be spread among others.
- respect and appreciate by establishing conditions for respecting dignity, appreciating students' responsibility for their own behavior or by appreciating their efforts they make in improving the situation. It is also worth expressing optimism for the future.
- treat criticism as the tool for development, a means of improvement and development of the student's competences.[24]

The teacher should always be interested in the causes of the problem from the student's perspective as well. Only then can all the factors involved in the situation be spotted, a proper solution found and a similar situation prevented in the future.

The principles and rules of forming feedback and its proper use in the educational process seem to be clear, easy and obvious, but their significance is seen when they are not properly used nor respected in practice. This is a very common cause of the disturbances in the process of communication and education. In order to find out about teachers' actual knowledge on feedback, research by A. Pawiak and K. Brągiel–Wardowska was conducted on a group of 148 primary and junior high school teachers within the cujavia–pomerania voievodeship. Due to the size restriction of the article only conclusions based

[23] G. Koć–Seniuch, Nauczyciel i uczeń w sytuacjach szkolnych, op. cit., s. 154.

[24] A. Grabka, Zmotywuj pracownika. Jak sprawić, aby twój zespół był wydajny i odnosił sukcesy, [in:] http://www.nlpnews.pl/wp-content/uploads/2010/08/zmotywuj-pracownika.pdf 2010, access: 10.05. 2012, p. 22.

on the part of the results will be presented. Respondents taking part in the research were asked about knowledge of different synonymous expressions connected with feedback. Based on the results it can be stated that the most popular was feedback (43.5%), while the less popular was the Polish version of English feedback (21.5%), even though it is a direct translation from English. A similar number of respondents (21%) understood feedback as constructive criticism. The remaining part did not give any answers. Where, then, do teachers know the definitions from?

The biggest group learnt about the notion of feedback during their studies (26%); a similar percentage of teachers learnt about it during different courses, and workshops (24%); 21.5% of respondents stated they know about feedback from private conversations and professional discussions; 10% found out about the issue from mass media, i.e. newspapers, radio, TV, the Internet, and also from books, films, and cinema. A high percentage (18.5%) gave no answer to any of the questions. Interestingly, only one fifth of the respondents learnt about feedback during their studies. Such data results may be rooted in the fact that more than half (65%) of the people involved in the research have been teachers for many years. We should hope that nowadays, while educating future teachers, constructive criticism is a part of the curriculum. Further research may provide an answer to this.

Analyzing ten tools of forming feedback, it was pointed out that it is crucial to recognize the type of the receiver of the information as far as their tolerance and individual predispositions to accept constructive criticism and behavior are concerned. Do teachers use this clue in their work with students? A high percentage of teachers (65%) said that they adjust the feedback to the student's individual needs. Less than one third (29%) admitted that they do so only sometimes, and only 4% said that they rarely pay attention to their student's needs concerning the form of feedback referring to their school achievement and behavior during classes and breaks. Two per cent of the respondents never thought about the problem. None of the teachers admitted that they do not adjust feedback to the student's needs. What does this state of things result from? Do teachers know the rules of forming feedback? In order to check this the respondents were given ten tools of feedback forming in the correct order. Three of them were changed on purpose in such a way that they were not formulated according to the assumptions of constructive feedback. The teachers' task was to mark the ones which, according to them, had a negative influence on the correctly given feedback. Only people who knew the theory and had experience in forming and giving feedback had no problem with the task.

The first false tool of feedback forming referred to focusing on reaching the aim at all costs, i.e. changing the behavior and student's conduct. Inconsistency with the rules of forming feedback was spotted by one fifth (16.5%) of the questioned teachers.

This may result from the fact that only a small percentage of teachers involved in the research tried to reach the set goal in a democratic way, taking students' feelings and reactions into account. Does this mean that 83.5% of teachers do not pay attention to the effects of destructive criticism?

Moreover, as much as 20% of respondents marked the next false tool, which was labelling students' behavior to be changed without showing empathy. It means that the remaining part of the teachers see nothing wrong in such behavior. They perhaps do this not realizing that it destroys a student's self–assessment and creates a gap between a student and a teacher, which in consequence makes good communication and cooperation impossible.

Many people marked imposing a solution as an inefficient step in forming feedback (30%), which means that these teachers take students' thoughts, feelings and opinions into account, and try not to impose their solution to the problem appearing in the process of education. All in all, the results of the surveyed teachers, a high percentage of whom could not spot the three wrongly formulated rules and would use them in forming feedback, allow us to conclude that teachers' knowledge about feedback is worrying. This is surprising when compared with the results received with reference to the necessity of adjusting the criticism to students' needs. It is puzzling as to whether a teacher who could not spot incorrect information in the list of the stages of feedback forming has the ability to give constructive criticism and adjust it to the student's needs.

Destructive criticism, as G. Koć–Seniuch states, 'makes sensitive people with low self–esteem believe even less in their own strengths and cognitive abilities, and decreases their activeness and creativity. There appears an additional problem concerning the significance of getting to know the students, their features of character and environmental conditions, as well as the teacher's life wisdom in his/her contacts with students'.[25]

In their response to open questions, the respondents emphasized that the opinion directed to students without third parties is the most effective as it "reaches" them the best. They declared that the opinion given by them describes students' achievement in learning, points out some knowledge gaps, and shows the methods of correcting mistakes and creating the necessary skills. One respondent claimed: 'I talk about my students work, tell them about their achievements and shortages. I suggest the methods and the ways of improving their skills and shortages in knowledge. I pay attention to what the student has already mastered, stressing that he/she does not need a lot to achieve success. Feedback is given in a positive atmosphere that motivates them to work'. Other teachers also pointed out the importance of the way information is given. They emphasized the significance of creating a good, friendly atmos-

[25] G. Koć–Seniuch, Nauczyciel i uczeń w sytuacjach szkolnych, op. cit., p. 135.

phere while giving constructive criticism. They pointed out that depending on the situation of the students they are given either praise or are reprimanded. There were also teachers who appreciated the importance of praise in the process of education, especially with weaker students. According to one of the surveyed teachers, 'Praise directed to the student in front of the whole class motivates and is especially important for weaker students'. As the research shows, teachers are aware of the importance of feedback in the process of effective and efficient education. Unfortunately, a high percentage has little knowledge about it. A large group of teachers has problems with proper feedback forming and has no idea about the rules. At the same time, many of the respondents stated that they use feedback and adjust it to the students' needs.

In light of the research results it is crucial to include information about feedback in the curriculum in future teachers' education.

Most of the surveyed (94%) think that the teachers' education should include information concerning proper feedback forming. A small percentage of the surveyed (6%) has no opinion about it. Apart from the above citied opinions, we should be aware that: 'teaching is a job that is not finished in any completed form of education, re–education, and additional courses. A teacher becomes the teacher not only due to their studies. The education a future teacher gets can only start the process of becoming a teacher ... A teacher becomes a teacher by doing the job. He/she becomes one due to their own effort in understanding and changing the person itself due to the self–reflection and changes in the personality it involves'.[26] Considering the dissatisfying results on teachers' knowledge of motivating students using constructive criticism, J. Kozielecki's statement should be remembered: 'any action can bring success, failure or so–called surprise (i.e. a surprising not an unintentional effect) ... A failure (feeling of failing in the performed activity) – as long as the teacher is competent enough and psychically strong enough – triggers so called task reaction, strengthening the motivation to overcome difficulties, expanding towards the areas of action that may compensate for the failure, and even make it a source of inspiration to change thinking and acting within the used methods of work.'[27]

It is very valuable and crucial in presenting the influence of constructive criticism on teachers' work to compare the answers received from teachers with students' answers. Only a research conducted among teachers and students could show the whole picture of the issue. However, E. P. Torrence's (1962) list

[26] R. Kwaśnica, Wprowadzenie do myślenia. O wspomaganiu nauczyciela w myśleniu, [in:] Z zagadnień pedeutologii i kształcenia nauczycieli, ed. H. Kwiatkowska, T. Lewowicki, Warszawa, 1995, p. 38.

[27] W. Komar, Dramat zawodności nauczycielstwa – dylematy, genezy i przyczyny, [in:] Z zagadnień pedeutologii i kształcenia nauczycieli, ed. H. Kwiatkowska, T. Lewowicki, Warszawa, 1995, p. 96.

of rules, "Directives for Teachers' Conduct in Working with Students in the Process of Creative Teaching", shows how important the issue by including the point: 'Develop constrictive criticism!'[28]

The notion of constructive feedback from the teacher is one of the most important elements in the process of good education.

REFERENCES

Banach C., My i nasze sprawy, SPES, Kraków, 2000.

Bee R., Bee F., Feedback, PETIT, Warszawa, 1998.

Domachowaski W., Kowalik S., Miluska J., Z zagadnień psychologii społecznej, PWN, Warszawa, 2004.

Grabka A., Zmotywuj pracownika. Jak sprawić, aby twój zespół był wydajny i odnosił sukcesy, [online], modified 5.08.2010, [access: 10.05.2012], [in:] http://www.nlpnews.pl/wp-content/uploads/2010/08/zmotywuj-pracownika.pdf 2010.

Grzesiuk L. (ed.), Umiejętności menedżera. Psychologia stosowana dla menedżerów, PWSH, Warszawa, 1997.

Jagieła J., Komunikacja interpersonalna w szkole, Krótki przewodnik psychologiczny, RUBIKON, Kraków, 2004.

Janowski A., Uczeń w teatrze życia szkolnego, WSiP, Warszawa, 1995.

Koć-Seniuch G., Nauczyciel i uczeń w sytuacjach szkolnych, TRANS HUMANA, Białystok, 1995.

Kwiatkowska H., Lewowicki T., Z zagadnień pedeutologii i kształcenia nauczycieli, WiZPITE, Warszawa, 1995.

Pease A., Język ciała, JEDNOŚĆ, Kraków, 1997.

Rzycka O., Feedback w pigułce [online], modified 11.04.2011, [access: 2.09.2012], [in:] http://manager.wieszjak.pl/zarzadzanie-zespolem/279636,2,Feedback-w-pigulce.html.

Solution of Human Resources [online], [access: 2.09.2012], Feedback na bieżąco w rozwoju kompetencji, [in:] http://www.solution.pl/feedback-na-biezaco-w-rozwoju-kompetencji.html.

Strycharska-Gać B., Za szkolnym progiem, WSiP, Warszawa, 2005.

Wikipedia: wolna encyklopedia [online], modified 31.12.2010, [access: 2.09.2012]. Krytyka, [in:] http://pl.wikipedia.org/wiki/Krytyka.

[28] G. Koć-Seniuch, Nauczyciel i uczeń w sytuacjach szkolnych, op. cit., p. 115.

Bianka Lewandowska
University of Wroclaw

A NON–STEREOTYPICAL IMAGE OF GENDER IN THE PROCESS OF EDUCATION: ISSUES, OBJECTIVES AND METHODOLOGY OF TRAINING FOR TEACHERS AND PARENTS

ABSTRACT

Education in the field of gender equality is now a compulsory part of school projects funded by the European Union. This subject, undertaken within the framework of training and workshops, is addressed to all of the participants of the project: teachers and, in many cases, parents. Knowledge of gender studies helps them implement the image of gender, free from stereotypes, into the process of teaching and upbringing. Training raises the awareness of the impact of verbal and non–verbal messages, the psychological and cultural attributes of gender, student's social roles, realizing personal goals and functioning in interpersonal relations. This chapter presents the problems and methods of training as well as the insights and reflections gathered during its course. It also describes the results of research on defining the traits of gender of a child by its parents – the participants of the training.

KEYWORDS: communication, education, stereotype, gender, teachers, child, parents.

"Who does not like to think, is impatient about the variety, which forces one to think".[1]
Janusz Korczak

Masculinity and femininity are complex, multidimensional concepts that – simplified and reduced to the cultural traits or behavior patterns – begin to act as a rigid form. Then – with social expectations, often unconscious messages and responses – we attach to them the behavior and self–concept of a growing girl or boy. As long as the stereotypical, polarized images of a woman and a man were fit to divide the social world into a masculine public sphere and a family domain of women, they marked a model of adaptation and provided a recipe to prepare the child for life (at the same time maintaining the negative phe-

[1] J. Korczak, Prawidła życia, Ezop, Warszawa, 2012, p. 124.

nomena such as inequality and violence based on gender). Now, however, images of the causal and insensitive, "real" men and passive, emotional women present in everyday thought and popular culture are little adaptive relics of the past – dangerous in restricting the life aspirations and skills of women and men, and often generating tension, guilt and violence in the relations between them.

Education, aimed at developing non-stereotyped thinking about the differences between the sexes among teachers and educators, is now a compulsory part of school projects funded by the European Union. According to the strategy of "gender mainstreaming", starting from the definition of ten existing social barriers that hinder the equal living conditions of men and women, the European Commission sets before the funded educational projects a requirement to take specific action in order to make the beneficiaries aware of the above-mentioned barriers and reduce them. It is worth recalling that specified, still active barriers include: 1) horizontal and vertical segregation of the labor market, 2) the differences in wages between men and women, 3) low availability of flexible working arrangements, 4) low participation of men in family responsibilities, 5) low participation of women in decision-making, 6) violence based on gender, 7) invisibility of gender issues in health care, 8) inadequate childcare systems, 9) gender stereotypes in all areas, and 10) multiple discrimination.[2]

This chapter presents a theoretical foundation of psychological equality workshops, aimed at primary and high school teachers and parents. Presented here are the objectives and the expected directions of impact and the connected methodology, and content issues are also analyzed. The chapter presents the results of research on parents' attitudes towards the generic typification of their children, conducted during 2010–2012 in a number of schools in Lower Silesia.

1. WHAT IS THE PURPOSE OF "EQUALITY" PSYCHOLOGICAL TRAINING?

According to EU guidelines, the aim of education projects in the Human Capital Program should be the weakening of the barriers of equality, including "preparing teachers to teach non-stereotypically and equally – enabling both boys and girls for all types of activities". In this, "the teachers should be aware of the impact of stereotypes on both the method of teaching, as well as the selection of educational materials", the "non-stereotypical message addressed to girls and boys, or extra-curricular equality activities for children of both sexes – presenting an attitude of respect towards each other and building awareness of possible choices, regardless of the social expectations of their gender", and

[2] Zasada równości szans kobiet i mężczyzn w projektach Programu Operacyjnego Kapitał Ludzki. Poradnik – aktualizacja, Ministerstwo Rozwoju Regionalnego. Departament Zarządzania Europejskim Funduszem Społecznym, Warszawa, 2010, p. 11.

"parental involvement in the lives of both nursery and school."[3] The above instructions set targets for psychological training.

On the other hand, the objectives and their specific content should be based on the current state of scientific knowledge – the results of research on psychological differences in sexes, the social and biological origins of these differences, the role of social stereotypes of gender roles in the individual development, shaping attitudes towards others and reinforcement of social inequalities as well as the individual development. The introduction of the idea of equality into educational interaction requires the inclusion of a wider knowledge of the formation of mental health. Training should therefore aim to:

1) familiarize participants with modern scientific knowledge about mental difference between the sexes and the origin of these differences, thus considering the possibilities of reducing some differences and the merit of including others in the educational design process, and
2) show the negative, psychological and social consequences of stereotypical images of sex – the limitations of self-fulfillment and justification for the unequal treatment of individuals and key areas of human activity, such as career and building relationships;

The participants of the training should also develop the following skills:

1) understanding of the complex biological and cultural origins of some psychological gender differences and an understanding that the statistical nature of scientifically measured differences between populations of boys and girls is only a quantitative advantage, not a normality or universality,
2) understanding of the nature of harmful gender stereotypes – the patterns of traits and preferences *a priori* attributed to individuals and restricting them, their origins and ways of impact,
3) detection of the above in school textbooks, acts of verbal and nonverbal communication, and media transmissions,
4) designing equality classes devoted to gender that develop mindfulness on individual differences between people, teach respect for different fields of human activity (work, housekeeping) and promote different patterns of success in life,
5) sensitivity and decisive response to any (even symbolic) socially sanctioned forms of gender-based violence in school life, and
6) motivating parents (especially "absent" fathers) to participate in the life of the school.

At this point it is worth pointing out that the results of sex-related psychological research and its interpretations do not constitute a coherent system, but rather a panorama of various, often conflicting positions heavily involved in ideological disputes.

[3] Ibidem, p. 69.

Next to the European Union requirements and the need to present the most current state of knowledge, the third factor, important in the design of the training, is the awareness of the problems among those taking part, i.e. teachers and parents. The available evidence suggests that in Polish society there prevails a belief in the lack of gender equality; however, it is accompanied by a low level of awareness of its barriers and concrete manifestations wherein the attitude of teachers their educators to gender is often conservative and reproduces stereotypical ideas and expectations.[4] Teachers are confident that they treat their students equally while they in fact systematically focus on the boys, treating them more harshly while girls are perceived as trustworthy and obedient. Teacher's messages stimulate passivity and conformism in girls, and independence, individualism and a greater degree of freedom in boys. In contrast to many EU countries, in Poland the theme of gender is not a part of teacher's training or professional development.[5]

2. THEORETICAL BACKGROUND OF TRAINING: SEX AND GENDER IN A PSYCHOLOGICAL PERSPECTIVE

Common beliefs on gender, established in culture, are not only rich in strong stereotypes and distorting simplifications, but are also significantly different from modern scientific models. On the one hand, human sex, in a popular opinion a binary category, and at the same time easy to recognize at first glance, is a complex scientific construct, multi–layered and dynamic. The "layers" in question are: genetic sex (a healthy person born with a certain system of sex chromosomes), hormonal (from the prenatal stage of development, reproductive glands produce hormones that determine secondary sexual characteristics, and according to some researchers, a specific gender–organization of the brain, although this theory has not been clearly established[6]), somatic (body structure, male or female in principle, yet these features are not divided with mathematical precision, and the ultimate nature of our sex is determined not only by biology, but also a number of culturally sanctioned auto–creational mechanisms), socio–cultural gender (in other words: the type of sexual or social role), and finally psychological gender or sex role (a distinctive system of

[4] Comp.: C. Magno, I. Silova, Teaching in transition. Examining school–based inequities in central/southeastern Europe and the former Soviet Union, International Journal of Educational Development, 27, 2007, p. 652; E. Górnikowska–Zwolak, Nauczycielskie koncepcje ról społecznych kobiety i mężczyzny – czynnik wzmacniający czy osłabiający szanse rozwojowe dziewcząt i chłopców?, [in:] Płeć i rodzaj w edukacji, Łódź, 2005, p. 85–91.

[5] A. Dzierzgowska, E. Rutkowska, Ślepa na płeć. Edukacja równościowa po polsku. Raport krytyczny, Fundacja Feminoteka, Warszawa, 2008, p. 79.

[6] S. Lipsitz Bem, Męskość, kobiecość. O różnicach wynikających z płci, GWP, Gdańsk, 2000, p. 35–37.

characteristics of a person and their severity, socially evaluated as feminine or masculine). Separate, but related to gender categories, are sexual orientation and gender identity (the sense of being a woman or a man).

Dynamism is mainly an attribute of the socio–cultural gender, described as genre and often understood as the totality of economic, social, political and cultural attributes and opportunities associated with being male and female. It is based on changes in the course of living, but also on the on– going negotiation of its manifestations in interactions. Harris notes the diversity of the standards and requirements adherent to the social role of a girl, teenager or a woman.[7] Each of us, by changing his/her social status, the environment or identifying with a new professional role, accents a variety of attributes assigned to our gender.

2.1. EVOLUTION OF THE VIEWS AND MEASUREMENT TOOLS IN GENDER PSYCHOLOGY

Research on the psychological differences between men and women have developed in the context of the emancipation of women and the feminist critique of patriarchal culture.

Initially, gender psychology, formed in accordance with the patriarchal division and opposition of the categories of masculinity and femininity, helped to create this image, accumulating evidence of the vast difference between male and female psychology. This difference, previously inferred from natural sources only, such as the construction of the brain or specificity of the physiology, justified the social limitations placed on women's access to education, or the incompetence of men in childcare, for example. This approach was reflected by the first tools measuring psychological gender, and femininity and masculinity were the extreme poles of a common continuum.[8] The results showed the test person as feminine, masculine, or undifferentiated. A high level of femininity for women and a high level of masculinity for men was considered the standard – everything else meant disorder. In the nascent feminist movement, different views on what type of gender portrayal would support the emancipation of women arose. Along with the feminist ideology, psychological theories also evolved – from the complete denial of earlier accented differences in experiencing the world, aptitudes and abilities, to re–recognizing them. The modern psychology of gender proves the existence of some statistical differences. Whereas feminist psychology intensively investigates how the social world of the West still favors a psychophysical structure typical for men by adapting the dominant culture, customs and mental health model (e.g. in psychology) to it. In the face of knowledge in its present state, we know now that men and women differ as a group much less, and as individuals within their biological

[7] J. Harris, Geny czy wychowanie?, Wyd. Czarna Owca, Warszawa, 2000, p. 243.

[8] S. Lipsitz Bem, op. cit., p. 103.

sex a lot stronger than assumed by the traditional views[9] (one could say here that "it was dreamed of by philosophers", because the views on the differences between the sexes are usually embarrassingly naive among recognized thinkers). Psychology also explores the specificity of women's and men's experiences connected to the primary and indelible difference, which is the difference of the flesh, especially the diversity of the reproductive function.

Common beliefs on female and male psyches are not only saturated with stereotypical images, but also the illusion of its natural origin and "normality". What's more, in the face of widespread changes in behavioral patterns and politically correct opinions proclaimed in the mass media, in the common reception the illusion of gender equality in modern culture, upbringing, education and work is being marked. This illusion is contradicted by empirical indicators of social inequality obtained in sociological research and surveys,[10] as well as qualitative analysis of the experience of modern men and women. The large discrepancy between common views on the image of sex and that obtained by this study could be the source of potential cognitive resistance and strong emotions accompanying discussions during equality training. It also means that it is necessary to organize experience and provide accurate arguments for the participants, showing the schematics and illusions of many assumptions.

2.2. FEMININITY AND MASCULINITY, OR COMMUNION AND CAUSAL TENDENCY?

Moreover, according to the views of some scholars,[11] the effective contribution of psychology to the weakening of the barriers of equality requires more than awareness and the disarming of harmful stereotypes. Schields and Bem state that what is needed is a "psychological revolution" – hence the abandonment of the categories of femininity and masculinity, considered as symptoms of psychological traits and emotional patterns, and tools for the "typification" of individuals, supporting the unequal conditions of their lives. What is this socially defined femininity/masculinity that reaches beyond the physical features? Every social division of masculinity and femininity is rooted in the traditional division of tasks within the family. In most cultures, "femininity", as a set of traits and interests, has a collective nature – tailored to caring for and controlling emotional needs of family members. And masculinity – the instrumental character – is geared to meet the needs of the family in the outside world. The "masculine" instrumental attitude is reflected in the orientation to achieve the

[9] J.S. Hyde, The gender similarities hypothesis, "American Psychologist" 2005, 60 (6), p. 581–592.

[10] Comp.: Krajowy System Monitorowania Równego Traktowania Kobiet i Mężczyzn. Raporty eksperckie, t. 1 i 2 (2006), Warszawa: Wydawnictwo Naukowe "Scholar", M. Grabowska (ed.), W drodze do Unii Europejskiej. Przewodniczka nie tylko dla kobiet. Fundacja im. Heinricha Bolla, Warszawa, 2002.

[11] S. Lipsitz Bem, op. cit., s. 184; S.A. Schields, Mówiąc od serca. Płeć i społeczny wymiar uczuć, Wyd. Literackie, Kraków, 2004, p. 235.

goal, while the "feminine" collective tendency is focused on interpersonal relationships and sensitivity, and the reactions and feelings of others. According to many authors,[12] what in Western culture we call feminine and masculine is in fact a development of two basic complementary tendencies, characteristic for all living organisms. One of them can be described as a causal tendency, both behavioral and selfish (agency). The second is responsible for building relationships with others and being sensitive to their reactions (communion). The behavioral tendency enables the organism to survive as an individual, and the communion tendency allows for integration with the environment. The first manifests itself in the protection of the self, emphasizing one's own identity, and the pursuit of expansion and competition. The manifestations of the other are altruism, the desire for contact and cooperation. Identifying causal orientation with masculinity and its social strengthening with males only, and the collective (communion) with femininity and its stimulation in women particularly, was somewhat adaptive in the culture of the past centuries. However, it has become a cumbersome limitation for individuals living today. The changes in society tend to decline the division of occupations or tasks for males and females. The functioning of women in the full spectrum of the world of work requires them to adopt the "causal" features – communicating assertively and promoting their achievements. The wave of emancipation causing the professional involvement of women initially entailed operation on "two levels" (both masculine and feminine), which soon turned out to be a "false path" of the feminist movement.[13] As life practice shows, the equality of men and women functioning in the world of work is only possible thanks to the making of a new "gender contract"[14] comprising social contracts and legal regulations allowing or even forcing spouses to share the housework. This is followed by the prevalent participation of men in the upbringing and nurturing of children, as well as new patterns of intimate–partner relationships assuming the loyal division of responsibilities and overt, effective communication. It requires subtle social skills and competent participation in domestic activities, traditionally regarded as "unmanly". A frame for the development of life competences free from the stereotypical constraints, preferably in the early stages of education, must be the equalization of the rank of career and the quality of the construction of close relationships. Henceforth the educators must believe that happiness and success in life can mean the fulfillment in each of these areas, regardless of gender.

An illustration of these "revolutionary" approaches is a new method of measuring psychological gender. The first change is the recognition of femi-

[12] Comp.: D. Bakan, The duality of human existence. Isolation and communion in Western man, Beacon Press, Chicago, 1966; C.G. Jung , O naturze kobiety, Brama, Poznań, 1992.

[13] Comp.: E. Badinter, Fałszywa ścieżka, W.A.B., Warszawa, 2005.

[14] Różnice w wynikach nauczania a płeć uczniów, op. cit., p. 21.

ninity and masculinity as two separate dimensions.[15] The subject of the examination can now diagnose both the level of femininity and masculinity. It is possible that one's results will show a typical psychological gender – that the concept of self is firmly adhered to the cultural pattern. It might also be that the result is characterized by high levels of both the femininity and masculinity psychological dimensions. Bem describes such cases as psychological androgyny and considers them part a modern model of optimal adaptation.[16] Unfortunately, most studies have not confirmed this view – the most adaptive, both in men and women consistently, is a high level of masculinity. In the modern Western world, characteristics and "causative" attitudes still provide better performance and lower levels of distress.[17] Another change is that the traditional notions of femininity, masculinity and androgyny are being gradually eliminated from the mental health discussions and swapped with concepts of the dependence or independence of the cultural patterns of gender.

This situation raises the question of whether the "typical", psychological gender patterns are the result of the duplication of archaic schemes through social learning. What is known about the biological determinants of "feminine" fragility and dependence, and the "male" desire to dominate or to indulge in violence? In the face of these complex requirements of modern life, if such conditions exist they are interesting rather as barriers to the adaptation of the individual than the natural justification for traditional gender roles. It is better to specify the area of biological determination and modify educational treatments accordingly than to "ideologically" deny the existing circumstances. If there are statistically significant differences between girls and boys in the area of psychological traits or predispositions, then – blind to these differences – the common education of both sexes could result in unequal effects.

As indicated by the results of empirical studies,[18] girls and boys, and then men and women (as groups), have different average levels of (at least) four mental functions: verbal ability (girls have a statistical advantage over boys), visualspatial ability, mathematical aptitude and level of activity and physical aggression (higher in groups of boys). In addition, studies show typical differences in the sensorial sensitivity (visual acuity greater in men, a higher sensitiv-

[15] S. Lipsitz Bem, op. cit., p. 116.

[16] Comp.: B. Lewandowska, Androgynia psychiczna jako model „zdrowej' płci psychologicznej człowieka, [in:] M. Reut (ed.), Człowiek, kultura, edukacja, t. 1, Wrocław, Wydawnictwo Politechniki Wrocławskiej, p. 89–99.

[17] J.S. Hyde, L.A. Frost, Metaanalizy w psychologii kobiety, [in:] B. Wojciszke (ed.), Kobiety i mężczyźni: odmienne spojrzenia na różnice, GWP, Gdańsk, 2002, p. 40.

[18] J. Miluska, Przyczyny różnic płciowych. Dylematy i rozstrzygnięcia, [in:] J. Miluska, P. Boski, Męskość – kobiecość w perspektywie indywidualnej i kulturowej, Wyd. IP PAN, Warszawa, 1999, p. 40.

ity to noise and less noise tolerance in women), non-verbal communication skills (higher in women), efficiency in the area of motility (mostly girls), hand-eye coordination (better for boys) and the differences in taste preferences. For the majority of the above-mentioned statistical considerations of gender differences, specificities in the functioning of the central nervous system and endocrine were detected. However, studies and meta-analysis also demonstrate the importance of the development of social reinforcement (parental, cultural, peer), social status or ethnicity. The reports indicating the possibility of reducing typical differences in the manner of early stimulation are crucial for the school's practices,[19] which means that it is possible to organize a teaching process in order to enhance typically "weaker" features in both sexes, e.g. support the development of mathematical skills in girls and stimulate the manual abilities and reading habits in boys. This type of action takes place in the educational systems of many EU countries and results in a systematic decrease of the differences in the results.

Additionally, typical temperamental differences (e.g. initially biologically determined) between men and women may reinforce the effectiveness of the social formation of gender. According to a study conducted with the use of the Cloninger[20] temperament test, men and women are different in the two – important predispositions conditioned by neurophysiology. Women systematically gain higher scores on tests of "harm avoidance" and "reward dependence". Avoiding injury is a tendency to inhibit the action in response to negative stimuli and is associated with the activity of neuropeptide serotonin. This dimension determines the high sensitivity of an individual to negative social signals. It is this tendency that can make most girls easier to discipline and teach "politeness" to, and thus limit their activity or aggression early. Hence, an illusion may arise that they are "by nature" more passive and gentle. Yet the dependence on the prize, associated with noradrenergic activity, is a tendency to maintain the behavior in response to a positive, especially social, reinforcement from outside. People with a high level of "addiction to awards" are defined as sympathetic individuals, ready to help others, dependent on support and acceptance. This feature also indicates susceptibility to excessive socialization and obedience to the pressures of others. Therefore, if such trends occur more intensely in girls/women than in boys/men, then they can cause closeness and acceptance starvation. Such girls/women display stronger community attitudes, at the same time being more sensitive to social impact. This results in the faster "absorption" of the rules of civility, relevance to the requirements, eager fulfillment of the orders in the family or school, and copy-

[19] Różnice w wynikach nauczania a płeć uczniów, op. cit., s. 81.

[20] J. Miettunen, J. Veijola, E. Lauronen, L. Kantojärvi, M. Joukamaa, Sex differences in Cloninger's temperament dimensions – a meta-analysis, "Comprehensive Psychiatry" 2007, Mar–Apr, 48(2), p. 161–169.

ing other models when a peer group or subculture becomes the dominant reference point.

It is easy to see that – the knowledge about the primarily biologically determined psychological differences – complicates the concept of educational activities that promote educational equality. This results in a differentiation of the treatment of both sexes, in order to not worsen the innate differences, and at the same time, through early training, supply the complementary skills. Such a situation requires respect for sensitivity to social punishment in the education of girls and boys with "typical" tempers, and a special emphasis on the formation of social competences – empathy and sensitivity to reactions. It does not end there as the tendencies in question are of a statistical nature, thus depending on the majority. Therefore, in addition to the typical majority, the population also entails a certain number of individuals with the characteristics typical for the opposite sex. Educational models should demonstrate sensitivity to the needs of those students who deviate from the typical pattern. Finally, an educator must carefully recognize the individuality of each child. Not being misled by the stereotypical images, one should exercise the pupil's competencies to their fullest possible extent, yet in a way that respects individual predispositions.

In order to meet these tasks, the parent and the teacher must reflect upon their own concept of education. Among other things, one must determine what kind of image of a healthy, well–functioning man underlies one's actions. One must face the question of whether – given an understanding that a man is a being of a variety of patterns of adaptation, sentenced to an active and intelligent search for the most appropriate personal formula for happiness – one respects the individuality of a pupil and shows them a different way of leading a good life, giving them a wide range of life skills, or whether one divides patterns of success and fulfillment in life into those appropriate for women and men. Or, perhaps, whether one adopts individualistic efficiency and rivalry as comprising the only model of health.

For it is here that we find the two cultural and political contexts of the equality training conducted at schools differing. The program of equalizing chances for men and women, carried out by the countries of the European Union, in addition to the related idea of a gender contract and development of broad life competences, is consistent with the assumptions of the feminist movement. However, in the post–communist countries where the ideology of capitalistic competitiveness dominates, the equalization of chances becomes a de facto promotion of the traditional male pattern, with professional and financial success as the only model of fulfilled living, and independence and entrepreneurship being the dominant dimensions of mental health for both men and women. Characteristics and life tasks traditionally considered "feminine" are valued low in consumer capitalism. In Polish schools, not only are the development of social competencies and the preparation for a family life denied to boys – as required by the model of equalizing chances – but are also frequently not developed at all.[21]

The elimination and neglect of the "PSHE" classes and universal sex education can be interpreted as an expression of depreciation of the traditionally "feminine" skills and problems. The school, like the reality in which it is embedded, is saturated with the feeling of rivalry and geared towards promoting individual achievements, frequently related to "shaping the appearances", instead of developing the skills necessary in private life. Schools are subjected to such expectations not only by the authorities, but also by parents and students. This is well illustrated by an example from school praxis, put forward during one of the equality workshops. Due to an observed decline of, formerly common, peer to peer support in the learning process, teachers at a certain school suggested a program for encouraging helpful behavior among children. At the beginning, the given help was not even to be selfless. In order to encourage it, a scoring system was introduced as positive reinforcement. Students responded very positively; however, the reactions of a few parents who had protested against wasting their children's time and energy on activities that are the teacher's responsibility, either in person or in writing, left the educators in a stupor.

3. 'THE SCHOOL AND THE SPIRIT OF INEQUALITY' – THE SIGNIFICANCE OF GENDER IN EDUCATION

The school, as an environment that shapes attitudes and skills, has a chance to be a place of effective disarmament of stereotypes and the formation of a new "gender contract" – mainly through the content of teaching and the principle of the equal and non-stereotyped treatment of sexes in the hidden program and in informal peer relations. It may be, however, also a place to reproduce schemes and reinforce social inequalities. This is done in at least two ways. The first possibility includes the generalization of the statistically more frequent characteristics of one sex. They are assigned to each particular individual, and by doing so give rise to rigid educational practices that limit choices and aspirations of the students and harm those who have less or none of the typical predispositions. The second way results in denying the existing differences in education, being "blind" to the problems of sex and having a low awareness of how the organization of the teaching process favors one of them.

[21] M. Wieczorek, K. Kucewicz, O (nie)wprowadzeniu powszechnej edukacji seksualnej, [in:] A. Dzierzgowska, E. Rutkowska, op. cit., p. 33–39.

3.1. THE SCHOOL PERPETUATING GENDER STEREOTYPES

If a woman wants to be something for someone, a man wants to be just "someone" – this is a maxim derived from the school textbook.[22] It is the wisdom of a calendar aphorism and a schematic differentiation, and yet it appears under the guise of scientific outlook, and may therefore be taken seriously by a young recipient searching for practical tips. Analysis of Polish school textbooks has revealed an abundance of verbally and nonverbally displayed stereotypes about gender–specific activities, aspirations, strengths and weaknesses of character and patterns of coping with emotions, often resulting in shockingly low levels of awareness of gender issues in their authors. The analysis of the already published teaching materials,[23] as well as examples from the media and popular culture, provide a rich exemplification, allowing the teacher, together with the participants, to explore the logic of stereotypes and reflect on the range of their negative impact. It is also worth showing the hidden assumptions which lay behind the stereotypical messages formulated by some teachers, e.g.: "I hope that the boys understood and the girls remembered". Reflecting on how the false stereotypes – creeping into the method of assessment, formulation of commands or student discipline – re–create reality is an important topic of training.

Why is the stereotypical message so dangerous in communicating with children? This is explained by the research showing their particular susceptibility to stereotypical perceptions of the social world, especially sex. Deaux and Kite write: "In order to cope with potentially impossible to understand amounts of information, people learn to improve their processing process by grouping people, objects and events into clear categories based on the similarity of the group members. Despite its effectiveness, this system is rich in all kinds of flaws".[24]

This definition shows the original source of the formation of gender stereotypes in the tendency to simplify reality, which is the nature of our knowledge. The less aware of the world we are and the less efficiently we use our minds, the more likely to resort to schemes we will be. This is why children, overwhelmed by the abundance of information and the rules that govern the world around them, are so eager to acquire the stereotypical, polarized gender models. The second reason for the demand of children and teens for gender stereotypes is a growing need to follow their peer groups being gradually stronger than the need to imitate their parents. As demonstrated by Harris,[25] from the

[22] M. Ryś, Wychowanie do życia w rodzinie. Książka dla młodzieży, CMPP–Ped MEN, Warszawa, 1999, p. 60.

[23] A. Wołosik, Edukacja do równości czy trening uległości? Czy polskie podręczniki respektują zasadę równości płci?, Stowarzyszenie „W stronę dziewcząt", Warszawa, 2009; R. Siemieńska (ed.), Portrety kobiet i mężczyzn w środkach masowego przekazu oraz podręcznikach szkolnych, Wyd. Naukowe „Scholar", Warszawa, 1997.

[24] K. Deaux, M. Kite, Stereotypy płci, [in:] B. Wojciszke, op. cit., p. 358.

[25] J. Harris, op. cit., p. 248.

moment when children begin to identify with a group they rigidly follow the rules. From the early formed feeling of being girl or boy comes a stereotypical perception of the unacceptable and required attributes and behaviors, no matter how egalitarian the attitudes of parents and teachers are. Therefore, the projects focused on "preparing for life" proposed by feminist psychologists have been ineffective. These concepts implied the protection of children from exposure to the gender models and the consequent presentation of behaviors alternative to stereotyping by the parents. The formation of a self–concept, free from sexual patterns in children, was unsuccessful. The actions resulted only in a feeling of confusion and disorientation.[26] From the moment the child understands that it is a boy or a girl, in fact throughout its whole adolescence, it is very interested in all the attributes of its kind. That is why it is very susceptible to stereotypes reproduced in media, primitive entertainment or educational content. The consequence of this susceptibility is the typification of both emotional expression and communication[27] style and deformation of aesthetics (e.g. monotone pink clothes and accessories for younger girls). This also causes the spread of stereotypes that threatens the health of girls (e.g. anorexia through copying standards of female attractiveness) and boys (e.g. drinking themselves into a stupor as a form of male initiation). Teachers and educators should therefore understand the developmentally normal (and very important for building a position in the group) need to be "typical" girl or boy, while remaining aware of the level of absorption of the stereotypical messages among the minors, as a factor for the risk of disorder. The task of the parents and teachers is to develop a reflective and critical attitude in children and adolescents, especially towards primitive and harmful stereotypes.

3.2. THE SCHOOL AS BLIND TO GENDER

As indicated by Moir and Jessel,[28] denying the statistical differences between the sexes may contribute to (in the course of education) favoring one of them or underestimating the specific problems of the other. For example, at the stage of initial training the school apparently favors the female sex, requiring from all children activities in which the girls statistically do better. Patiently sitting and listening with attention, coordination and motility used in drawing and writing, verbal expressiveness, and quiet and peaceful behavior means it is more difficult for a typical boy to master these tasks (e.g. a first–year student who, at this stage, often causes trouble and is undervalued). However, after a few years of school training, boys master these skills and "catch up" with girls. Meanwhile, visualspatial thinking, spontaneously practiced by boys from the

[26] Comp.: E. Badinter, XY – tożsamość mężczyzny, W.A.B. Warszawa, 1993, p. 148.

[27] Comp.: S.A. Shields, op. cit., s. 175–213.

[28] A. Moir, D. Jessel, Płeć mózgu. O prawdziwej różnicy między mężczyzną a kobietą, PIW, Warszawa, 1993, p. 34.

early stages of development (e.g. with playground construction games) and less stimulated in girls, appears only in the higher grades of primary school at the stage where it is harder to stimulate the growth of this ability. The girls, confronted with tasks requiring spatial imagination, can experience significant difficulties that reduce their sense of efficiency. This is especially because the situation is often accompanied – as communicated by teachers more or less explicitly – by an expectation of the lower performance of girls in maths and, as frequently reported in the research, attributing their success to effort rather than ability.[29] Therefore – paradoxically – girls can be rated higher in Natural Sciences while steadily losing faith in their abilities.

Newsweek magazine published an article entitled: "Today, education favors girls",[30] describing the phenomenon of the formation of private, male schools. The author points out that in such schools it is easier to include the dominant needs and characteristics of this sex in an account of the process of learning. The lower sensitivity of boys for various bans and disapprovals is the norm and there is no comparison with "polite girls", resulting in the opinion of their being bullies or the suspicion of psychomotor hyperactivity. More time is therefore spent on sport activities. It is assumed in advance that the implementation of social skills, less forced by innate factors, will require systematic efforts. The author refers to the words of a prominent developmental psychologist: "In Poland, there is no talk about how much boys are different from girls. It's a taboo, politically incorrect topic. I think that some may believe that the differences between the sexes disappear if we pretend they do not exist … The current educational system 'prefers girls' for a simple reason – because it prefers politeness. In a large mass, girls are more obedient and more focused on cooperation. It is easier to lead them as a group and admonition brings faster results"[31]. Perhaps it is so one can still look for an analogy to the phenomenon described by Moir and Jessel. Again, the girls who are usually considered more polite and have better behavior grades are seemingly favored. But is it not that the school, disciplining boys, requiring them to restrain their impulses and behave politely, forces the development of new skills safe for the personality of the "typical" boy who, because of temperamental predispositions, has a higher resistance to social punishment? In the same situation, "typical" girls and boys with "untypical" psychological construction for their gender become even more polite in the school environment. They don't develop such complementary competencies as resistance to negative social signals or emphasize one's individuality; on the contrary, school strengthens the lack of assertiveness and introduces the risk of over–socialization. One can assume that girls have a temper "not matching" the requirements of the school.

[29] R. Unger, Seksizm: perspektywa zintegrowana, [in:] B. Wojciszke (ed.), op. cit., p. 265.

[30] K. Święcicka, Dziś edukacja faworyzuje dziewczynki, "Newsweek" 2009, nr 18.

[31] Ibidem, p. 14.

It is worth paying attention to the psychological effects of the physical differences. Boys, statistically stronger and more physically active, develop more quickly in this area. The girls develop mental abilities quicker and mature sexually much earlier, which are of great importance to their way of being and experiencing the world. This is also the main argument put forward by opponents of co–educational schools in which peers operating at different levels of development are commonly measured, and which contributes to the production of intellectual helplessness and anti–school attitudes in mentally "younger" children (usually boys).

To sum up, the fact that children have different predispositions, which cannot be deduced *a priori* from their biological sex and at the same time require additional training, is another argument that supports the individualized learning process and non–schematic treatment of students. Magno and Silova propose replacing the concept of gender equality with the category of "gender fairness", assuming the "guarantee of equitable outcomes, regardless of gender".[32]

This attempt to organize topics which are important for gender education enforces the choice of training content. The described subjects motivate the non–stereotyped attitudes and practices among teachers and parents. Firstly, it is the knowledge about the change and customization of patterns of optimal adaptation to life that should be included in education programs. Secondly, it is the awareness that children are not a blank slate waiting for upbringing and education, and that their predispositions are certainly related to gender. However, this relationship has a merely statistical character, which means that biological sex does not provide one with simple guidelines for the process of socialization and a recipe for life fulfillment. And finally, although customs and lifestyles have long ago changed the traditional, rigid gender roles, children and young people have a naturally strong willingness to absorb stereotypes and submit to them. It is adults' goal to avoid such patterns in education as the thoughtless categorizing of students and routinely dividing the sexes, sending messages reinforcing stereotypical limitations, and schematically, "ideologically" denying differences. Education should also refer to the harmful stereotypes used by consumer culture, allowing for criticism, reflection and courage to go beyond the set patterns. The primary task of training for teachers and parents is to propose and test a "different perspective" – the non–schematic, complex recognition of the issues of gender. This can motivate a systematic change in practice and translate into effects releasing schools from stereotypes. Such practices include identifying stereotypes in various cultural contents, encouraging a pupil to reflect on them and give comments, counterexamples and raising discussions. Another practice is to observe one's communication with the child and release it from the reaction of surprise, disapproval or fear when

[32] C. Magno, I. Silova, op. cit., p. 649.

they manifest constructive behavior and reactions associated with the opposite sex, or do not show preferences associated with the scheme of gender.

4. PSYCHOLOGICAL TRAINING FOR TEACHERS AND PARENTS AS A FORM OF ADULT EDUCATION: METHODOLOGY AND PROGRESS OF THE MEETINGS

The specificity of educational actions involving adults is the intentional search for knowledge that is useful for them in everyday activities.[33] In order to ensure that the theoretical knowledge presented during training is absorbed, it must refer to direct experience and be seen as useful, allowing for a better understanding of oneself and one's life's tasks and solving important problems. Therefore, the demonstration of how the non–stereotypical, free from schemas understanding of gender problems supports the perception of a child's needs and daily educational practice helps to promote equality better than the simplified agitation, engaging all the differences between the sexes as a cultural illusion, and women as victims of patriarchy. This persuasive type of message can (sometimes) be mistrusted, especially in Polish society, being marked by the historical trauma of propaganda.

The plan of the "equality" training is based on the adult learning model formulated by Kolb[34] and including, for each introduced issue, four stages:

4.1. EXPERIENCE

At this stage, the trainer examines the experiences of the participants and seeks those who prove the validity of the problems, or (as an experiment) creates a new experience for the participants. The initial part of the equality training is usually an exercise aiming to raise awareness of the participants – both teachers and parents – that stereotypical images of male and female personality penetrate reality and that in their educational practices they relate to them in some way. Below, an experiment with a dual function in addition to the implementation of the training's aim will be described. This is being used to measure the attitude towards gender stereotypes in trained groups. At the beginning of the meeting, participants are invited, as parents, to participate in the questionnaire–survey, presented as "concerning parental attitudes and serving scientific purposes" (if someone is not a parent the task is to address the questions to an imaginary child of a chosen gender). In order to create the questionnaire, a Polish adaptation of the inventory for studying psychological gender[35] was

[33] Comp.: A. Andrzejczak, Projektowanie i realizacja szkoleń, PWE, Warszawa, 2010.

[34] D. Kolb, Experiential learning: Experience as the Source of Learning and Development, Englewood Cliffs, Prentice Hall, New Jersey, 1984.

[35] A. Kuczyńska, Płeć psychologiczna, podstawy teoretyczne, dane empiryczne oraz narzędzia pomiaru, "Przegląd Psychologiczny", 2, p. 237–247.

modified. Two sets of features identified as the most masculine and feminine (in the social context) are mixed and supplemented with several neutral features. The original question of the inventory was changed to "Below, 30 features that characterize people are listed. Mark how much you would like to support them in your child's development". Considering each of the characteristics, parents were asked to evaluate on the five–point scale the extent to which they would like to develop the features in their children. The completing of the questionnaire was followed by a brief discussion about the meaning of basic concepts such as femininity, masculinity and gender equality. Then, the design of the questionnaire was explained and the participants were presented with a list of "feminine" and "masculine" features. Participants could summarize their numerical results on the scale F (feminine) and M (masculine) – that is, figure out how much they would like to develop the personality of their children in accordance with the cultural pattern. This is done by first comparing and discussing the results in small groups and then by comparing the scores with the average results of the whole group (after counting). It is not an assessment of "normality" of parental aspirations by reference to the average result, but an experience of carefully looking at the important dimensions and patterns of human emotional reactions that are attributable to a certain sex in our culture. Delicacy and care are considered as "feminine", while a sense of humor, the desire to dominate and appetite for success as "male". This is accompanied by the following reflections on the different attributes: to which extent do I perceive them to be adaptive and would I like to reinforce them in my child? Do I strongly expect behaviors that are consistent with the gender stereotype or would I give the child traits that belong to both schemes? Sharing these thoughts in subgroups in a natural way leads to a discussion on the origin and function of psychological differences between the sexes. This is then the transition to the second stage of the cycle.

4.2. REFLECTING ON THE EXPERIENCE

By moderating and summarizing the discussion, the trainer helps in the analysis of the experience, realizing the assumptions behind it and drawing conclusions. On the basis of their own reflections on assumptions, participants engage more in the introduced educational problems and questions. What is the origin of gender stereotypes? To what extent does the psychological profiling of men and women serve or continue to serve their adaptation to social reality? Participants are free to decide whether to entrust the result of the test to the group and would like to support the development of the child's personality in a way more or less consistent with the scheme. The second phase of training is usually a stormy debate, not only about the patterns of gender roles but also the broader concepts like the definition of mental health and personality determinants of happiness. There is also the usual question of whether psychology as a science has empirical knowledge and theoretical models that can help to sort out these questions and reflections.

4.3. THE INTRODUCTION OF THEORETICAL KNOWLEDGE

At this stage, the trainer confronts the experiences and discussion results with reliable scientific knowledge, presented in an interesting way. The presented theoretical models and conclusions of the research, organizing the overall content, are studies on sex differences and their biological origins and susceptibility to social influence, the process of the formation of stereotypes and the ways they generate inequality. At this stage, the reflection on masculinity and femininity is treated as two social/collective and causal aspects of the human occurring in individual and varied proportions. In the next stage, the participants can see if the obtained levels of awareness and absorbed knowledge will help them to distinguish the statistically important trends from limiting stereotypes, identifying the latter and eliminating them from the practice of education.

4.4. TESTING THE ACQUIRED KNOWLEDGE IN PRACTICE

At this stage, the trainer offers participants exercises, during which they can apply the knowledge in analyzing and solving practical problems, identify the discussed phenomena and at the same time reflecting on them and discussing them. Practical exercises are usually performed in small groups that analyze the patterns of sexual examples taken from textbooks, texts, culture and everyday family situations. Participants decide to what extent these patterns can adversely affect the concept of self and the aspirations of children, and together create alternative ideas. Exercises also include designing the equality classes directed at students. The subjects of the classes are gender differences and stereotypes, causal and social competences development and the validity of both of aspects. The task of the trainer is to familiarize teachers with the range of materials that can help in the preparation of such activities at different stages of development.[36] The discussed sequence of steps repeats in a single educational meeting that introduces more themes, such as gender–based violence or specific behavioral problems associated with growing girls and boys. Training, as a whole, also includes a summary and closure element which aims to enable participants to formulate feedback on their internal states, mood, raised reflections and related content.

[36] E. Majewska, E. Rutkowska et al., Równa szkoła – edukacja wolna od dyskryminacji. Poradnik dla nauczycielek i nauczycieli, Dom Współpracy Polsko–Niemieckiej, Gliwice, 2008; A. Wołosik, E. Majewska, Napastowanie seksualne. Głupia zabawa czy poważna sprawa?, Difin, Warszawa, 2011; S. Buregren, Mała książka o feminizmie, Jacek Santorski & Co Agencja Wydawnicza, Warszawa, 2007; http://www.wstronedziewczat.org.pl, www.gender.pl

4.5. THE SPECIFICITY OF TRAINING AIMED AT PARENTS

Because Polish teachers are not trained in issues related to gender equality, they cannot provide substantive support to parents in this regard. In some EU countries the education about equality – even at the planning level – involves cooperation with parents. For example, in France, the Convention of 2006 states the avoidance of the connection of professional aspirations with the gender scheme "requires management of activities for young people, students, and parents – the whole education community".[37] Whereas in Portugal, parents are enrolled in the health education (including sex education) of students.[38] Equality, training performed with the involvement of parents is still a rarity in the Polish education, but – as demonstrated by the already carried out meetings and their evaluations – can be useful and effective. It is conducted similarly to the teacher training discussed here. Less space is devoted to the analysis of stereotypes in textbooks, concentrating on those that stiffen the division of responsibilities in the family and the principles of socialization of girls and boys. A specific topic (for the meeting with parents), introduced on the base of a Kolb's four–stage model – from sharing parenting experiences to new concepts of psychological applications – are traditional and contemporary models of fatherhood and motherhood and the possibilities of the division of responsibilities between parents.[39]

5. PARENTS TOWARDS THE GENERIC TYPIFICATION OF CHILDREN – RESULTS OF THE STUDY

Surveys examining the association of educational attitudes and gender schemas, completed by parents and teachers, have been subjected to a preliminary study. The study group is hardly representative for a wider population of Polish parents. The group also lacks a gender balance (108 women, 48 men). Thus, the results indicate only the extent to which the participants of the equality trainings (4 groups of teachers and 4 groups of parents) want their children to develop both stereotypically "feminine" and "masculine" characteristics, and how groups of mothers and fathers differ in this matter. The data is compiled from the properly completed questionnaires of the participants who referred the questions to girls or boys between the ages of 1 month and 18 years. Therefore, the results of 156 questionnaires were taken into account, of which 108

[37] Różnice w wynikach nauczania a płeć uczniów, op. cit., p. 70.

[38] Ibidem.

[39] Comp.: M. Sikorska, Być rodzicem we współczesnej Polsce. Nowe wzory konfrontacji z rzeczywistością, W.U.W., Warszawa, 2009; A. Pobojewska, Edukacja rodziców. Szkoła komunikacji międzypokoleniowej. Podręcznik dla trenerów, Wyd. WSHE w Łodzi, Łódź, 2006.

were fulfilled by mothers and 48 by fathers. Table 1 below presents the mean scores of scales F and M for all participants, indicating the emphasis on the typically female and male characteristics in the upbringing of boys and girls.

Table 1. The average values of F and M scales, indicating the degree of emphasis on typical patterns of femininity and masculinity in the education of girls and boys

Child sex	Average values of F and M scale	
	F	M
Girls	46	42
Boys	40	48

The results of the parents of boys and girls were statistically analyzed using the Mann–Whitney U test and for both scales the importance of the differences was demonstrated. Thus, in the examined group of parents, the expected level of femininity in daughters is significantly higher, and the level of masculinity is significantly lower than that of sons. Parents as a group tend to form the personalities of their children in accordance with the cultural pattern.

Does the sex of the parents affect their attitude towards the gender typification of children? Table 2 presents the mean scores of scales F and M, separately for mothers and fathers, listed by child's sex.

Table 2. The average values of F and M scales, indicating the degree of emphasis on typical patterns of femininity and masculinity by mothers and fathers in the education of girls and boys

	Mothers (n=108)		**Mothers in total**	**Fathers (n=48)**		**Fathers in total**
	Girls	Boys		Girls	Boys	
Scale "F"	45	41	43	48	38	43
Scale "M"	42	48	45	42	48	45

The statistical analysis (Mann–Whitney U Test), designed to compare the mean scores of scales F and M obtained by mothers and fathers of girls and boys, showed no statistical significance between these groups. Therefore, in this study the sex of parents seems to have no impact on the level of emphasis on gender patterns in the education of their children.

However, the results were also translated on the types of the child psychological gender expected by the parents. Because the original test questionnaire for measuring of the psychological gender was not standardized, and the individual results were evaluated in reference to the average results of the group for the feminine and masculine scale, this research was conducted in the same way. Setting high scores on both scales, the average value of F and M in the whole group was adopted as the norm (43 for the scale F, 45 for the scale M). In this way, the proportional image of the part in the group of mothers and fathers was obtained. Table 3 below shows what part of the surveyed group of mothers and fathers would like to shape the characteristics and behavior of their children in conformity with the typical (feminine for girls, masculine for boys) gender schema, and what part considers a more adaptive androgynous pattern (male and female characteristics in the high intensity in children of both sexes), crossed (standard "male" for girls and "feminine" for boys) and undifferentiated (the mild features of both schemes).

Table 3. Attitudes of parents towards the gender typification of their children, defined in terms of the "expected" psychological gender

	Mothers (n=108)	Fathers (n=48)	In total
Expected PP Girls	n = 53	n=23	n=76
typical (high F, low M)	32% n=17	39% n=9	34% n=26
androgynous (high F, high M)	26% n=14	30% n=7	28% n=21
crossed (high M, low F)	25% n=13	17% n=4	22% n=17
undifferentiated (low F, low M)	17% n=9	14% n=3	16% n=12
Expected PP Boys	n=55	n=25	n= 80
typical (high M, low F)	51% n=28	40% n=10	48% n=38
androgynous (high F, high M)	18% n=10	24% n=6	21% n=17
crossed (high F, low M)	18% n=10	12% n=3	14% n=11
undifferentiated (low F, low M)	13% n=7	24% n=6	17% n=14

As shown in table 3, the largest group of parents, both mothers and fathers, expects a typical pattern in girls and boys, called here a psychological gender (consistent with gender stereotype). However, in the group of fathers this expectation appears equally often towards daughters and sons, while in the group of mothers of boys the emphasis on the typical pattern of gender is significantly more numerous (51%) than in the group of mothers of daughters (32%). On the other hand, half of the parents of daughters expects them to have a high level of masculinity in the standard androgynous form (28%) or crossed (22%), while only 36% of parents want to strengthen the high level of femininity in their sons. One can say that in the group of parents, especially mothers, there is a tendency to favor the male characteristics pattern. Half of the responding mothers declared that a boy has to be typically male. Also, half of the mothers of daughters would like to develop a high level of male characteristics in their offspring. As discussed earlier, this trend perhaps reflects the understanding of gender equality through the development of the personality of girls and boys in the "masculine" direction as causal and instrumental. Parents are guided by the higher adaptability of the male model in the world, and that is still far from equal.

The trends shown in the mentioned study are prevalence of educational attitudes consistent with gender stereotype and – especially in the group of mothers – the predominance of the male model in the education of girls, requiring verification in a representative group of parents. In groups of the participants of the described trainings, the following study, carried out during the introduction meeting dedicated to gender equality – shows the presence of two psychological barriers to equality: the stereotypical perception of gender and the preference for the masculine aspect in education.

REFERENCES

Badinter E., Fałszywa ścieżka, W.A.B., Warszawa, 2005.
Badinter E., XY tożsamość mężczyzny, W.A.B., Warszawa, 1993.
Bem Lipsitz S., Męskość, kobiecość. O różnicach wynikających z płci, GWP, Gdańsk, 2000.
Brannon L., Psychologia rodzaju. Kobiety i mężczyźni: podobni czy różni, GWP, Gdańsk, 2002.
Buczkowski A., Dwa różne światy, czyli jak socjalizuje się dziewczynkę i chłopca, [in:] Od kobiety do mężczyzny i z powrotem. Rozważania o płci w kulturze, J. Brach-Czaina (ed.), Trans Humana, Białystok, 1997.
Buregren S., Mała książka o feminizmie, Jacek Santorski & Co Agencja Wydawnicza, Warszawa, 2007.
Chybicka A., Kosakowska-Berezecka N., Między płcią a rodzajem, Impuls, Kraków, 2010.
Dzierzgowska, A., Rutkowska, E., Ślepa na płeć. Edukacja równościowa po polsku. Raport krytyczny, Fundacja Feminoteka, Warszawa, 2008.
Harris, J., Geny czy wychowanie?, Wyd. Czarna Owca, Warszawa, 2000.
Jones, L., Moore, R., Równość szans. Program szkolny i przedmiot, [in:] Z. Kwieciński (ed.), Nieobecne dyskursy, vol. V, Wyd. UMK, Toruń, 1997.
Kolb, D., Experiential learning: Experience as the Source of Learning and Development, Englewood Cliffs, Prentice Hall, New Jersey, 1984.
Kuczyńska, A., Płeć psychologiczna, podstawy teoretyczne, dane empiryczne oraz narzędzia pomiaru, "Przegląd Psychologiczny", 2.
Lewandowska, B., Androgynia psychiczna jako model "zdrowej" płci psychologicznej człowieka, [in:] Reut M. (ed.), Człowiek, kultura, edukacja, vol. 1, Wrocław, Wydawnictwo Politechniki Wrocławskiej.
Magno, C., Silova, I., Teaching in transition. Examining school-based inequities in central/southeastern Europe and the former Soviet Union, "International Journal of Educational Development" 2007, 27.
Majewska, E., Rutkowska, E., Równa szkoła – edukacja wolna od dyskryminacji. Poradnik dla nauczycielek i nauczycieli, Dom Współpracy Polsko-Niemieckiej, Gliwice, 2008.
Mazurkiewicz, G., Kształcenie dziewcząt i chłopców. Naturalny porządek, nierówność czy dyskryminacja, Centrum Edukacji Obywatelskiej, Kraków, 2005.
Miettunen, J., Veijola, J., Lauronen, E., Kantojärvi, L., Joukamaa, M., Sex differences in Cloninger's temperament dimensions – a meta-analysis, "Comprehensive Psychiatry" 2007, Mar-Apr, 48(2).
Miluska, J., Boski, P., Męskość – kobiecość w perspektywie indywidualnej i kulturowej, Wyd. IP PAN, Warszawa, 1999.
Miluska,, J., Psychologia płci jako wyzwanie dla edukacji, [in:] J. Brzeziński, L. Witkowski (red.), Edukacja wobec zmiany społecznej, Wyd. Edytor, Toruń, 1994.
Moir, A., Jessel, D., Płeć mózgu. O prawdziwej różnicy między mężczyzną a kobietą, PIW, Warszawa, 1993.
Pankowska, D., Wychowanie i role płciowe, GWP, Gdańsk, 2005.

Pobojewska, A., Edukacja rodziców. Szkoła komunikacji międzypokoleniowej. Podręcznik dla trenerów, WSHE w Łodzi, Łódź, 2006.
Shields , S. A., Mówiąc od serca. Płeć i społeczny wymiar uczuć, Wydawnictwo Literackie, Kraków, 2004.
Siemieńska, R. (ed.), Portrety kobiet i mężczyzn w środkach masowego przekazu oraz podręcznikach szkolnych, Wyd. Naukowe "Scholar", Warszawa, 1997.
Sikorska, M., Być rodzicem we współczesnej Polsce. Nowe wzory konfrontacji z rzeczywistością, W.U.W., Warszawa, 2009.
Wojciszke, B. (ed.), Kobiety i mężczyźni: odmienne spojrzenia na różnice, GWP, Gdańsk, 2002.
Wołosik, A., Edukacja do równości czy trening uległości? Czy polskie podręczniki respektują zasadę równości płci?, Stowarzyszenie "W stronę dziewcząt", Warszawa, 2009.
Wołosik, A., Majewska, E., Napastowanie seksualne. Głupia zabawa czy poważna sprawa?, Difin, Warszawa, 2011.

Bożena Matyjas
Jan Kochanowski University in Kielce

MEDIATION: A METHOD OF CONFLICT RESOLUTION IN THE SCHOOL ENVIRONMENT

ABSTRACT

The increasing number of different conflicts in modern schools have provided a challenge for educators. There are different types and sources of conflicts experienced at school. The most common seem to be student – student and student – teacher disagreements. One of the problem–solving strategies is mediation, a technique of soft intervention. Mediators show impartiality, respect and empathy to the parties. Educators, teachers, head teachers as well as students who received training in problem–solving skills can act as mediators. The purpose of mediation is to help two parties resolve their dispute with a mutually acceptable agreement. It should be emphasized that participation in mediation is typically voluntary which helps parties reach an agreement. The purpose of this chapter is to distinguish and discuss school–based conflict and present mediation as a method to manage and resolve disputes.

KEYWORDS: communication, education, mediation, school, school–based conflict.

INTRODUCTION

Living and functioning within society, people create different interpersonal relationships. As individuals they have to coexist and cooperate in order to accomplish their goals or plans and achieve their dreams. The school seems to be a place where students, teachers and parents meet to take up various activities for the pupils, at the same time meeting their own needs.

In the process of teaching and education, complex relationships are developed through interpersonal interactions between pupils, teachers and parents. In society, people are not alike in their nature, attitudes, levels of education, values, interest and aspirations. These differences among the group may cause tension and lead to conflict (Moore, 2009, pp. 31–32).

CONFLICT: ITS DEFINITION, CAUSES AND MANAGEMENT STRATEGIES

The word "conflict", from the Latin *conflictus*, denotes fighting (synonyms: disagreement, struggle, clash). In human society, conflict refers to a struggle or a clash of two (or more) individuals resulting from: 1) incompatible or opposing needs, drives and wishes or 2) antithetical value systems (Gordon, 2004, p. 195).

Conflict is a situation in which one or two parties attempt to frustrate the other's goals and needs attainment. Conflict also means a perceived divergence of interest. Common sources of interpersonal conflicts are differences in:

- attitudes,
- interests,
- needs,
- and expectations (Gordon, 2004, p. 195).

Conflict always involves such elements as parties, different causes and types (Moore, 2009, p. 76). Christopher Moore identified causes and types of conflict commonly known as The Circle of Conflict based on five categories: 1) values 2) relationships 3) information or data 4) interests and 5) structure that are typical for every person (ibid. p. 76).

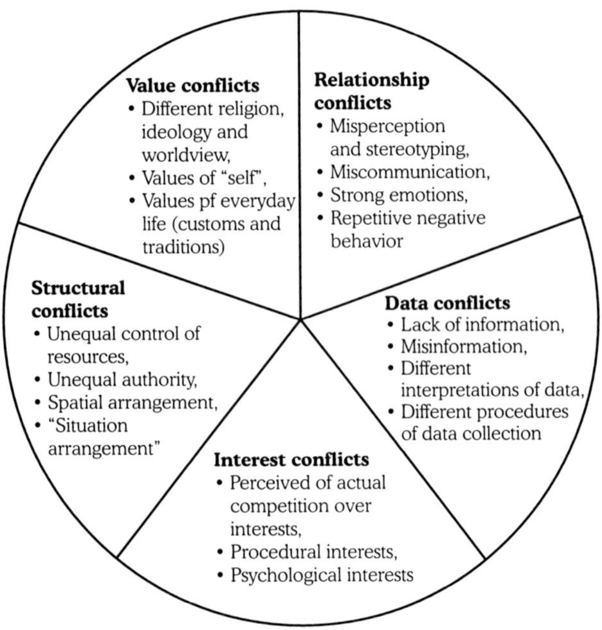

Figure 1. The Circle of Conflict – causes.
Source: M. Kuszyk, Koło konfliktu, available at: http://www.kuszyk-mediacje.pl/procedury1.php,on 10.04.2010.

Conflicts typically occur in different areas and are caused by the following factors:

1. Value conflict arises over actual or perceived differences in values or differing standards on the evaluation of ideas or behaviors;
2. Data conflict, which involves lack of information, as well as incomplete or wrong data, results from disrupting information (sender – receiver) and causes misinformation, lack of information or information delay, manipulation or withholding of information that may lead to relationship problems;
3. Relationship conflict results from poor communication or miscommunication and strong emotions; inaccurate or incomplete perceptions or stereotypes of others as well as repetitive negative behavior are common causes of relationship conflicts;
4. Structural conflict is caused by unequal or unfair distributions of power and resources, unequal control or authority, time constraints, as well as geographical or environmental factors that hinder proper communication and cooperation contributing to structural conflict;
5. Interest conflict is caused by competition over perceived or actual incompatible needs when one party believes that the needs of an opponent must be sacrificed to satisfy its own needs. At school, interest–based conflict occurs primarily over psychological issues such as unsatisfied needs, e.g. the desire for participation, respect and success, and perceptions of trust and fairness (Moore, 2004, p. 76).

Interpersonal conflict can also have a positive side that promotes positive changes and development. The analysis of specialist literature proves that conflict may lead to the following positive changes:

- The motivation of the conflict parties increases. The differences between the sides of conflict may increase their involvement in task accomplishment;
- The conflict may stimulate human development as it drives individuals to find innovative solutions by looking for new ideas;
- The conflict can contribute to improving self– and partner–awareness; it gives the chance to identify partner's needs, important issues and objectives. This knowledge seems to be indispensable for cooperation in order to achieve goals;
- The positive conflict resolution may increase confidence in the former opponent and gives the feeling of mutual understanding; finding positive solutions may bring conflict parties closer to each other and consequently improve problem–solving skills;
- If conflict resolution satisfies the expectations of the parties, it creates favorable conditions for the sense of justice or fairness which can motivate conflict parties to help others;
- The conflict can be an early warning sign of problems in an educational institution concerning, for example, its structure, or exchanging or sharing information.

Unfortunately, school authorities receive warning signs of the situations that need to be changed when conflict already exists or even arises.

Lack of or poor conflict management skills may lead to an increase in negative emotions which:

- create tensions and anxiety, and disorganise and delay work; all the parties involved tend to suffer from the effects of unresolved conflict;
- cause stress among pupils who are exposed to negative emotions; this may lead to learning difficulties, anger, aggressive (hidden or open) behavior; avoiding confrontation, as well as emotional escape from problems or difficulties will not bring about conflict resolution and negative emotions will not disappear;
- emotional tension can result in additional problems such as hostility or reluctance that hinder communication and cooperation within a group; such a situation may exist until conflict is resolved or conflict arises.

Taking the above into consideration, it is necessary to prevent conflict between pupils; that is, to eliminate factors which directly lead to possible conflict situations. It should be emphasized that this is one of the most significant tasks of the modern school for resolving conflict when it arises.

Conflict typically proceeds through different phases. The handling of conflict requires awareness of its various developmental stages. To describe the conflict process Louis Pondy (Słaboń, 1995, p. 19) identified five distinct but interrelated stages (or phases):

1. Latent conflict
2. Perceived conflict
3. Felt conflict
4. Manifest conflict
5. Conflict aftermath.

Although each type of conflict is different, its particular stages tend to be interrelated. Different kinds of conflict are characterized by various factors. In short-term conflicts the successive phases develop so quickly that they can sometimes hardly be identified (unless the division into particular conflict phases is arbitrary). On the other hand, in long-term conflicts transition between particular stages tends to be imperceptible (which is a different type of difficulty compared with short-term conflicts). It is worth noticing that the above mentioned types of social conflict can be recognized as various phases of the same process. This is illustrated by the division into latent and manifest (open) conflicts. It frequently happens that latent conflict initially occurs as a kind of introductory phase to be further developed into open conflict within the conflict process. Various types of conflict can be interrelated.

David J. Lieberman, in *Sztuka rozwiązywania konfliktów* (2004, p. 27), identifies various sources of conflict as filtered through their psychological mechanisms. According to Lieberman, conflict proceeds through four different phases:

1) an unexpected situation occurs;
2) as a result, control of the situation is lost;
3) an individual loses their sense of freedom and becomes dependent, which results in fear or anxiety;
4) fear or anxiety releases anger which not only compensates for the loss of control, but also conceals such emotions as envy, shame or guilt.

School–based conflict involves two types of conflicts:

1) intrapersonal conflict refers to the discord that occurs within an individual when a person internally argues with themselves and has trouble choosing between two or more goals; pupils often experience ideological conflicts, as well as conflicts concerning their future life or career;
2) interpersonal or group conflict, also called external conflict, refers to the disputes that arise between individuals; they may be directly fighting against each other, or may be opponents competing for the same goal. This kind of struggle happens between at least two interdependent parties who perceive incompatible goals, insufficient resources, and interference from others in achieving their goals (EP XXI w., 2003, p. 74). This conflict can be illustrated by the choice of the form/school captain, where only one person can be selected from among a group of several candidates.

Interpersonal conflict can refer to role and value conflicts. "The conflict of role often occurs within pupil teams where different attitudes hinder establishing proper relationships and at the same time facilitate arising interpersonal conflict. Pupils can argue about ideology, orientation, way of life, morals and values, as well as attitudes towards other peer groups" (Encyklopedia pedagogiczna, 1997, p. 286). According to W. Dobrołowicz (1996, p. 12), conflict occurs in the situation of intentional, contradictory plans, intentions, activities etc. performed not only by one, two or more persons, but also by social groups. Conflict is the natural struggle between individuals over differences in their interests, beliefs and values.

There are three basic categories of school–based conflicts which occur between school community members:

- teacher – student: the most frequent and varied, and can take different forms;
- teacher – teacher: typical workplace conflicts;
- teacher – parent: these are happening more and more frequently and represent high proportion of all school–based conflicts (Stachyrska, 1996, p. 34).

The categories of conflict described above refer to the whole school community including parents who more frequently participate in school life.

The problem of school–based conflict has been discussed by many researchers. Where people meet, communicate and interact, sooner or later differences between them occur and inevitably lead to conflict. Along with increasing confidence or trust in others, the differences in views, values, preferences, habits and customs are revealed (Balawajder, 1994, p. 94). This situation appears to be natural since people have always differed in many respects, accepting different values, and have had various interests and priorities which can be unacceptable for others. The bigger the differences that occur in a group, the more difficult it is to deal with the problems (Dana, 1993). This situation can be illustrated by the nature of conflicts between pupils at school. It should be remembered that the school not only relies on teachers tasked with transmitting knowledge to the students – the most important are the students, along with their feelings, experiences, problems and worries; that is, the internal world of a young person which cannot be measured and evaluated, or changed and tailored like a school curriculum (cf. Stańkowski, 2009, p. 23).

Although conflict is a natural part of school life, it has only recently been openly discussed by media and teachers. It is probably associated with the issue of mediation which is growing in popularity with its all undeniable advantages (discussed in the next part of the article) and disadvantages, i.e. long–term conflict resolution. Such problems as a classroom and lesson–based school system, overloaded school curriculum and tutors' excessive responsibilities do not facilitate mediation as a method and strategy for school–based conflict resolution.

MEDIATION: A METHOD OF SCHOOL–BASED CONFLICT RESOLUTION

Numerous school rules mention the issue of conflict resolution. Primarily, conflicts should be reported to the headmaster, as illustrated by the following quotation: "It is strongly recommended that any kind of disputes are settled through negotiation, mutual agreement and respect to the conflict parties. It is suggested that conflict (overt or open) should be primarily settled by the head teacher (Stańkowski, 2009, pp. 68–69).

In the literature, it is the head teacher who plays the key role of mediator with all the necessary competences. The teacher's personality is emphasized as an important factor when working with pupils. In psychology, the emotional maturity of a teacher or head teacher is referred to as the power of ego which denotes "high self–esteem and confidence, as well as the ability to deal with problems calmly and objectively" (Fonatana, 1998, p. 411). It is also important that "Every teacher should have the ability to encourage students to speak, and then should listen to them with patience and interest, interrupting only when it is really necessary" (ibid., p. 411). The ability to speak and listen to their audience tends to be essential for teachers to do their job well. Many authors consider these abilities to be significant and point out that they should be discussed in guidebooks for students in the fields of pedagogy or teaching.

Learning and teaching in the classroom take place through interpersonal communication between teachers and students. G. Kowalska (2003, p. 41) discusses verbal and non–verbal messages from the teacher as a matter of great importance in communication process. The sense of friendliness and confidence in the classroom has a significant impact on the students' and teacher's well–being.

T. Gordon (2003, p. 184) emphasizes the need for active listening which occurs when a teacher listens and reflects back to a student their understanding of the conflict. This process communicates to the student that the teacher cares and is engaged in the conversation. T. Gordon offers a No–Lose Method of Conflict Resolution which enables both teacher and student to find a mutually acceptable solution to a given problem. The goal is to find a solution that is acceptable to both parties involved in the conflict, where no one loses. Students should be encouraged to speak openly while teachers should listen actively. Active listening lets the students know that the teacher understands and accepts what they are saying and feeling. On the other hand, teachers have the right to meet their needs, too. They can do this through I–message, which is a non–blameful and non–judgmental way of letting the student know what they have done to cause a problem for the teacher. An I–Message makes students respect the teacher's needs.

It appears that a good teacher needs to be an active listener, focused on the student and open to their point of view. Although not always easy, it is undoubtedly worth trying to refrain from immediately commenting on the subject. Such behavior helps students express their thoughts and feelings, as well as build their confidence. What is more, during active listening the teacher can apply useful phrases or expressions, such as "yes", "I see" etc. Many authors specializing in the issue of mediation emphasize that active listening involves both verbal and non–verbal messages.

Before I focus on the issue of school–based mediation, I would like to discuss the term "mediation" as such. Mediation – (from the Latin *mediare*, meaning "to be inside") is a voluntary and confidential way to resolve a dispute with the help of a neutral person – the mediator. Mediation differs from other institutional conflict resolutions in that it aims not to establish who is right or wrong, but to reach a mutually agreeable solution satisfying both conflict parties. A mediator does not resolve the charge or impose a decision on the parties. Instead, the mediator helps the parties to agree on a mutually acceptable resolution. Conflict parties are perfectly aware of their needs. That is why in the process of mediation they are considered to be experts in conflict resolution. As a result, the final agreement depends mostly on the parties (Moore, 2009, p. 15). Mediators use appropriate techniques and skills to open and support dialogue between disputants, aiming to help the parties reach an agreement. They help the parties identify the important issues in the dispute and decide how they can resolve it themselves. They will also accept the lack of agreement according to the will of the parties. Mediation focuses on the needs and interests of the conflict parties, enabling the parties to express their views and rights in a calm and well thought out way. This is possible thanks to the participation of the third party, the mediator. The decision to begin mediation depends only on the conflict parties. Each of the parties, including the mediator, can break the process of mediation if they cannot see any chances to reach a final agreement or they simply do not want to continue the mediation.

The process of mediation involves the following rules:

1. Voluntary participation – no party can be forced or manipulated to participate against its will. This rule refers to each stage of mediation; each party can stop the mediation at the beginning or in the middle of the process without bringing about any negative consequences. The parties should agree to participate in mediation at the beginning of the mediation process; this approval should be also confirmed when the parties are fully aware of the process they are involved in.
2. Confidentiality – the mediator is obliged to keep the information they learn during mediation confidential. All mediation–related communications between the parties or from the parties to the mediator and any information and evidence presented to the mediator during the proceedings are confidential unless the parties and the mediator mutually agree otherwise. The mediator's files and records are also closed to all persons and are not admissible as evidence in any action. The mediator's report and the information or recommendations contained in it cannot disclose the course of the mediation process or the judgment of the parties behaviors. However, as the Council of Europe agreed, in the case of serious crimes the mediator should balance the rule of confidentiality and the need for preventing serious harm or injustice, in particular when it is required to ensure the protection of the best interests of children or to prevent harm to the physical or psychological integrity of a person. In such cases, the mediator should report to the relevant public services.
3. Impartiality – this means that the mediator does not support any of the parties but helps them both fully participate in and benefit from mediation. The mediator cannot be engaged in the conflict through personal relationships with one or both conflict parties or through earlier efforts to resolve the dispute. The mediator, as an independent third party to the dispute, is there to assist the opponents to communicate with each other in a rational and problem solving way, to identify and clarify disputed issues, and consider the available options for reaching a settlement that is acceptable to both parties. It is the mediator's responsibility to control the mediation proceedings and to treat each party in a balancing way. There should be no advocating for or against one party, nor taking of sides for one party against the other.

4. Neutrality – this focuses on the idea that mediators cannot intervene in the substance of the dispute or impose conflict resolutions on the parties, even if they are convinced that a certain solution could be the best for the parties. The mediator should be free of bias and should set aside his or her opinions and feelings. The role of the mediator is to guide the parties to the essence of the conflict and its acceptable resolution.
5. Acceptability – this offers the parties the possibility to not accept the mediator, who might be perceived as not impartial or neutral, giving them the right to change mediator. In order for any settlement to be concluded the parties must voluntarily agree to accept the mediator. It is important for the mediator to be accepted by both parties of the conflict prior to the mediation proceedings (Waluk, 2001, p. 27).

The mediator's main tasks are to:

- facilitate effective communication,
- give the parties essential information about the legal system they are involved in,
- apply techniques to support conflict resolution,
- assist in defining relevant issues and priorities,
- remain in formal control of mediation sessions,
- educate, explore the problem, extend sources of information through the help of experts,
- initiate and conduct negotiations (Moore, 2009).

The role of the mediator is to facilitate the process of communication between the parties. The mediator helps those involved in the dispute talk to each other, thereby allowing them to resolve the dispute themselves. In spite of stereotypes or negative emotions expressed by the parties, the mediator assists them in reaching a mutually acceptable agreement, as well as helps to remove those negative factors which hinder conflict resolution. The mediation session is intended to identify important issues, clarify any misunderstandings, explore solutions and finally negotiate an agreement.

School mediation is based on the principles of general mediation discussed above, and has adopted these to the school setting. According to B. Czarnecka–Dzialuk et al. (2001, p. 17), "school–based mediation is an alternative way to resolve disputes. It is sometimes referred to as 'negotiations involving three parties' which means to negotiate through the third party, mediator (a person or a group) who facilitates the process of conflict resolution rather than impose solutions".

The need to apply mediation at school was noticed after the 1st General Convention of the Polish Mediation Centre. Mediation as an important method of conflict resolution was mentioned in its Strategic Plan 2001–2004. In 2001 the Polish Mediation Centre organized a pilot all–Poland competition "I resolve disputes without violence, that is how much I know about the Restorative Justice". The second year students from lower secondary schools took part in the competition which aimed at making the competitors aware of the fact that disputes or conflicts should not be resolved through aggressive or confrontational actions. They can be resolved in a peaceful way in order to understand the reasons of the conflict party's behavior and present its negative effects to the aggrieved.

Mediation proceedings can be applied to almost all types of disputes that occur at school. The most important principle of mediation is the voluntary participation of the conflict parties. School–based mediation gives the students the possibility to serve as mediators, enabling them to control emotions and finally resolve conflict or disagreement. An offender has a chance to notice the harm and understand the need for compensation. The aggrieved party can control the fear of the offender and receive compensation. Thanks to mediation, the sense of safety at school increases and the school community has a chance to integrate. What is more, mediation promotes mutual respect and dialogue, which lead to peaceful, effective and thorough conflict resolution.

It appears that class tutors and school counsellors can play a very important role in conflict resolution. A class tutor is commonly the teacher who, on behalf of the school community, undertakes the role of caring for a class group and the responsibility for the education and welfare of pupils. "Apart from the passion for work with children, a class tutor should be a clever person equipped with expert knowledge in the field of pedagogy and psychology. The role of the class tutor requires constant support and improvements. Educational problems that may arise while working with students along with the duties and responsibilities imposed on the class tutor significantly influence the quality of his/her work" (Kopczyńska, 2011, p. 36).

J. Radziewicz (1986, p. 79) emphasizes the specific characteristics and competences of the class tutor who "sometimes on the same day and at the same time has to be a trustworthy tutor and an advocate or a spokesperson for his/her students, an organiser of their social, cultural or scientific life in the classroom, as well as an adviser and mediator in any disputes or arguments". The class tutor needs to meet very high, professional standards and requirements such as factual knowledge, competences in psychology and pedagogy, and an appropriate type of personality and commitment to work.

In her research on the efficiency of class tutor work, M. Kopczyńska (2011, p. 36) notices that 23% of students report confidence in their class tutors due to their readiness to help and resolve conflict, whereas 28% of respondents trust their tutors because they are able to keep secrets. The same research reveals that 12% of the students report that their tutors are helpful in solving school–based problems. It appears that a good mediator should possess all the qualities mentioned above.

The Committee on Pedagogical Sciences of the Polish Academy of Sciences outlined "standard professional competences for teachers based on five groups:

pragmatic, cooperative, creative, IT–media and communication competences" (Denek, 1998, p. 215). I would like to focus on communication– based competences since they are essential in the work of the class tutor who also acts as the mediator. They involve the ability to empathize and the unconditional acceptance of the other person, whereas empathic understanding, considered to be an essential element of the mediation process, is based on active listening, paraphrasing, etc.

J. Lukasik (2006, p. 40) proves in his research that communication competences play a significant role in the class tutor's activities. Teachers typically support their students through encouragement, a serious attitude to their pupils' problems so that they have confidence in resolving disputes or disagreements, as well as through verbal and non–verbal messages of help in each difficult situation. The author suggests that the class tutor's competences should be thoroughly discussed by students of teaching. Developing effective techniques of interpersonal relations, ethics and cultural awareness seems to be an important challenge for future teachers and educators.

A school counsellor can successfully play the role of mediator who contributes to resolving different types of conflict between students. The school, along with its students, will also benefit from a school counsellor trained in mediation skills who can facilitate the dispute resolution process.

The school counsellor – mediator should encourage students to talk openly about any problems as well as develop their ability and willingness to share information and insights. The mediator is not a judge and cannot force or impose any solution on the parties. The best course of action seems to be observation, understanding students' personal views and collecting their ideas to find an amicable solution that satisfies all parties involved in the conflict. The school counsellor – mediator is obliged not to disclose the information gathered during the proceedings. The role and function of the mediator end when the settlement agreement is signed, which may include apologies or a method of damage compensation.

The rules of school–based mediation are similar to other mediation proceedings which always involve such elements as voluntary participation, confidentiality, neutrality and impartiality of the mediator.

A good school counsellor – mediator is a neutral and impartial person who does not impose a solution on the parties or does not have the authority to decide about any issues for the parties. The role of the mediator, as an independent third party to the dispute, is to facilitate the process of communication, typically through assisting the parties so that they can reach a consensual settlement that is fair and acceptable to all the parties. Using various techniques to improve dialogue between disputants, the mediator remains neutral and impartial at all times. The mediator, always calm and self–possessed, should restrict any communication barriers, e.g. pressure or aggression, and demonstrate how to communicate through employing good speaking and listening skills. A good mediator should possess the ability to establish friendly relations between the parties, inspire confidence and create proper conditions for discussion. An important moment during the process of mediation tends to be a dialogue between the different sides. The mediator should direct the parties to focus on issues and stay away from personal attacks. The next step is to assist the parties in understanding the conflict and to make them aware of the advantages resulting from the dialogue. Then, the mediator facilitates a dialogue between the disputants.

The mediator must understand the reasons for the conflict to make the parties aware of the consequences, accept the decisions of the opponents and find out if they hold responsibility. It is important to reach the best solution that works for both parties involved. The mediator cannot make decisions for the disputants. Instead, they enable the parties to analyze their own experiences. Finally, the disputants reach conflict resolution through dialogue and mutual understanding.

School–based mediation may contribute to the decrease of conflicts at school and reduce the rate of aggressive behavior. By means of mediation, the school counsellor can discuss with teachers and students the reasons of conflicts, their possible effects, the ways of compensation and predictions concerning the future behavior of the disputants.

The fear of punishment does not prevent an aggressive student from improper behavior. However, direct confrontation with the student's actions and condemnation of aggressive behavior without rejecting and criticizing an individual result in understanding and accepting responsibility for their actions (Hauk, 2006, p. 11).

Mediation is not only an important but also a useful tool for managing different types of conflicts effectively, even if, in spite of the mediator's efforts, a final agreement is not reached. School–based mediation, as an alternative to a traditional way of conflict resolution based on the authority of teachers or head teachers, may bring about long–term positive effects such as the promotion of constructive conflict management at school.

CONCLUSIONS

The increasing number of different conflicts has recently been a challenge for modern schools. Since traditional methods of conflict resolution tend to fail, the teachers seek new and effective strategies to help the parties resolve disputes. At present, mediation in the education sector is the fastest growing alternative dispute resolution method. A mediated agreement is particularly valuable to parties who have an ongoing relationship, such as school–related relationships involving students, teachers and parents. According to the school rules and regulations, it is the head teacher who is responsible for providing students with psychological and pedagogical counselling. It should be emphasized that mediation also has a great educational value. Both adults and young people learn how to benefit from the dialogue and successful communication. They also learn to respect the other party's rights. Additionally, the opponents become aware of the fact that everyone makes mistakes as they are unavoidable. Therefore, the most important aspect is to understand and compensate for them. Mediation enables opponents to reach a compromise by negotiating an agreement. School–based mediation is a tool to overcome disputes in order to build a harmonious educational environment.

Class teachers and school counsellors should not only apply the techniques of mediation, but also encourage students, teachers and parents to participate, when advisable, in this method of conflict resolution. As a consequence, according to E. Kressel: "they have a chance to transform mediation from an often underestimated tool of conflict resolution into a popular and commonly adopted strategy to solve disputes or disagreements in everyday life" (quoted after: Deutsch, Coleman ed., 2005, pp. 519–543).

Nowadays, more and more teachers, class teachers or school counsellors participate in specialized trainings on the theory of conflict, effective communication, negotiation techniques and mediation. They are fully aware of the fact that conflict resolution skills are necessary for it to work effectively in a school environment.

Mediation programs can be implemented in schools in order to:

- react to different types of conflict through explaining the problem, building an understanding for the reasons of dispute and creating effective procedures;
- discuss controversial issues and facilitate the process of communication by means of active listening skills, that is to listen carefully to each others' opinions, feelings and needs, and finally work together to find solutions that address everyone's concerns;
- teach or improve conflict resolution skills;
- promote a useful conflict resolution method focused on reaching a mutually agreeable resolution and beginning negotiations, rather than punishment.

In addition to dispute resolution, mediation can function in schools as a means of dispute and aggression prevention. It also promotes cooperation within the school community. In primary and lower secondary schools aggressive behavior takes different forms. Therefore, any types of aggressive behavior cannot pass unnoticed, and even those considered as less serious should be revealed and discussed. Students will then be able to understand the problem of aggression and prevent it, or reckon with its consequences. It is necessary to teach children and young people that aggressive behavior, as a way to face obstacles or solve problems, should be successfully replaced by peaceful ways of conflict resolution.

As pedagogical research reveals, most peer conflicts remain hidden and grow unchecked. In these cases, students are left alone with their problems. Young people simply do not believe that someone can help them solve a conflict or disagreement. On the other hand, students are sometimes convinced that they are able to deal with a problem unassisted. It may result in the escalation of aggressive behavior and the isolation of victims of violence, especially when it comes to serious forms of aggression. Students sometimes ask friends for help as they are emotionally closer to their peers rather than adults. However, young people are not always able to help their friends in difficult situations.

According to the statistics (Kmiecik-Baran, 1999, pp. 96–117), the most common ways and strategies of school-based conflict resolution include:

- resolving disputes (100%) focused on problem explanation, and understanding and tension reduction; this is often implemented by class teachers;
- compromise (93%), that is a settlement of differences in which each side makes concessions;
- cooperation (53.3%) which brings the parties to an agreement they both feel comfortable with;
- negotiation and mediation (33.3%) based on techniques and strategies which facilitate communication and promote reconciliation between the parties which will allow them to reach a mutually acceptable agreement;
- avoiding conflict resolution (10%).

The statistics mentioned above indicate that mediation, as a method of conflict resolution, is not commonly implemented by teachers. This situation may result from the fact that teachers or class teachers are not professionally prepared to introduce it. Fortunately, more and more teachers are aware of the necessity of considering professional development as an integral part of their profession, becoming involved in postgraduate studies in mediation which contribute to effective school-based conflict resolution.

REFERENCES

Balawajder K., Rozwiązywanie konfliktów międzyludzkich, [in:] Psychologia w pracy menadżera, ed. Kożusznik B., Wyd. UŚ, Katowice, 1994.

Czarnecka-Dzialuk B., Wójcik D., Mediacja w sprawie nieletnich w świetle teorii badań, Wyd. Typografia, Warszawa, 2001.

Dana D., Rozwiązywanie konfliktów, PWE, Warszawa, 1993.

Denek K., O nowy kształt edukacji, PWN, Warszawa, 1998.

Deutsch M., Coleman P.T. (ed.), Rozwiązanie konfliktów, Wyd. UJ, Kraków, 2005.

Dobrołowcz W., Jak osiągnąć porozumienie?, [in:] Szkice w psychologii społecznej, ed. E. Stanisławiak, WSP, Warszawa, 1996.

Encyklopedia pedagogiczna, ed. W. Pomykało, Fundacja Innowacja, Warszawa, 1997.
Encyklopedia Pedagogiczna XXI wieku, ed. T. Pilch, Vol. II, Wyd. Akademickie "Żak", Warszawa, 2003.
Fontana D., Psychologia dla nauczycieli, PWE, Poznań, 1998.
Gordon T., Wychowanie bez porażek w szkole, Instytut Wydawniczy PAX, Warszawa, 2004.
Gordon T., Wychowanie bez porażek, PWN, Warszawa, 2003.
Hauk D., Łagodzenie konfliktów w szkole i pracy z młodzieżową. Poradnik do treningu mediacji, Wyd. Jedność, Kielce, 2006.
Kmiecik-Baran K., Młodzież i przemoc. Mechanizmy socjologiczno-psychologiczne, PWN, Warszawa, 1999.
Kopczyńska M., Specyfika pracy wychowawców klas 4-6, "Nowa Szkoła" 2011, No. 4.
Kowalska G., Kompetencje nauczyciela warunkujące efektywną komunikację interpersonalną, "Polonistyka" 2003, Vol. 55.
Kuszak M., Koło konfliktu, http:/www.kuszak-mediacje.pl/procedyry1.php on 10.04.2010.
Libermann D.J., Sztuka rozwiązywania konfliktów. Jak porozumieć się w każdej sytuacji, GWP, Gdańsk, 2004.
Łukasik I., Nauczyciel wychowawca we współczesnej szkole, "Nowa Szkoła" 2006, No. 7.
Moore Ch.W., Mediacje. Praktyczne strategie rozwiązywania konfliktów, Wolters Kluwer Polska, Warszawa, 2009.
Radziewicz J., Wychowawca i jego klasa, Młodzieżowa Agencja Wydawnicza, Warszawa, 1986.
Słaboń I., Konflikt społeczny i negocjacje, AE, Kraków, 1995.
Stachyrska B., Dialog negocjacyjny między nauczycielem a uczniem, "Nowa Szkoła" 1996, No. 2.
Stańkowski B., Konflikt nauczyciel-uczeń. Uzdrowienie relacji w świetle "Reguły 5R", WAM, Warszawa, 2009.
Waluk J., Problemy wprowadzania mediacji w Polsce, "Mediator" 2001, No. 19.

Barbara Jezierska
University of Wroclaw

COMMUNICATION IN A REHABILITATION INSTITUTION AS A CONDITION OF ITS FUNCTIONALITY IN THE ASSESSMENT OF EDUCATORS IN YOUTH EDUCATIONAL CENTRES

ABSTRACT

Youth socio–therapy centers are institutions that deal with children and teenagers in the intellectual norm who are maladjusted socially with behavioral disorders that hinder the realization of life tasks without special help and who, for emotional reasons, are unable to learn in a regular general education school. They were set up with the purpose of eliminating the reasons and manifestations of behavioral disorders and in order to prepare their inmates for life in accordance with the existing social and legal norms. Our research was aimed at determining a real and postulated functionality of youth socio–therapy centers in their communication aspect in the opinions of 98 educators employed in these institutions. The research was carried out in Lower Silesia with the use of a specially designed questionnaire containing questions referring to ways of communication inside and outside the institutions. The educators of youth socio–therapy centers participating in our research indicated the reasons for difficulties they had while discharging their educational obligations and put forth a number of postulates with regard to possible favorable changes in the functioning of rehabilitation institutions. The educators' opinions on the functionality of rehabilitation institutions indicate that the form and quality of communication connections in their structure have an influence on the adequacy of accomplishing their objectives.

KEYWORDS: communication, education, rehabilitation, socio–therapy centers.

INTRODUCTION

The social environment of a rehabilitation institution conditions the quality of the educational activities performed there. Its full recognition is a necessary determinant of the rational organizing and correcting behaviors of children and youths that are socially unacceptable as well as promoting appropriate behaviors.

The proper functioning of a rehabilitation institution is a condition of its development and an important factor in the appropriate course of the life of a rehabilitation group that functions within it. The effectiveness of an institution depends on the clear and unambiguous purposes that it specifies, its internal organization and division of work as well as on separating professional duties from the personal interests of its employees. Its effectiveness also depends on the objectively determined harmony with the aims and tasks for which it has been established as well as its internal integration and efficient cooperation with various associated institutions. It allows for the achievement of the intended, socially desired results and the pursuance of mutual goals in the process of determining and assigning various actions.[1]

The fundamental criteria of the assessment of the proper functioning of a rehabilitation facility are its ability to self–improve, cohesion of its social structure and harmony between various functions that it performs.[2]

All dysfunctions, both within the internal sphere of a rehabilitation institution as well as in its cooperation with a surrounding social environment, lead to clear discrepancies between its assumed and actual functioning.

OBJECTIVES, TASKS AND THE FORMAL ORGANIZATION OF YOUTH SOCIO–THERAPY CENTERS

With regard to minors for whom educational or reformatory means must be applied, total institutional care is used.[3]

Reformatories, youth educational centers, shelter–homes for minors, state emergency upbringing centers, police rooms for children, social adaptation centers[4] and youth socio–therapy centers are among those institutions whose organizational structures, curriculums and systems of education are totally subordinated to the rehabilitation objectives 24–hours a day.[5]

Youth socio–therapy centers are institutions designed for children and teenagers in the intellectual norm who are maladjusted socially with behavioral disorders that hinder the realization of life tasks without special help and who, for emotional reasons, are unable to learn in a regular general education primary or secondary school.

[1] C. Czapów, Wychowanie resocjalizujące, Warszawa, 1978, pp. 85–93.

[2] A. Podgórecki, Patologia życia społecznego, Warszawa, 1969, pp. 16–31.

[3] Act on procedures with minors of 26 October1982, Diary Acts No 35, item 228, as amended, Diary Acts 2010, No 33, item 178.

[4] Ordinance of Minister of National Education dated 13 August 1999 on types and operation of public educational, care and rehabilitation institutions and framework statutes of these institutions, Diary Acts No 67 item 758.

[5] Ordinance of Minister of Education and Sport dated 7 March 2005, on types and detailed rules of activity of public institutions, conditions of stay of children and youths in these institutions and cost of stay in these institutions borne by the children's parents, Diary Acts No 52, item 467.

They are also designed for children and teenagers who, because of developmental disorders, difficulties in learning and disorders in social functioning, may be in danger of social maladjustment or an addiction, and therefore require the special organization of learning processes, methods of work and education as well as specialist psycho–educational help.

They were established with the purpose of eliminating reasons and manifestations of behavioral disorders and to prepare their inmates for life in accordance with the existing social and legal norms.

The main aims of youth socio–therapy centers are as follows: organization of didactic classes; preventative, educational as well as socio–therapeutic activities enabling the acquisition of life skills which facilitate proper functioning within a family and society; assistance in planning educational and professional carriers, taking into account the abilities and interests of inmates; and aiding parents or legal guardians with regard to the improvement of skills that are necessary in supporting the development of children and youths, especially in the scope of developing their potential abilities and avoiding risky behaviors.[6]

Children and youths are admitted to youth socio–therapy centers on the basis of decisions of psychological and pedagogical service centers, the applications of parents or rulings of family courts. A basic organizational form of work in the youth social therapy centers is a rehabilitation group numbering 8 to 12 pupils. At least two educators supervise the activities of a rehabilitation group. The scope of therapy depends on what spheres of functioning of a given pupil should be corrected, and on their readiness to participate in this process.

The youth socio–therapy centers include a school which provides possibilities for its inmates to continue education on an appropriate level; however, in the light of the existing law, a socio–therapy institution may function without a school as part of its organizational structure. The centers organized in this way do not admit minors in most cases, fearing that they cannot guarantee their proper functioning in a regular school.

MODEL FUNCTIONING OF REHABILITATION INSTITUTIONS

The basic goal of rehabilitation institutions' activity is the corrective socialization of people who are socially maladjusted. This process takes place by means of an intended educational procedure with the use of specially selected methods and means of impingement in a given environment.[7] Both the people sub-

[6] Ordinance of Minister of Labour and Social Policies dated 1 September 2000 on care and educational institutions, Diary Acts No 80, item 900.

[7] B. Urban, J. Stanik, *Resocjalizacja. Teoria i praktyka pedagogiczna*, Warszawa, 2007, vol. 1, pp. 225–226.

ject to rehabilitation as well as the carers remain in interpersonal mutual relations, as described by theoreticians.[8]

In other words, the teachers and their mutual relations in a given physical and social environment create the upbringing reality. This is described or characterized by rehabilitation systems, exposing its total character through the use of all its elements with the relations that take place between them.

The course of rehabilitation activities usually comprises the following four directions:

- eliminating reasons for the personality disorders of inmates,
- removing the negative changes in personality,
- consolidation of the achieved corrective results,
- inspiring an individual who is being rehabilitated to self–education.[9]

On the level of the rehabilitation institution these directions are determined on the basis of criteria which refer to:

- system of action,
- interpersonal bonds,
- flow of information,
- management,
- work evaluation.[10]

Each institution constitutes a system for realizing particular purposes. Aims and tasks as well as principles, rules and models of activities of particular people and institutions as a whole are standardized and formalized, which limit the freedom of behavior and create a general organizational framework of people's actions.

The condition of interpersonal bonds developed in the institution is determined on the basis of their formal and informal features. A formal bond, which is full of kindness and mutual help, strengthened by an informal bond developed through accordance with the basic purposes of the institution, ensures the efficient achievements of these goals.

A flow of information takes place both inside the institution and as a result of exchange with the environment outside. This enables cooperation with other institutions as well as help and cooperation within the institution, maximizing the effects of activity.

Different systems of management can be variously distributed on a continuum whose extremes constitute an autocratic style and a democratic style. It is impossible to state which style is the best and which is defective without taking

[8] J. Kurczewski, Patologia interakcji międzyludzkich, [in:] Zagadnienia patologii społecznej, (ed:) A. Podgórecki, Warszawa, 1976, pp. 281–316.

[9] C. Czapów, S. Jedlewski, Pedagogika resocjalizacyjna, Warszawa, 1971, pp. 27–40.

[10] A. Podgórecki, Socjotechnika: funkcjonalność i dysfunkcjonalność instytucji, Warszawa, 1974, pp. 39–67; J. Staniszkis, Patologia struktur organizacyjnych, Warszawa, 1972, pp. 32–47; P. Tyrała, Kierowanie, organizowanie, zarządzanie. Zarys prakseologii, Toruń, 2002, pp. 114–121.

into consideration a particular situational and social system which is subject to management. In order to find appropriate rules, it is necessary to take into account the element of relativity of management styles with reference to relations which are supposed to be managed.

The process of evaluation, reflected in gratifications that are granted in the course of work, facilitates planning and controlling the process of managing a given institution. Evaluation has an integrative and motivating value, contributing to the behaviors which serve the purpose of an institution and eliminating those which are undesirable.

Appropriate rehabilitation activities are carried out in three stages:

- communicative integration,
- permanent belonging based on normative integration,
- formal membership based on functional integration.[11]

A consequence of the proper course of these stages is the optimal functioning of an educational institution described in three aspects:

- interpersonal relations within a rehabilitation institution,
- orientation of the teaching staff towards satisfying the needs and aspirations of participants in an educational situation;
- organizational system expressed in the structural aspects of activities of an institution.[12]

The efficiency of the rehabilitation institution system activities is determined by the features of its members and its structure in mutually striving for established goals and the process of arranging integration, cooperation and communication.[13]

COMMUNICATION IN A REHABILITATION INSTITUTION AS A CONDITION OF ITS FUNCTIONALITY

The functionality of an institution depends on its integration, cooperation and communication levels. The form and quality of communication connections of an institution influence the realization of the goals of this institution , and its integration and efficient cooperation make it possible to achieve the expected and socially desired results.[14]

In the conditions of rehabilitation institutions, processes of integration, cooperation and communication take place by means of an educational relation-

[11] W. Kieżun, Krytyczna teoria organizacji: wybór zagadnień, Warszawa, 2004, pp. 211–231; T. Kotarbiński, Traktat o dobrej robocie, Wrocław, 2000, pp. 56–72.

[12] L. Pytka, Pedagogika resocjalizacyjna. Wybrane zagadnienia teoretyczne i metodyczne, Warszawa, 2005, pp. 164–165.

[13] C. Czapów, op. cit., p. 91.

[14] A. Podgórecki, Zagadnienia patologii społecznej, Warszawa, 1976, pp. 188–195.

ship, and the formal and informal social organization.[15] Thanks to this, it is possible to perform tasks which correspond to social expectations and are accepted by the educators of an institution, constituting a result jointly achieved by a team of people with material resources ensuring the successful performance of their tasks.

The cooperative structure of an institution comprises management and executive tasks. These consist of activities preparing for final actions referred to as designing, deciding and controlling processes. The process of designing takes place within the structure of actions, functions and objectives as well as their optimal applications. It consists in determining goals which can be achieved in particular conditions, proper diagnosing, establishing executive teams and functions, assigning partial tasks and elaborating the coordination of activities of teams and individuals. The results of designing are presented in the form of decisions on rules of performance, while controlling processes deals with the consistency of realized tasks with their assumed design and criteria, as well as correcting any possible deviations from the assumed plan of action.[16]

The system of communication and information working in an institution results in interactions between its participants and is dependent on their appropriate distribution. This distribution ought to ensure efficient organizational communication enabling the positive cooperation of actions and well organized collaboration, so that it is possible for every member of the system to receive and send all information. As a matter of fact, the information flow conditions the common accomplishment of a task. The meaning of information constituting the communicative institutional structure is twofold. Firstly, by communicating what should be done and what consequences follow from a failure to act, information directs the actions of institutional system members and by arousing emotions it encourages action.[17] There are four main types of communication: those connected with work and tasks; those connected with an institution and its functioning, enabling feedback and the mutual stimulation of thinking that lead to changes and improvements; integration, connecting people and making their work significant and leading to greater involvement; and ordering, which refers more to people and places than to their work; for example, being transferred to another task or deciding when the canteen will be renovated.

The process of information flow occurs within an institution as well as through exchanges with an external environment. It enables cooperation with other institutions as well as assistance and cooperation within an institution, which increases the effects of activities of a given institution. Communication problems cause disturbances in sending and receiving information that are sig-

[15] V. Będkowska-Heine, Społeczna percepcja instytucji resocjalizacyjnych przez ich wychowawców i wychowanków, Wrocław, 1998, p. 179.

[16] L. Pytka, op. cit., p. 195.

[17] K. Zimniewicz, Współczesne koncepcje i metody zarządzania, Warszawa, 2009, pp. 106–117.

nificant for the appropriate functioning of an institution and the lower adequacy of objectives that it assumes. The efficiency of communication channels enables the mutual use of experiences and knowledge, mutual help and cooperation, transmitting information, recommendations, remarks as well as discussion and the evaluation of activity. More importantly, communicating with people means appreciating their value as human beings. In the conditions of an educational institution it means that people are appreciated not only for the roles they perform, but also for their whole personalities. The quality of communication in an institution has an impact on the motivation of employees and their work satisfaction, their engagement and energy as well as their performance and efficiency. Information flow problems are connected with blocking or otherwise impairing information channels within an institution, which in turn causes disturbances in sending and receiving information that are significant for its employees.

Factors influencing the uniformity, integration and effective functioning of a social organization within the scope of its internal communication follow from the principle of the effective information flow. A given organization can function effectively only when it has a reliable and relevant system of information flow, obtaining and processing. Any disturbances, obstructions, breaks, shortages or information noise existing in any element of the system contribute to a lower efficiency of actions than assumed.

The defectiveness of the information flow within an institution, as well as problems with ways of selecting outside information and transmitting information, constitute significant features of dysfunctionality. This phenomenon is particularly evident in the disturbances or failures of so called two–directional information flow, which secures information exchange between the managing and managed bodies of a given institution.

The functionality of an institutional organizational system is an effect of communication dependencies on the one hand and a stimulating value of information received by members of an institution on the other. Apart from stimulation processes, it also involves the performance of particular tasks which constitute a response to stimulation. The institutional structure is determined by the division of labor which results in organizational roles played by members of the system. In this aspect of the institutional structure, we can distinguish its vertical division where partial tasks are carried out and a horizontal division in which, when cooperating in order to attain a common goal, particular phases of a uniform process of carrying out a task are completed.[18]

The basic factor of functionality of an institution is communication between its participants and a system of communicating with other institutions, expressed through an increased dependence with regard to the mutual exchange

[18] C. Czapów, op. cit., pp. 90–91.

of services resulting from the division of labor, performing social roles, combining functions and tasks carried out by group institutions with roles and functions attributed to them as well as their harmonious performance. Disturbances in information flow and communication lead to isolation and marginalization as regards the norms and standards of procedures recognized as obligatory in the system of institutional impingements.[19]

PURPOSE AND REALISATION OF THE RESEARCH

Our research was aimed at determining a real and postulated functionality of rehabilitation institutions in the communication aspect in the opinions of their educators, indicating the educational tasks they are able to carry out, the quality of educational actions, the level and range of postulated changes and possibilities of further reformatory actions in this regard.

The research was carried out in youth socio–therapy centers in Lower Silesia where there are 19 institutions of this type, 32% of the national total. The research comprised 98 educators employed in these institutions.

A specially designed questionnaire was used in our research containing questions referring to a general assessment of an institution, the possibilities of rehabilitation impingements, staff taking part in the rehabilitation procedures, the educational environment influencing the activity of its participants, actual possibilities for carrying out educational tasks and problems with their realization, possibilities of introducing changes improving the efficiency of functioning youth socio–therapy centers in the existing reality and an estimated scale of a level (high, average, low) of functionality of a rehabilitation institution. Indexes of the internal functionality of an institution were taken into consideration in this scale, which referred to the following aspects: levels of achieving institutional objectives, a system of actions, management and work evaluation as well as communication within and outside an institution in the scope of:

- types and intensity of social relationships and contacts between participants in a rehabilitation institution,
- communication structure of a rehabilitation institution,
- coordination of information flow in the institution structure,
- organizing the activity of information flow inside an institution and with the external environment.

[19] J. Turowski, Socjologia. Małe struktury społeczne, Lublin, 2001, pp. 130–132.

RESEARCH RESULTS

The examined educators employed in youth socio–therapy centers indicated their reasons for difficulties in discharging educational obligations. They referred to several clearly defined areas:

- inmates diagnosed with mental and neurological disorders as well as somatic illnesses and disorders,
- the professional preparation of educators,
- management, communication and cooperation within an institution,
- cooperation with external institutions,
- system of gratification and professional promotion,
- institutional formalism and ritualism.

Youth socio–therapy centers are designed to provide their inmates with health care in accordance with the relevant regulations. However, educators have observed a considerable growth in the number of inmates who require medical treatment. This is even more alarming because the health conditions of many inmates make it impossible to subject them to educational procedures, such as hearing and eyesight problems that prevent them from formal education. Neurological and emotional speech impediments as well as speech problems resulting from physical distortions impair their articulation. Such things as faulty postures, orthopedic anomalies, a deformed skeleton and juvenile scoliosis eliminate them from participating in physical classes. Almost all inmates have dental diseases, many have eczema, scabies and other dermatological illnesses.

Youth socio–therapy centers are intended for young people with disorders that hinder their proper functioning at school and in the social environment. According to the participating educators, the young people have such serious disorders that they should be treated in hospitals, including those specialising in addiction therapy and mental diseases. The lack of possibilities to fully communicate with inmates due to their mental and somatic defects and frequent consciousness disorders caused by pharmacological or narcotic substances, apart from serious problems in the educational process, constitutes a real danger to their health and lives, along with those of the educators. It is even more alarming that the examined educators have observed a significant growth in the number of inmates requiring medical treatment, while the appropriate funds for that purpose are more and more limited.

Most of the educators are not prepared to meet challenges of youth socio-therapy centers. They believe that the social significance of the institutions in which they work is small, and even that their purposes are socially harmful. They see no sense in working with inmates because “they are good for nothing”, “they will cause problems again when they go back home”, “here, they can only learn from those who are more demoralized than they are themselves", "instead of spending money on them, we'd better organize labor camps". It is often the case that they themselves suggest lowering the age of criminal responsibility for their inmates and "the like", especially because this is what "the society demands", which in any case "does not appreciate us or our work".

Many educators have worked out specific defensive mechanisms against the inconveniences of their work. Some of them are characterized by a high reactivity level – "they walk around with a stick in their hand and look for an occasion to react to improper – in their opinion – behaviors of the inmates". Frequently, they do not want to notice educational problems and consequently do not take any action aimed at solving them. They deny the existence of problems, do not report any events that took place while they were on duty such as escapes or "playing with a fire extinguisher, producing snow". They create a specific autonomy for themselves and escape into their intellectual development. There are really few educators who truly look for sources of problems and try to engage in an appropriate rehabilitation activity.

There are some insignificant differences among the educators in their assessment of features of the information flow in particular centers. The majority think that the information flow existing in their institution shows few characteristics of dysfunctionality. The information about inmates is treated seriously and a system of communication among teachers, educators and pedagogues is appropriate. However, other educators think that the information transfer in their institution is hampered, and many educators therefore have no idea about the significant events and decisions taken in their center, or learn about them "after a given event" or when "they are no longer so important". Information is not "patent", and educators do not cooperate with one another for the good of their institution. On the contrary, they often get satisfaction from the fact that "the event did not happen while she/he was on duty but somebody else got the blame", and they are happy about their colleagues' failures because they "put on airs". There is no good information flow between them, they do not keep the necessary documentation, and "they do not write anything in their duty records" in order to avoid any troubles, or simply excuse themselves because "bureaucracy is considered to be more important than their work".

These disturbances occur mostly in relation to the teacher – educator, and to a lesser extent in the processes of communication with the institution's authorities and superior institutions. In this regard, the autocratic style of managing an institution was emphasized; however, this was not assessed negatively when referring to ensuring a high level of material functioning of an institution. A negative aspect was observed in the case when the realization of the assumed plans was hindered and their decisions with regard to an educational group were undermined. This situation often caused aggression or apathy of "autocratically controlled" educators.

All educators emphasize the fact that there are disturbances in the information flow from external institutions, which makes it difficult to make decisions as to the educational procedures in relation to newly admitted inmates, because "opinions about inmates are trite", "nothing results from them" and "a community interview is totally useless".

The educators give some negative opinions on cooperation with some of the external institutions, stressing their incompetence, lack of orientation in a given situation and knowledge about the real problems of rehabilitation institutions. They often complain about the ignorance of judges, length of court proceedings, incomplete and incorrect diagnosing of inmates in psychological and pedagogical service centers, tardiness of the police when responding to notifications sent from institutions and finally the fact that the institutions that are designed to cooperate with the centers ignore information which is of key importance.

The employees of all researched institutions were not satisfied with the obtained gratifications, considering them to be incommensurable with work input and their duties. All participating educators noticed a low prestige of the profession, a great turnover of staff, low salaries which had not increased for years as well as limited career possibilities in this profession. "Educators have worked in the same institution for years, often until they are retired" and at best "a former educator is promoted to the post of headmaster of a center". Due to "ridiculously low salaries" "young people escape to other jobs", and often go abroad. They claimed that rehabilitation institutions would be much more efficient if motivation for work was stimulated by "substantial awards" and fair promotions on "salary scales". An appropriate system of incentives promotes talented and efficient employees and has an integrative and motivating value. Less importance was definitely attached to awards without financial gratification and other non–financial privileges, and the educators did not consider these awards as encouragement to "increase pedagogical efforts".

According to the educators, their institutions have too many and too detailed organizational regulations in relation to their real needs, and some of the regulations defining models of behaviors are too strict or rigorous. They feel they are forced to strictly observe some functional diagrams with no creative invention and possibilities to communicate beyond the existing regulations. For example, the rule of maintaining discipline in a group may be in conflict with an intention to keep an inmate who causes behavioral problems but, despite a breach of discipline, shows a potential for improvement due to their personal bond with an educator. Another contradiction can be observed in the rule of working with the whole group contrasted with the requirement to introduce individual educational impingements.

The requirement to observe the literal meaning of organizational regulations and the fact that educators know exactly what they have to do and what is beyond the scope of their duties cause them to stick only to a minimum as defined by the regulations. The procedures of dealing with affairs and methods of actions are subject to change. The system of actions becomes more and more conservative, rigid and anti–innovative. Consequently, it is often the case that educational tasks remain merely a record in paper documentation to please external controllers without being reflected in actual activities.

The educators submitted the following postulates referring to the possibilities of introducing favorable changes in the functioning of youth socio–therapy centers:

- limiting the number of inmates in a group,
- organizing another system of selection of members of educational groups so that a group does not imitate the school class structure,
- creating a transitional group for newly admitted inmates, thus enabling the educator to observe and get to know them,
- appropriate placement of inmates in groups with a possibility to change the group during the inmate's stay in an institution,
- decreasing (not increasing) the number of educators in charge of a group so that they are able to follow a procedure of continuous educational impingements, similar to parental care and not limited to short periods of being on duty,
- establishing a special therapeutic center for inmates with disorders,
- compensating hard working conditions with decent salaries and retirement after 20 years,
- observing "clear rules of the game" in both formal and informal contacts,
- taking care of a good atmosphere at work and mutual kindness as well as help from colleagues,
- an appropriate shape of the communication network, in particular within an institution, because "we can perfectly deal with a lack of information about a young person from external sources",
- introducing activities supported by ideas and innovations as a dominant tendency of organizational behaviors, which would facilitate the process of accepting the major objectives of an institution by its employees.

Educators think that the basic way to ensure the efficiency of actions of a rehabilitation institution is the full, exhaustive and rational distribution of tasks between various institutions designed for taking care of young people who require help with their school duties and proper functioning in society, simultaneously ensuring information flows between these institutions. If one institution is assigned various diagnostic, caring, educational, therapeutic and didactic tasks, there is a danger of preferring some tasks and neglecting others. Defining tasks accepted by educators in a different way than the assumed institutional tasks may lead to refraining from some tasks or carrying out only those recognized by educators as feasible in the particular institutional conditions.

According to educators, the functionality of an institution is facilitated by clearly determining the rights to make decisions in the process of organizing educational impingements. Clear and explicit communication of what should be done when and to what extent, without the excessive blurring of responsibility in educational procedures or making decisions at a higher level and not within a rehabilitation institution, prevents exercising full control over the process as well as contributing to avoiding responsibility or appropriate involvement, tardiness in making decisions and the accumulation of unresolved issues which significantly lower the efficiency of educational procedures.

In educators' opinions, the desired functionality of a rehabilitation institution also depends on its relations with other cooperating institutions. The intensity and quality of communication connections ought to comprise, *inter alia*, transmitting all information required by participants and exclude situations in which institutions work only for their own benefits and needs, do not serve each other and do not cooperate to achieve a common superior goal, i.e. the good of an inmate.

Educators emphasized that to increase the functionality of sociotherapy centers it would be purposeful if they were excluded from provisions of the act in cases dealing with minors as places where an educational means is exercised and applied towards minors on the basis of provisions of this act by making this institution only for those children and young people who require specialist help. A differential factor ought to be the level of demoralization of minors. Youth socio–therapy centers are designed for children and young people who are in danger of social maladjustment or drug addiction and not for children and young people who are already demoralized, socially maladjusted or in conflict with the law. However, these borders are often crossed and largely depend on a subjective assessment of a given judge. A phenomenon that is quite often encountered is the change of verdicts concerning an educational means by family judges who assign minors to sociotherapy centers and, particularly alarming, allocate minors towards whom the execution of reformatory means was suspended in those institutions. This situation leads to introducing changes in institutional objectives; i.e. in an attempt to improve conditions of achieving wrongly ascribed tasks and formal success in an educational process, these institutions increase their staff and material resources, protect themselves against control, and engage in informal contacts and relationships to enhance the possibilities of achieving their tasks and attaining the best results within the role imposed on them. It takes place without noticing the consequences for other institutions, brings about problems that make it impossible to perform their appropriate functions and leads to open or hidden conflicts among them.

Educators think that in the process of the educational impingements it is important to determine the rules of performing educational tasks and to outline methods of their accomplishment which would exclude excessive arbitrariness, for example, the use of performed roles which are not in accordance with the educational objectives of a rehabilitation institution. However, in practical terms it cannot limit the natural course, creative contribution and initiative of these institutions. According to educators, it is particularly important to have responsible management which ensures the functioning of a rehabilitation institution in accordance with the assumed plan and introduce a sensible system of gratification, motivating engagement in an appropriate activity.

BIBLIOGRAPHY

Act on procedures with minors of 26 October 1982, Diary Acts No 35, item 228, as amended, Diary Acts 2010, No 33, item 178. (Ustawa o postępowaniu w sprawach nieletnich z dnia 26 października 1982 r., Dz. U. Nr 35, poz. 228, ze zmianami Dz. U. 2010, Nr 33, poz. 178.)

Będkowska-Heine V., Społeczna percepcja instytucji resocjalizacyjnych przez ich wychowawców i wychowanków, [in:] J. Semków, M. Wawrzak-Chodaczek (ed.), Od szkoły pamięci do szkoły rozwoju, Wydawnictwo Uniwersytetu Wrocławskiego, Wrocław, 1998.

Czapów C., Wychowanie resocjalizujące, PWN, Warszawa, 1978.

Czapów C., Jedlewski S., Pedagogika resocjalizacyjna, PWN, Warszawa, 1971.

Kieżun W., Krytyczna teoria organizacji: wybór zagadnień, Wydawnictwo Wyższej Szkoły Przedsiębiorczości i Zarządzania im. Leona Koźmińskiego, Warszawa, 2004.

Kotarbiński T., Traktat o dobrej robocie, Zakład Narodowy im. Ossolińskich, Wrocław, 2000.

Kurczewski J., Patologia interakcji międzyludzkich, [in:] Zagadnienia patologii społecznej, (ed.) A. Podgórecki, PWN, Warszawa, 1976.

Ordinance of Minister of National Education dated 13 August 1999 on types and operation of public educational, care and rehabilitation institutions and framework statutes of these institutions, Diary Acts No 67 item 758. (Rozporządzenie Ministra Edukacji Narodowej z dnia 13 sierpnia 1999 r. w sprawie rodzajów i zasad działania publicznych placówek opiekuńczo-wychowawczych i resocjalizacyjnych oraz ramowych statutów tych placówek, Dz. U. Nr 67 poz. 758.)

Ordinance of Minister of Education and Sport dated 7 March 2005, on types and detailed rules of activity of public institutions, conditions of stay of children and youths in these institutions and cost of stay in these institutions borne by the children's parents, Diary Acts No 52, item 467. (Rozporządzenie Ministra Edukacji i Sportu z dnia 7 marca 2005 r., w sprawie rodzajów i szczegółowych zasad działania placówek publicznych, warunków pobytu dzieci i młodzieży w tych placówkach oraz wysokości i zasad odpłatności wnoszonej przez rodziców za pobyt ich dzieci w tych placówkach, Dz. U. Nr 52, poz. 467.)

Ordinance of Minister of Labour and Social Policies dated 1 September 2000 on care and educational institutions, Diary Acts No 80, item 900. (Rozporządzenie Ministra Pracy i Polityki Społecznej z 1 września 2000 r. w sprawie placówek opiekuńczo-wychowawczych, Dz. U. Nr 80, poz. 900.)

Podgórecki A., Patologia życia społecznego, PWN, Warszawa, 1969.

Podgórecki A., Socjotechnika: funkcjonalność i dysfunkcjonalność instytucji, Książka i Wiedza, Warszawa, 1974.

Podgórecki A., Patologia działania instytucji, [in:] A. Podgórecki (ed.), Zagadnienia patologii społecznej, PWN, Warszawa, 1976.

Pytka L., Pedagogika resocjalizacyjna. Wybrane zagadnienia teoretyczne i metodyczne, Akademia Pedagogiki Specjalnej im. Marii Grzegorzewskiej, Warszawa, 2005.

Serafin K., Procesy w organizacji, Wydawnictwo Górnośląskiej Szkoły Handlowej, Katowice 2002.

Staniszkis J., Patologia struktur organizacyjnych, PWN, Warszawa, 1972.

Tyrała P., Kierowanie, organizowanie, zarządzani. Zarys prakseologii, Wydawnictwo Adam Marszałek, Toruń, 2002.
Turowski J., Socjologia. Małe struktury społeczne, Towarzystwo Naukowe KUL, Lublin, 2001.
Urban B., Stanik J., Resocjalizacja. Teoria i praktyka pedagogiczna, Wydawnictwo Naukowe PWN; Pedagogium Wyższa Szkoła Pedagogiki Resocjalizacyjnej, Warszawa, 2007.
Zimniewicz K., Współczesne koncepcje i metody zarządzania, Polskie Wydawnictwo Ekonomiczne, Warszawa, 2009.

Ivana Poledňová
Masaryk University, Brno, Czech Republic
Jindřiška Šmejkalová
Regional Charity of Třebíč, Czech Republic
Jana Borůvková
College of Polytechnics, Jihlava, Czech Republic

THE RELATION OF PERSONALITY FACTORS TO CLASSROOM SOCIOMETRIC STATUS IN SECONDARY SCHOOL STUDENTS

ABSTRACT

This chapter deals with the relationship between the personality characteristics of students and their sociometric status in the classes of secondary technical school. Its main aim is to reveal whether the personality characteristics of students in late adolescence affect their sociometric status from the point of view of influence and popularity. Also verified is how school competences (results and praise) affect sociometric status in connection with personality dimensions. Sociometric status (influence and popularity in the school class) was gained through the sociometric method SO–RA–D and individual personality dimensions were measured by NEO–PI–R. Results of the research show that a higher degree of agreeableness affects the popularity of an individual in the class and the evaluation of schoolmates. A higher degree of extraversion increases authority in the class, while a higher degree of conscientiousness decreases it. Individual components of neuroticism also influence the degree of authority in the class, while depression and self–consciousness decrease authority and impulsiveness increases it. School results do not affect sociometric status in connection with personality characteristics, but praise decreases the popularity of introverts. Students in late adolescence are able to reflect their personality characteristics and development in time. They are also able to evaluate the positives and negatives of their personality in a school group.

KEYWORDS: communication, education, sociometric status, method SO–RA–D, NEO–PI–R.

1. INTRODUCTION

In the course of life all individuals become members of many social groups, with classroom peer groups being the most important ones. During adolescence in particular, the school class becomes a platform for the mutual exchange of opinions, impressions and behaviors, a space mediating the acquisition of different social skills, prestige and values. The peer group serves to satisfy basic psychological needs, including the needs of achievement, security or safety. One's social status within the peer group is determined by many factors, and personality traits remain the most elemental.

The school class is a representation of a very complex, multi–layered social world. It is a distinctive, in a sense unrepeatable, assemblage of individuals, constituting itself through the personalities and original social configuration of the individual students. The position one occupies in such a group is the measure of one's social interaction skills and, to a certain extent, also a possible predictor of one's later success at work or in other significant social environments (Lašek, 2001). The school class's original function is educational. It is an institutionally established unit with the students having no influence on its formation. Regulation is provided by a formal set of school rules. One special feature of classroom peer groups, however, is that they also develop an informal structure, arising from the way each student is liked or disliked by their classmates. This informal framework pervades every aspect of the group and affects its structure and dynamics. For most members, the school class becomes a referential group. This means that students enjoy being a part of the group and wish to belong in it (Hrabal, 1992, 2003). On one hand, the class is dependent on the kinds of students who join it, which is a determining factor of its structural development. Conversely, class membership shapes and affects the personalities of individual students. Some of the most significant factors having an impact on the nature and shaping of the classroom peer group are the **personalities of the students with their subsequent development and maturation, the personality of the teacher, and the curriculum together with the institutional conditions underlying the teaching process**. However, a whole range of other variables can also contribute to the shaping of the class, these often being relatively independent from the classroom group dynamics (Prokop, 1996; Hrabal, 1992).

The different development of classroom peer groups is expected in connection with **gender differences**. Dynamics in mixed classes will not be the same as in all–female or all–male classes, especially with the onset of adolescence. Group relationships are particularly strong and more integrated in all–male classes. This is, however, probably linked to a higher index of influence which is primarily based on psychological and physical capabilities as dictated by the group values and norms. In the name of general principles or group solidarity, boys tend to be more confrontational towards the teachers and the school. Girls, meanwhile, appear more mature in their adherence to the established school norms, and also tend to be less confrontational and more conformist (Hrabal, 2003).

Another variable projecting onto the structure and dynamics of school classes is **age**. In late adolescence, the period we focus on in our research, which roughly covers the time of secondary school studies in the Czech Republic, classroom peer groups slowly shift away from the center of the teenagers' social development contexts. This is, among other things, caused by the gradual transformation of one's personality as well as the integration of adolescents in a broader context of social relationships. Adolescence is marked by an increased need of autonomy, independence and self–assertion, but also the need of mutuality and reciprocity in personal relationships. The informal structure of the school class becomes more pronounced and largely independent of the institutional values and norms. Interpersonal relationships grow deeper, and the status system of the class becomes more stable. The connection between school performance and student's popularity and influence in the class grows weaker. The way individuals are judged by their peers tends to be more universal and complex; important factors are the students' social and moral maturity, the degree of their personality integration and autonomy, but also their achievement – and work–related characteristics which are important for one's future successful functioning. Class differentiation in secondary schools is affected by educational specialization with regard to students' selected future occupation. Specific types of secondary schools attract students of similar intellectual capacities, interests and demographic profiles, which are all potential factors affecting group development within the classroom (Hrabal, 2003).

The informal position of an individual in the class is represented by their **social status**. A method traditionally used for the assessment of sociopreferential relations and students' social status within the class is **sociometry**, a methodological approach developed at the beginning of the 20th century by J. L. Moreno. A sociometric test consists to a small extent of questions regarding interpersonal relationships which are presented to the members of a particular group who are mutually well–acquainted. The respondents are typically asked to make positive or negative choices from among the group members according to certain criteria connected to particular social situations (Kulka, 1983). Madarasová–Gecková, Orosová and Madaras (2004) distinguish between two types of sociometric tests. The first is referred to as "peer nomination" tests, which involve positive or negative nominations of peers according to a preselected criterion. The second is called "peer ratings" and uses scale–based mutual assessments of the group members.

The impact of personality on the sociometric status of the individual has been studied numerous times. The results, however, have often been contradictory. The research has focused mainly on those aspects of personality involved in the interaction process with other people, and was mostly concerned with temperament traits. It was found that both **introversion and neuroticism** influence one's status within the group. Extroversion is an important factor at an early stage of group formation. At this stage, extroverts tend to receive more nominations compared to the rest of the group; later on, their popularity gradually ebbs away. Still, it is more likely for extroverts to assume leading positions within the groups, which means they are considerably influential and often serve as norm creators. It has been evidenced that sociability, a facet of extroversion, correlates positively with sociometric status, which is viewed as an outcome of the emotional expansiveness of sociable individuals expressed by the number of received nominations. In contrast, introverts are likely to be isolated in small groups, and their status tends to be rather negative. In larger groups, however, their status changes, often turning positive, and in many cases these individuals even become favored among their peers (Kolominskij, 1980).

Research has also found positive correlation between sociometric status and **intelligence**. It has been documented that the upper 25% of people in the sociometric hierarchy possesses significantly higher intelligence than the lower 25%. In the opposite direction, however, this relationship was not confirmed. Additionally, sociometric leaders and popular individuals usually stand just slightly above the group average concerning their intellectual abilities – the difference must not be overly pronounced (Petrusek, 1969). Personal attributes which students of higher grades value most in their peers include honesty and helpfulness, alongside volitional capacities and intellect (Kolominskij, 1980). **Other personality traits** studied in relation to the sociometric status include, for example, sociability, self–confidence, sense of humor, emotional stability, and mental health. Significant associations have been found, but it is not clear whether these attributes in themselves give rise to higher positions in the sociometric hierarchy, or they more likely become better developed in the context of higher social status (Petrusek, 1969). High sociometric status is apparently more accessible to those individuals who possess characteristics highly regarded by the rest of the class and corresponding to their value orientations (Kolominskij, 1980).

Newcomb, Bukowski and Patee (1993) provided a meta–analysis of four types of peer status (popular, rejected, neglected and controversial) in relation to aggression, sociability, cognitive abilities and social withdrawal, comparing them to average school children. According to their findings, **popular children** are less aggressive, less withdrawn, more sociable and possess higher cognitive abilities. They are better predisposed for forming and maintaining interpersonal bonds, and for others positive relationships with these individuals constitute a gain, which results in better trust and maintenance of their high social status. These children have good social skills in conflict resolution, are prosocially oriented, possess predominantly positive personal traits, and enjoy many friendships. **Rejected children**, on the other hand, are less sociable and more aggressive, show greater inclination toward social with drawal, and their cognitive abilities are below average. Aggressive tendencies are not compensated for by prosocial behavior. These children are also more likely to suffer from depression and anxiety. To win a position inside the peer group, they often resort to risk behaviors which might lead to further rejection, even ostracism. All this constitutes a threat for their further development. Later in life their social deficit might result in various pathologies. **Neglected children** are least different from average children in their personality disposition. They are usually quite anonymous for their peers and are little involved in the peer group's affairs. They are less aggressive and less sociable than average children. They are also more withdrawn, but in this group this particular feature does not become a cause of depressive symptoms. Their prosocial orientation and friendship networks are similar to those of average children. The last studied group is **controversial children** whose behavior is a combination of that of popular and rejected groups. Like rejected children they tend to be more aggressive but they also possess much better cognitive abilities and social skills. Their aggression, therefore, is compensated for by prosocial behavior, positive personality traits and friendliness.

Similar findings describing individual sociometric statuses have been reported by Ollendick, Weist, Border and Greene (1992), and Cantrell and Prinz (1985). In their studies, the above mentioned groups have also been analyzed from other perspectives, using teachers' and school reports. Rejected children showed more problematic behaviors; were viewed as hyperactive; suffered from attention deficit disorders; achieved worse grades; and were more likely substance abusers. Similarly to their neglected peers, they possessed an external locus of control. Neglected children were seen by their classmates as less popular and more withdrawn. Teachers, however, observed no difference in their behavior compared to their average classmates.

Our study focuses on the relationship between sociometric status and selected personality attributes in secondary school students. The personality traits chosen for the study were the five personality factors identified within the Big Five model.

2. RESEARCH OBJECTIVES AND RESEARCH HYPOTHESES

The aim of our study was to address three main **research questions**:

1. **Is there a connection between personality traits and classroom sociometric status in late adolescence?**

   From this first research question we derived the following six hypotheses:

   - **H1: Agreeableness is positively correlated to students' popularity in the class.** We assume that highly agreeable individuals believe in honorable intentions in others, are ingenuous and compassionate and unselfishly help other people. They show modesty and humbleness and seek to avoid conflicts (Hřebíčková, 2004). All these characteristics contribute to their greater peer popularity and likeability, because they make them less confrontational and help them maintain positive relationships.

- **H2: Agreeableness is positively correlated to the positive evaluation of others within the classroom peer group.** We expect that individuals who are more obliging and kind to others and strive to promote harmonious relationships will be more indulgent and positive in their ratings of others than less agreeable individuals.
- **H3: Extroversion is positively correlated to student's influence within the class.** Extroverts are individuals who enjoy the company of other people, are self–assertive, active and more likely to assume leading positions (Hřebíčková, 2004). Therefore, they should not have problems getting involved in group affairs and are more or less predetermined for leading roles.
- **H4: Neuroticism is negatively correlated to a student's influence in the class.** We hypothesize that emotionally unstable individuals tend to be more insecure, are more prone to feelings of guilt, shame and embarrassment and have greater difficulties coping with stressful situations (Hřebíčková, 2004). As a consequence, these individuals lack the ability of self–assertion and interaction regulation among the group of peers (Hrabal, 2003). Their influence on their classmates should therefore be limited.
- **H5: Conscientiousness is positively correlated to the student's influence in the class.** Late adolescence is the time of identity formation, establishment of one's self–confidence, increase in personal responsibility, and development of conscientiousness, which are associated with better social competence and skill (Macek, 2003). These features are all potential predictors of greater influence and the ability to successfully assert one's ideas and opinions.
- **H6: All–male classes report higher average influence indexes than mixed classes.** This assumption is based on different dynamics in co–educational and all–male classroom peer groups. A higher average influence in all–male classes is expected due to the greater emphasis on physical strength, self–assertion ability and stricter norm enforcement (Hrabal, 2003).

2. **Does school achievement in interaction with personality attributes also predict classroom sociometric status in late adolescence?**

The second research question can be subdivided into the following hypotheses:

- **H7: Introverted boys with good grades are more popular with their class than introverted boys with poor school performance.** This hypothesis assumes that in introverts school achievement would have an impact on peer popularity. It has been evidenced that individuals who are introverted, i.e. rather non–assertive, quiet, reserved and passive and, in addition, with poor school performance, tend to be less popular in the class than others (Ollendick, Weist, Border, & Greene, 1992).
- **H8: Non–conscientious students with good academic performance are more popular than non–conscientious students achieving poor academic results.** Again, the impact of academic performance on popularity is hypothesized, this time in relation to low conscientiousness levels. If the student is negligent, indifferent, uninterested and aimless, and at the same time their grades are low, their popularity will be lower. Good grades, on the other hand, would increase their likeability.
- **H9: Students open to experience who achieve good grades are more influential among the classroom peer group than open students achieving poor academic results.** Some concepts related to the Big Five draw a connection between the personality dimension of Openness to Experience and intelligence (Goldberg, 1990, cf. Hřebíčková, 2004) and suggest that Openness is a predictor of the achieved level of education (Ostendorf & Angleitner, 2000, cf. Hřebíčková, 2004). Intelligence is correlated to the sociometric status: sociometric leaders, i.e. the greatest sources of influence, possess higher intelligence than the group average (Petrusek, 1969). Thus, we hypothesize that students who make use of this personal potential in achieving better school results increase their influence within the peer group.
- **H10: Neurotic boys with good grades have more influence within the class than neurotic low–achievers.** We elaborate on the finding that rejected children tend to be more depressed and anxious and have lower cognitive abilities compared to their peers (Newcomb, Bukowski, & Patee, 1993). If neuroticism has a negative impact on one's school achievement, it should also have a negative impact on one's influence among the peer group.
- **H11: Introverted students who have been officially praised by the class teacher or headmaster for their achievements are less popular than introverts who have not been officially praised.** Withdrawn, taciturn, non–assertive and passive students who have been officially praised by the school authorities are expected to be less popular among their peers. Their social withdrawal in connection with official praise, which might be perceived as an indicator of conformity

with the established school authorities, makes them less likeable for their classmates.

3. **How do students with distinctive personality traits perceive their own classroom social status in late adolescence?**
This question will be addressed using qualitative methodology. In this manner, the opinions of different students with particularly strong personality dispositions concerning their classroom social status are contrasted with "objective" indicators obtained in the quantitative part of the study.

3. METHOD

The instruments and other measures used in the study included the following:

1) **The Sociometric Rating Questionnaire (SO–RA–D)** designed by V. Hrabal (1979) is used for the assessment of relationships and interactions in small groups, especially school classes. On a five–point Likert–type scale each individual rates his or her peers with regard to their popularity and influence from most (1) to least (5). This quantitative assessment is then complemented by a free verbal description/assessment of one's perceived peer popularity. During administration, the terms "popularity" and "influence" are explained to the students. Influential people are those whose opinions and behaviors serve as models and reference for others, regardless of whether the influence is good or bad. Popular people are those whom we find likeable and whose company we enjoy. Hence, data collected from the Sociometric Rating Questionnaire provide information about popularity and influence of every single group member, about everyone's general status within the group and, to a certain extent, also about the relationship of every individual to the others. Quantitative results are represented by indexes of influence, popularity and friendliness. The fourth index – impressionability – was added later on in 2005 with the development of a new electronic version of the scale with new norms for the Czech population (Hrabal, 1979; Slavíková, Homolová, & Doležel, 2005).
2) **NEO Personality Inventory – Revised (NEO–PI–R)** is a multidimensional personality inventory developed by P. T. Costa and R. R. McCrae measuring five general dimensions of personality: Neuroticism (N), Extroversion (E), Openness to Experience (O), Agreeableness (P) and Conscientiousness (S). Each factor comprises six subscales (Hřebíčková, 2004) – see Table 1 below.

Table 1. Summary of individual scales and subscales of NEO–PI–R (Hřebíčková, 2004)

Scale/Subscale	Brief Description
N: Neuroticism	Measure of coping with psychological stress
N1: Anxiety	Worries and fear about future consequences
N2: Angry Hostility	Feelings of anger and hostility
N3: Depression	Feelings of dejection and despair
N4: Self–Consciousness	Feelings of embarrassment, shame and unease
N5: Impulsiveness	Succumbing to temptations (food, cigarettes, alcohol, drugs, shopping, etc.)
N6: Vulnerability	Proneness to getting carried away by pressing or stressful situations; tendency to panic
E: Extraversion	Measure of sociability, activity and vitality
E1: Warmth	Friendliness and enjoyment of company of others
E2: Gregariousness	Sociability; seeking of social contacts
E3: Assertiveness	Dominance and self–assertion
E4: Activity	Vitality; preference for rapid pace of life
E5: Excitement Seeking	Preference for thrilling experiences and strong sensations
E6: Positive Emotions	Optimism and feeling of happiness
O: Openness to Experience	Measure of openness to new experiences
O1: Fantasy	Creation of interesting inner fantasy world; imagination
O2: Aesthetics	Sense of art and beauty; sensitivity
O3: Feelings	Ability to appreciate and experience a great variety of positive and negative emotions both for oneself and with others
O4: Actions	Preference for novelty and diversity over the well–known and ordinary
O5: Ideas	Intellectual inquisitiveness; openness to novel, unconventional ideas
O6: Values	Readiness to test established social, political and religious values; non–dogmatic thinking
P: Agreeableness	Measure of agreeableness towards other people
P1: Trust	Tendency to trust others
P2: Straightforwardness	Honest and sincere treatment of others
P3: Altruism	Generosity, thoughtfulness and helpfulness
P4: Compliance	Preference for cooperation over competition
P5: Modesty	Modesty towards other people
P6: Tender–Mindedness	Tender–Mindedness, sympathy and compassion for others
S: Conscientiousness	Measure of how people deal with their responsibilities
S1: Competence	Readiness and ability to effectively accomplish tasks
S2: Order	Art of staying well–organized and making systematic progress
S3: Dutifulness	Adherence to rules; reliability
S4: Achievement striving	Readiness to set challenging tasks and accomplish them
S5: Self–Discipline	Ability of self–motivation for task accomplishment and keeping away distractions
S6: Deliberation	Ability to think things over in advance

3) School databases provided two kinds of information about students participating in the study: **average grades** obtained in the last completed semester and reports of **official praise** by class teacher or headmaster. Apart from praise, student's disciplinary sanctions (reprimands and reduced "manners grades", which are a part of the certificate at the end of each school year in the Czech Republic) were originally planned for inclusion in the analysis as well. However, since there were no reduced manners grades and only four official reprimands, disciplinary sanctions could not be taken into account in the present study.

4) A semi-structured interview was used with selected respondents with particularly prominent personality traits. The questions covered three basic areas: respondents' capacity of self-reflection; the impact of one's personality dispositions on one's functioning in the classroom peer group; and the way respondents perceived the class and their own status within it.

4. PARTICIPANTS

The research sample consisted of **124 students** from six classes in the fourth year of secondary school with a technical specialization concluded by Maturita examination (i.e. the official certification exam taken by students in higher-order secondary schools in the Czech Republic). The age varied between 18 to 22, with an average of 19. Due to the educational specialization, the vast majority of respondents (N = 113) were male; only very few (N = 11) were female.

In the qualitative part of the study, **6 respondents** were interviewed. The group, selected on the basis of the quantitative data, included individuals who obtained either extremely high or extremely low scores on one of the personality scales in the NEO Personality Inventory.

5. RESULTS

5.1. RESEARCH QUESTION NO. 1

First, the six hypotheses derived from the first research question were tested, i.e. whether there is a relationship between personality dispositions and classroom sociometric status (determined by influence and popularity) of students in late adolescence. Data was analyzed using Pearson correlation coefficients and Student's t-tests for two independent samples. With regard to the interpretation of correlation coefficients it has to be taken into consideration that one of the instruments used in the study – the Sociometric Rating Questionnaire – employs reverse scoring. Both influence and popularity scales in the questionnaire yield scores ranging from 1 to 5, with 1 standing for greatest influence/popularity and 5 standing for lowest influence/popularity. This is in contrast to the personality inventory NEO–PI–R where higher T–score values represent higher degrees of the personality disposition measured. Consequently, negative correlations needed to be interpreted as positive associations and vice versa.

The distribution of individual personality dimensions measured by NEO–PI–R in the research sample was tested using confidence intervals and histograms showing frequencies for individual intervals of the scores. An interval of ten T–scores was used, which was possible due to the fact that the conversion of raw scores into T–scores is achieved through linear transformation. For all five personality dimensions both confidence intervals were found within the range between the 25th and 75th percentiles, hence we may conclude these variables were all approximately normally distributed.

The first two hypotheses regarded the expected positive relationship of the personality dimension of Agreeableness to both student's popularity and his/her positive evaluation of others. The correlation coefficient $r = -.20$ ($p \leq .02$) indicates that there is a statistically significant connection between Agreeableness and peer popularity. This means that **Hypothesis 1 has been supported** – a higher level of Agreeableness is associated with higher popularity with one's classmates. Similarly, we have **found support for Hypothesis 2**: Students who are more agreeable make more positive nominations, which means they find their classmates more likeable and are more likely to express a friendly attitude ($r = -.23$; $p \leq .01$). This pattern is in agreement with several earlier studies (Newcomb, Bukowski & Patee, 1993; Cantrell & Prinz, 1985) which concluded that popular students tend to exhibit more positive social behavior and possess a greater degree of positive personal attributes. Since the image of a highly agreeable person more or less corresponds to the image of prosocial personality, given that the peer group does not promote pathological behavioral norms, these individuals should enjoy the greatest popularity with their peers.

The remaining hypotheses suggest associations between student's influence among the classroom peer group and three other personality dimensions: Extroversion, Neuroticism, and Conscientiousness. **Hypothesis 3**, regarding a positive relationship between Extraversion and personal influence, **was** also **confirmed**. The correlation $r = -.34$ is highly significant ($p \leq .00$). We have also found highly significant correlations with three out of six Extraversion subscales – Warmth, Gregariousness and Assertiveness (see Table 2 below). As an important personality disposition, Extroversion is taken into account by most leadership theories. Extroverts are more likely to assume the roles of leaders, exercise greater influence on the group and are more involved in group decision–making, organization and management issues (Kolominskij, 1980; Slavíková, Homolová, & Doležel, 2005; Giberson, 2004). Extroversion has an impact on the number and quality of interpersonal relationships, as well as the time spent in mutual interaction (Asendorpf & Wilpers, 1998). In the classroom the sociometric status improves with higher degrees of assertiveness, sociability and friendliness, which are all facets of Extroversion (Newcomb, Bukowski, & Patee, 1993).

Table 2. Correlations between personal influence index and subscales of Extroversion

	Warmth	Gregarious-ness	Assertive-ness	Activity	Excitement Seeking	Positive Emotions	Extroversion
Influence	**–.30**	**–.32**	**–.39**	–.14	–.16	–.12	**–.34**
	p = .00	**p = .00**	**p = .00**	p = .13	p = .08	p = .19	**p = .00**

Hypothesis 4 suggested that higher Neuroticism is associated with lower influence in the classroom peer group. This hypothesis **has not been supported** (r = .07; ns). However, in 3 out of 6 subscales of Neuroticism relationships with influence, negative associations were detected with Depression and Self–Consciousness, and positive association was found with Impulsiveness (see Table 3 below). It is possible that these three characteristics are the most noticeable ones during peer interaction in the school environment. Self–conscious individuals tend to avoid public appearances because they fear being ridiculed by others. A higher level of depression, on the other hand, is expressed as proneness to the feelings of sadness, despair and a hopeless perspective of the future. In the school environment, these tendencies are not easily concealed, which can lead to a diminished potential of exercising influence on others. Impulsiveness as an inability to regulate one's desires and impulses, and a tendency to seek immediate need satisfaction, could predispose individuals to certain socially undesirable behaviors like substance abuse, which is relatively common among Czech teenagers and can often be found among valid group norms. Behavior connected to the group norm system subsequently becomes associated with greater personal influence within the peer group.

Table 3. Correlations between personal influence index and subscales of Neuroticism

	Anxiety	Angry Hostility	Depression	Self–Consciousness	Impulsive-ness	Vulner-ability	Neuroti-cism
Influence	–.00	–.04	**.21**	**.28**	**–.24**	.11	.073
	p = .99	p = .64	**p = .03**	**p = .00**	**p = .01**	p = .26	p = .44

Hypothesis 5 predicted a positive association between Conscientiousness and the student's influence in the class. Although the correlation (r = .19) proved statistically significant ($p \leq .04$), the hypothesis **has not been confirmed**, since the relationship was in the opposite direction than that expected. Three subscales of Conscientiousness also showed negative associations with influence: Order, Dutifulness and Deliberation. The greater the level of these three dispositions, the weaker the influence of the student among his/her classmates (see Table 4 below). These results indicate that in late adolescence

a certain degree of irresponsibility, carelessness and lack of structure is considered a standard, and those who possess these attributes are more likely to achieve more influential positions within the class. This conclusion is in accordance with a more recent perspective on the challenges of adolescence and transition to adulthood. An even more prevailing opinion today is that identity formation is not finished with the passing of adolescence, and the development continues in the subsequent stages. The period of psycho–social moratorium becomes extended, providing young people with more time to try out various life experiences, focus on entertainment and distractions, and postpone the establishment of binding long–term commitments (Macek, 2005).

Table 4. Correlations between personal influence index and subscales of Conscientiousness

	Competence	Order	Dutiful-ness	Achievement Striving	Self–Discipline	Delibera-tion	Conscientious-ness
Influence	–.022	**.20**	**.232**	.089	.15	**.22**	**.19**
	p = .80	**p = .03**	**p = .01**	p = .33	p = .11	**p = .02**	**p = .04**

Hypothesis 6 predicted a higher average influence score in all–male classes as compared to mixed–sex classes. Due to the homogeneity of variances the average values of sociometric and dispositional indicators could be used to test the differences between these two types of classes. The difference regarding average peer influence, however, did not prove statistically significant (t = –0.93; p = .35). The hypothesis was therefore **not supported**. In Table 5 below, average values of all four sociometric indicators (popularity, influence, friendliness and impressionability) are summarized for both all–male and co–educational classes. No significant differences were found in any of these indicators. This might be due to the fact that the number of female students attending the school chosen for the study, as well as their representation in the individual classes, was so small that their impact on the overall classroom climate was too low to be traceable in the mixed classes. In order to fit in, girls are probably forced to conform to the rest of the class.

Table 5. Differences in sociometric indicators between all–male and mixed classesdf

	Mean Mixed	Mean All–Male	t–value	df	p	N Mixed	N All–Male	SD Mixed	SD All–Male
Popularity	2.38	2.48	–1.18	122	0.24	59	65	0.45	0.50
Influence	3.14	3.26	–0.93	122	0.35	59	65	0.80	0.63
Friendliness	2.40	2.52	–1.59	112	0.11	55	59	0.42	0.43
Impressionability	3.16	3.29	–1.10	112	0.28	55	59	0.62	0.60

A dispositional comparison of the two types of classes, however, indicates that all–male classes are on average significantly more neurotic (N). This can be ascribed mainly to two subscales of Neuroticism: Depression (N3) and Self–

Consciousness (N4). Conversely, Warmth as a facet of Extroversion (E1) and Straightforwardness as a facet of Agreeableness (P2) were significantly higher in mixed classes. Table 6 below shows the comparison of the two types of classes regarding personality indicators. Significant differences are highlighted in bold.

Table 6. Differences in the Big Five personality dimensions between all-male and mixed classes

	M Mixed	M All-Male	t-value	df	p	N Mixed	N All-Male	SD Mixed	SD All-Male
N1	49.24	52.68	-1.94	122	0.06	59	65	9.80	9.94
N2	48.61	51.14	-1.56	122	0.12	59	65	9.42	8.62
N3	**47.92**	**53.32**	**-2.85**	**122**	**0.01**	**59**	**65**	**9.35**	**11.53**
N4	**48.14**	**52.75**	**-2.24**	**122**	**0.03**	**59**	**65**	**10.44**	**12.31**
N5	49.61	52.18	-1.53	122	0.13	59	65	9.82	8.98
N6	47.59	49.89	-1.49	122	0.14	59	65	8.41	8.72
N	**48.15**	**52.95**	**-2.83**	**122**	**0.01**	**59**	**65**	**9.42**	**9.48**
E1	**54.88**	**51.80**	**2.27**	**122**	**0.03**	**59**	**65**	**7.73**	**7.40**
E2	53.31	51.32	1.07	122	0.29	59	65	10.46	10.24
E3	49.25	47.94	0.68	122	0.50	59	65	11.33	10.09
E4	46.97	47.66	-0.37	122	0.71	59	65	10.96	9.91
E5	50.69	52.74	-1.18	122	0.24	59	65	9.89	9.43
E6	51.22	48.51	1.51	122	0.13	59	65	10.35	9.59
E	52.22	50.71	0.81	122	0.42	59	65	10.16	10.60
O1	50.32	47.18	1.60	122	0.11	59	65	10.42	11.29
O2	48.88	49.00	-0.07	122	0.94	59	65	8.54	9.83
O3	50.46	50.17	0.16	122	0.87	59	65	9.35	10.55
O4	46.15	47.78	-0.90	122	0.37	59	65	10.30	9.78
O5	47.47	47.82	-0.19	122	0.85	59	65	9.20	10.69
O6	50.49	49.40	0.63	122	0.53	59	65	9.55	9.73
O	48.76	48.28	0.28	122	0.78	59	65	8.67	10.41
P1	50.36	47.62	1.334	122	0.19	59	65	11.77	11.18
P2	**53.85**	**49.38**	**2.35**	**122**	**0.02**	**59**	**65**	**10.08**	**10.99**
P3	55.42	53.25	1.64	122	0.10	59	65	8.04	6.78
P4	51.14	49.83	0.83	122	0.41	59	65	9.39	8.22
P5	50.19	52.35	-1.17	122	0.24	59	65	10.67	9.93
P6	52.95	50.55	1.40	122	0.16	59	65	10.15	8.91
P	53.95	51.29	1.75	122	0.08	59	65	8.80	8.08
S1	52.66	49.34	1.89	122	0.06	59	65	9.64	9.90
S2	49.59	50.69	-0.59	122	0.56	59	65	10.72	10.14
S3	52.54	50.78	1.09	122	0.28	59	65	8.37	9.48
S4	49.36	47.94	0.76	122	0.45	59	65	11.01	9.89
S5	50.66	49.49	0.71	122	0.48	59	65	9.14	9.07
S6	52.00	48.66	1.78	122	0.08	59	65	11.01	9.89
S	51.97	49.68	1.23	122	0.22	59	65	10.91	9.88

5.2 RESEARCH QUESTION NO. 2

The second set of hypotheses was derived from the second research question, i.e. whether classroom sociometric status in late adolescence is also affected by students' school performance in interaction with personality variables. For this purpose the research sample was divided according to the standard scores yielded by the individual personality scales into two groups ($T < 50$ and $T > 50$). Each of these groups was then further divided into two subgroups with respect to average semester grade or obtained praise. First, an F–test was used to verify the equality of variances across the groups. After that, a Student's t–test was employed to test the significance of differences between both group averages.

Hypothesis 7 proposed that introverted boys with good school performance are more popular than introverts with lower grades. To test this hypothesis, the group of introverted boys ($E < 50$) was divided according to their school achievement into a subgroup of high–achievers and low–achievers (as compared to the class average). The average popularity index in the former group was 2.54 with a standard deviation of 0.42. In the latter group the average was also 2.54, SD = 0.16. An F–test was used to test the variance comparability of both groups ($p \leq .02$), followed by a one–tailed t–test for independent samples with unequal variance. The result was statistically insignificant ($p \leq .50$), which means that **Hypothesis 7 was not supported**.

Hypothesis 8 assumed that non–conscientious students with good school performance are more popular than those showing poor school performance. Students with low levels of Conscientiousness ($S < 50$) were taken out of the sample and divided into two groups according to their average grades as compared to the class average. In the first group the average popularity score was 2.32, SD = 0.30; in the second group the score was 2.48, SD = 0.10. An F–test was used to test the variance comparability of both groups ($p \leq .01$), followed by a one–tailed t–test for independent samples with unequal variance. The result did not prove statistically significant ($p \leq .13$), and therefore **Hypothesis 8 was not supported**.

Hypothesis 9 suggested that high–achieving students with high levels of Openness to Experience are more influential among their peers than their lowachieving counterparts. Students with high levels of Openness to Experience ($O > 50$) were extracted from the sample and divided into two groups according to their average grades as compared to the class average. In the first group, the average influence score was 3.05, SD = 0.60; in the second group, the score was 3.23, SD = 0.50. An F–test was used to test the variance comparability of both groups ($p \leq .66$), followed by a one–tailed t–test for independent samples with equal variance. The result did not prove statistically significant ($p \leq .20$), and therefore **Hypothesis 9 was not supported**.

According to Hypothesis 10, neurotic boys with good grades should have more influence among their classmates than those with poor grades. Students with high levels of Neuroticism (N > 50) were taken out of the sample and divided into two groups according to their average grades. In the first group the average influence score was 3.19, SD = 0.49; in the second group the score was 3.33, SD = 0.69. An F–test was used to test the variance comparability of both groups ($p \leq .36$), followed by a one–tailed t–test for independent samples with equal variance. The result did not prove statistically significant ($p \leq .25$), and therefore **Hypothesis 10 was not supported**.

Hence, our study found no significant impacts of school performance on the classroom sociometric status, even though in the studies by other authors such associations were reported (e.g. Eronen & Nurmi, 2001; Ollendick, Weist, Border & Greene, 1992). It has to be noted, however, that these earlier results were obtained with primary school samples. In contrast, our findings indicate that in late adolescence mutual peer evaluation is much less likely to be affected by the perception of the other's academic performance. It is generally considered normal not to study, and low grades therefore have little impact on one's sociometric status. Macek (2002) performed a structure and frequency analysis of individual activities adolescents engage in on a daily basis and found that time spent at home studying shortens with age.

Hypothesis 11 suggested that introverted students who were formally praised by the class teacher or headmaster are less popular than introverts who were not formally praised. Students with low levels of Extroversion (E < 50) were extracted from the sample and divided into two groups according to the records of formal praises. In the first group, the average value of the popularity index was 2.05, SD = 0.09; in the second group the score was 2.55, SD = 0.30. An F–test was used to test the variance comparability of both groups ($p \leq .34$), followed by a one–tailed t–test for independent samples with equal variance. The difference proved statistically significant ($p \leq .04$). Hence, **Hypothesis 11 was supported**. Formal praise, which might be considered a representation of the student's acknowledgement by the official school authorities and an expression of his/her support and conformity to their value system, is perhaps perceived as a symbol of betrayal of the group norms and consequently results in diminished popularity with one's classmates.

5.3 RESEARCH QUESTION NO. 3

Regarding the third research question, interviews with three respondents with particularly pronounced personality traits were analyzed. Table 7 below shows basic quantitative data for each respondent. Scores in those personality dimensions which were particularly marked in each individual are highlighted in bold.

Table 7. SO-RA-D and NEO-PI-R scores obtained by respondents included in the qualitative part of the study

Code of the respondent	**A12**	**B17**	**C15**
Influence Index	3.1	2.25	2.38
Influence Percentile	24	5	16
Popularity Index	1.85	2.05	3
Popularity Percentile	7	13	77
N: Neuroticism (T-score)	62	65	**20**
E: Extraversion (T-score)	**23**	51	53
O: Openness to Experience (T-score)	**32**	77	50
P: Agreeableness (T-score)	56	47	**25**
S: Conscientiousness (T-score)	45	**30**	**80**

All three respondents participating in the interviews were informed about their personality inventory results. Sociometric results could not be revealed due to ethical concerns. All interviews were recorded using a digital voice recorder and fully transcribed. Three general topics were covered in the interviews: 1) self-reflection (perception of one's personality characteristics; development of one's traits in time; external factors influencing personality development); 2) dynamics between one's personality and the class (positive or negative impact of one's personal characteristics on one's classroom functioning); and 3) perception of the class (student's perception of the classroom peer group and their own social status within the class).

The data obtained from the interviews were analyzed using a clustering method. The overall status of individual students in the class is illustrated by square diagrams showing influence and popularity scores of the respondents in relation to their classmates' results obtained from cluster analysis. A light green line marks the boundary of the class nucleus; a dark green line represents the broader classroom peer group. If the individual is positioned outside these two boundaries, it means that his/her influence, popularity or both differ widely from those of his/her peers.

Respondent A12

The first interviewed respondent, identified by the dataset code A12, was an 18-year-old male. His average final grade in the last semester was 1.75, as compared to the class average of 2.47. He was neither formally reprimanded nor praised. According to the personality inventory, his most distinguishing traits included very **high Introversion** and very **low Openness to Experience**. The respondent belonged to the three most popular students in the class. Regarding influence, he was positioned in the center of the peer group.

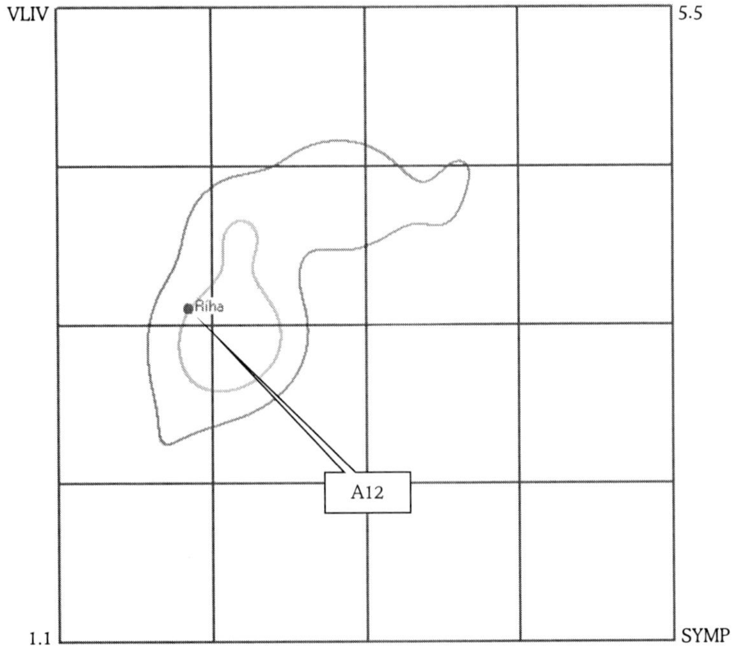

Figure 1. The status of respondent A12 within the classroom peer group

Self-assessment of personality traits: The respondent is only partly aware of his personality disposition. He describes himself as introverted but does not perceive himself as an extreme introvert. Concerning his inclinations towards conservatism, these were reflected upon for the first time during the interview.

Trait development: The respondent describes the development of his most distinctive trait, i.e. introversion, as a shift from a more extreme to milder disposition. In early childhood he generally preferred solitude; with the onset of adolescence (between 13–14 years of age) his solitariness began to ease off. After entering secondary school it took him a bit longer to fit in with the rest of the class.

Influence of personality traits on functioning within the classroom peer group: The respondent believes his distinctive traits do not particularly influence his position and functioning in the classroom peer group. He does not have any problems expressing his opinion or getting his way. He has several good friends in the class. One thing that makes him different from the others is the fact that it is more difficult for him to make new acquaintances. However, this is something which is more likely perceived as a problem by his peers, not by himself.

Classroom social status: The respondent views his status as average; he would most likely localize himself in the center of the class.

Peer assessment: Classmates perceive the respondent as a friendly person who does not particularly differ from the rest of the class, who is willing to help and is nice to talk to. Sociometric indicators of general classroom social status positioned him in the upper 25% of the class, with his popularity ranking higher than his influence. This means that the respondent most likely underestimates his position in the class.

Respondent B17

The respondent coded as B17 is a 19-year-old male. His last average final grade was 1.85 (as compared to the class average 2.36). He did not receive any formal reprimands or praise. In the personality inventory he scored **very high in Openness to Experience** and **very low in Conscientiousness**. His classmates rate him as one of two **most influential** students in the class. Concerning **popularity**, he ranks among the first 33% of the class. From the combination of both of these sociometric indexes and verbal assessments, respondent B17 emerges as an effective leader of the class.

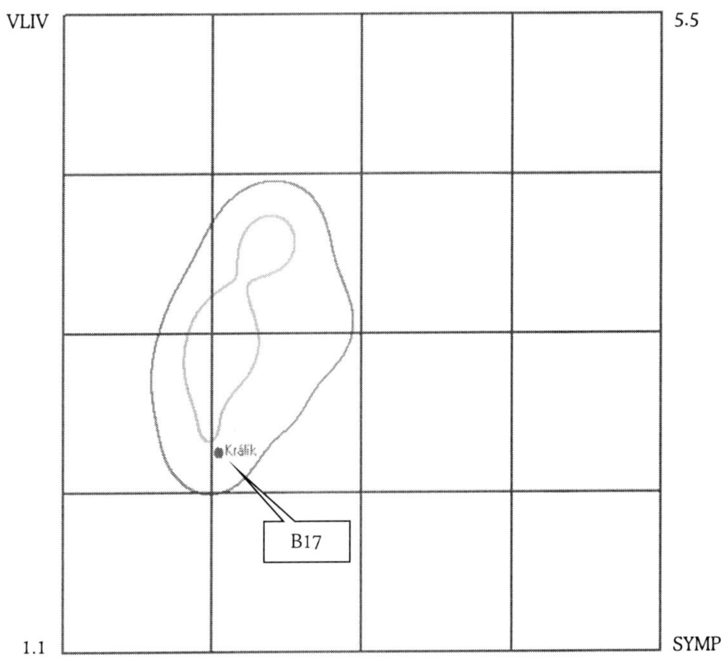

Figure 2. The status of respondent B17 within the classroom peer group

Self-assessment of personality traits: The respondent knows about his two most distinctive dispositions. He considers himself an individual open to new things and experiences. He is especially interested in humanities and intends to study psychology and sociology at university. He is also aware of his own lack of conscientiousness and refers to his inability to self-motivate on finishing tasks.

Trait development: According to the respondent his personality traits started to become more accentuated in early adolescence.

External factors influencing personality development: Reflecting on his personal characteristics in childhood the respondent mentions the influence of his mother.

Positive impact of personality traits on peer group functioning: The respondent shows ambivalence concerning his lack of conscientiousness and responsibility in relation to the peer group. In certain situations the lack of conscientiousness helps him win more popularity with his classmates, who see him as a hero. He believes that this particular trait is quite characteristic of his age as well as the social status of a secondary school student. A high degree of openness to experience is perceived as very positive. The respondent sees it as beneficial to interpersonal relationships and as an asset in debates with classmates.

Negative impact of personality traits on peer group functioning: Sometimes the respondent encounters situations when his lack of conscientiousness becomes a weak point in his own eyes, either with regard to his classmates or with regard to the attainment of his own academic achievement goals.

Perception of the classroom peer group: The class is perceived positively as a peaceful and balanced group of peers where everyone communicates with everyone else. At the same time, however, it is viewed as a rather phlegmatic community with no one willing to organize things or step out of the crowd.

Classroom social status: The respondent is aware of his prominent position and influence among his classmates. He knows he is usually in the middle of things and finds himself where the action is or where decisions are being made.

Peer assessment: Classmates' assessments are not completely unequivocal. Some perceive the respondent as a strong leader, which also follows from the sociometric data. Others appreciate his sense of humor and intelligence. Several classmates point out his rather chaotic behavior, and one of them even accused the respondent of arrogance and treachery. Indisputably, however, the respondent belongs to the leading personalities and appears to be the main source of action in the class.

Respondent C15

The respondent coded as C15, also a male, was 20 years old. His average final mark from the last semester was 1.82 (as compared to the class average 2.4); he received no reprimands or praise. His personality profile showed three prominent traits: **very low scores in** both **Neuroticism and Agreeableness**, and a **very high score in Conscientiousness**. According to his popularity index, he seemed rather unpopular. As far as influence is concerned, he was ranked among the **25% most influential** students in the class.

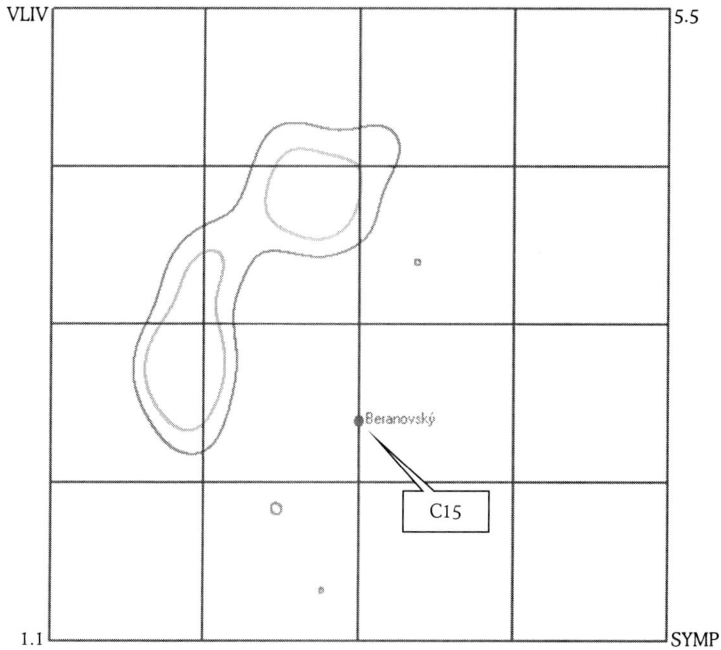

Figure 3. The status of respondent C15 within the classroom peer group

Self-assessment of personality traits: The respondent's perception of his own personality disposition is in accordance with the results from the inventory. He knows he is very emotionally stable, calm and level-headed, and not easily disconcerted by stressful situations. He regards himself as a determined person who keeps working on himself; when he wants to achieve something he does his best. Regarding interpersonal relationships, he describes himself as rather detached.

Trait development: The respondent does trace the development of his personality dispositions in time. During adolescence the individual traits grew more extreme. At the beginning of adolescence he acquired much autonomy and freedom since his parents were very liberal. The next stage, around 16 years old, is perceived rather negatively as a short period of wasted time when he neglected and failed to pursue his important personal objectives. As he turned seventeen, his conscientiousness started to push through with his determination and strong desire to achieve something.

External factors influencing personality development: One of the most important factors was parental influence. The parents allowed the respondent much autonomy at quite an early age, which meant he could make most decisions by himself. Another significant influence in the formation of his personality, as perceived by himself, was his general life experience; his interpersonal relationships were strongly affected by negative feelings. His responsible approach to duties is also partly a result of the extended period of secondary school studies and deferred school entry.

Positive impact of personality traits on peer group functioning: As positively regarded attributes, the respondent refers to his reliability and dutifulness which help him achieve academic success and attain his goals. His purposefulness is reflected in his answers to all interview questions. He frequently refers to the fact that he works hard on himself, and his entire daily schedule is completely filled and organized.

Negative impact of personality traits on peer group functioning: The respondent understands that his personality disposition is more of a disadvantage for his functioning in the peer group. Nevertheless, he does not seem particularly bothered by this. He is an idiosyncratic, individualist personality and does not feel the need to fit in. He knows his opinions and lifestyle are different from those of his classmates, which does not do much good to their mutual understanding. Although he normally talks to his peers and tries to avoid judging them, he does not have close friends among the class, and this situation probably suits him best. His classmates do not understand his approach to responsibilities; they believe it is just a pose – a means to show off. The student's responses indicate a strong desire to distinguish himself from others, a strong self–focus, and a high opinion of his own personal exceptionality, which are all characteristic of a narcissist personality. Distrust and skepticism towards classmates correspond to the respondent's low level of Agreeableness.

Perception of the classroom peer group: The respondent's view of the classroom peer group is predominantly negative. He finds them intolerant and prefers to keep his distance.

Classroom social status: The respondent perceives himself as someone who prefers to hold back, not because he could not push himself forward, but rather because his opinions and attitudes differ from the rest of the class, and so he does not even seek to express them. He does not conform to the established class norms. However, his belief that his views are generally neglected is not shared by his classmates, who ranked him among the 25% most influential students.

Peer assessment: Classmates consider the respondent primarily from the perspective of his distinct ideas and opinions. Although they do not associate with him, some of them appreciate that he is not afraid to be different from the rest. They also welcome the opportunity of interesting debates with the respondent. The students also point out his self–centeredness, considering him an egoist. The sociometric results present him as an influential but rather unpopular student. His exclusion from the classroom core group is also illustrated by the square diagram.

In summary, the three interviews tell us the following:

Respondents B17 and C15 perceived their personalities in accordance with the inventory. Respondent A12 was only partially aware of his personality disposition; as a rather pragmatically oriented individual, he did not focus too much on his inner experience. **All three respondents, however, demonstrated considerable abilities of self–reflection.** Their profiles were usually in correspondence with classmates' assessments.

The respondents also perceive the development of their own personality traits in time. They have noticed increments in Openness to Experience (B17) and Conscientiousness (B17, C15). Introversion, on the other hand, grew milder with age (A12). Two respondents (A12, B17) localized the time when their traits had started to become more pronounced in early adolescence, i.e. aged 12–13. Respondent C15 also identified such a turning point in his personal history, but associated it with the age of around 17.

The most frequently mentioned **external factor** affecting personality development was the influence of one's parents (B17, C15), especially as behavioral models or sources of a particular parenting style. One respondent (C15) also referred to the impact of interpersonal relationships; however, he did not elaborate on the issue.

One of the respondents (A12) did not perceive any connection between his personality and his social status in the class. The other two **assessed both advantages and disadvantages of their personality disposition for their peer group functioning correctly**. Respondent B17 viewed costs and benefits as relatively equal; in student C15 the impact was rather negative. The benefits of accentuated traits included higher empathy (B17), more friendships and popularity (B17), easy communication (B17) and academic success (C15). Negative consequences associated with a distinctive personality involved anxiety affecting school performance (A12, B17), being unable to meet one's academic aspirations (B17), being unpopular with certain classmates (C15), having few friends (C15) and pushing oneself into the foreground at the expense of other students (C15).

The perception of the individual classroom peer groups was not unanimous, but was highly influenced by the personalities of the respondents. Student B17 viewed his peer group very positively. In contrast, respondent C15's opinion of the class was quite negative – he found it intolerant and unfavorable with regard to his individuality. Respondent A12 did not directly touch on the topic, but considering that he reported having good friends among the class, it might be expected that his view would be rather positive.

The respondents found it difficult to assess their **own status within the classroom peer group**. Again, the comments were influenced by personality dispositions. Respondent B17 regarded his position as focal. Student A12 assumed he did not differ widely from the rest of the class. Finally, student C15 saw himself at the periphery of the group and personally did not show much interest in it.

6. CONCLUSION

The results of our study have confirmed the connection between particular personality dimensions and sociometric indicators of classroom social status in students. On the other hand, the relationship between school performance and sociometric status was not confirmed. The main findings of the study can be concluded as follows:

- **Highly agreeable students not only enjoy greater popularity with their classmates, but also find their classmates more likeable.**
- **Higher levels of Extroversion are associated with higher influence among the classroom peer group.** Extroverted individuals are better at getting their way in the group; they are more assertive in decision-making, and more active than their classmates. Individual components of Extroversion (Warmth, Gregariousness and Assertiveness) were also correlated to personal influence at school.
- Neuroticism as such does not have an impact on the level of influence; yet, three out of its six components do. **Whereas Depression and Self-Consciousness are associated with decreased personal influence, Impulsiveness is associated with increased influence.**
- **Higher levels of Conscientiousness serve to reduce one's influence among classmates.** This connection was also found in three facets of Conscientiousness: Order, Dutifulness and Deliberation.
- Average influence indexes do not differ significantly in all-male and mixed classes. **However, all-male classes score higher in Neuroticism, Depression and Self-Consciousness. Mixed classes, on the other hand, show higher levels of Warmth and Straightforwardness**, which are both characteristics related to interpersonal relationships.
- School performance does not have any significant impact on the classroom social status in relation to personality dispositions.
- **Formal praises by the class teacher or headmaster diminish introverted students' popularity** with their classmates.

- Students in late adolescence seem to be capable of self–reflection concerning their personalities and the **development of their personality traits in time**. The turning point in the development is likely to be localized in early adolescence at 12–13, when some of the traits become more pronounced.
- The students do perceive **the impact of their personality on their functioning in the classroom peer group** and are apparently able to identify both **costs and benefits** associated with their traits in relation to the class.
- The student's **assessment of** both **the classroom peer group and** their own **status** within the class seems to be **marked by** their **personality** in late adolescence.

REFERENCES

Asendorpf J.B., Wilpers S., Personality Effects on Social Relationships, "Journal of Personality and Social Psychology" 1998, 74, 6, 1531–1544.

Cantrell V.L., Prinz R.J., Multiple Perspectives of Rejected, Neglected, and Accepted Children: The Relation Between Sociometric Status and Behavioral Characteristics, "Journal of Consulting and Clinical Psychology" 1985, 53, 6, 884–889.

Eronen S, Nurmi J.E., Sociometric Status of Young Adults. Behavioural Correlates, and Cognitive–Motivational Antecendents and Consequences, "International Journal of Behavioral Development" 2001, 25, 3, 203–213.

Hrabal V., Sociometrický test, příručka T–118, Bratislava, Psychodiagnostické a didaktické testy 1979.

Hrabal V., Sociální psychologie pro učitele, Praha, Karolinum 1992.

Hrabal V., Sociální psychologie pro učitele, Vybraná témata, Praha, Karolinum 2003.

Hřebíčková M., NEO osobnostní inventář, Praha, Testcentrum 2004.

Kolominskij J.L., Psychológia vzájemných vzťahov v malých skupinách, Bratislava, Slovenské pedagogické nakladatelství 1980.

Kulka J., Sociální psychologie pro učitele, Praha, SPN 1983.

Lašek J., Sociálně psychologické klima školních tříd a školy, Hradec Králové, Gaudeamus 2001.

Macek P., Adolescence, utváření identity a současní čeští dospívající, [in:] Smékal V., Macek P. (eds.), Utváření a vývoj osobnosti, Brno, Barrister&Principal 2002.

Macek P., Adolescence. Praha, Portál 2003.

Macek P., Kde končí dospívání a kde začíná dospělost?, [in:] Macek P., Dalajka J. (eds.), Vývoj a utváření osobnosti v sociálních a etnických kontextech, Brno, FSS MU 2005.

Madarasová–Gecková A., Orosová O., Madaras T., Vybrané problémy použitia sociometrie v školské praxi, "Československá psychologie" 2004, 3.

Newcomb A.F., Bukowski W.M., Patee L., Children's Peer relations: A Meta–Analytic Review of Popular, Rejected, Neglected, Controversial, and Average Sociometric Status, "Psychological Bulletin" 1993, 113, 1.

Ollendick T.H., Weist M.D., Border M.Ch., Greene R.W., Sociometric Status and Academic, Behavioral, and Psychological Adjustment: A Five–Year Longitudinal Study, "Journal of Consulting and Clinical Psychology" 1992, 60, 1.

Petrusek M., Sociometrie, Praha, Svoboda, 1969.

Prokop J., Škola jako sociální útvar, Praha, PedF UK 1996.

Slavíková I., Homolová K., Doležel P., Sociometricko–ratingový dotazník V. Hrabala, st., Praha, IPPP ČR 2005.

Teresa Bogacz
College of Management "Edukacja" in Wroclaw
Beata Konopska
Institute of Geodesy and Cartography, Warsaw

A MAP AS AN INSTRUMENT IN THE EDUCATIONAL COMMUNICATION PROCESS AT SCHOOL LEVEL

ABSTRACT

Cartographic compilations, in the form of maps and atlases, are one form facilitating communication in a teacher–student relationship in the process of knowledge transfer, especially in the fields of geography and history. Spatial information referring to objects, phenomena and events, both natural and socio–economic, occurring today and in the past, is represented on maps in the form of cartographic signs. After meeting certain conditions geographical and historical maps are an effective communication instrument. These conditions include the conformity of the map content with the curriculum and information capacity of a scale (in which the map is presented) and the elaboration of map graphics in accordance with cartographic semiotic principles. Both conditions – the first related to the map content and the second to the graphics – are closely related to the characteristics of the user who, depending on their age, may have different perceptions and experiences. This applies mainly to the recipient of school maps. Separate requirements are imposed by students with vision defects (partially blind or blind). In the first stage of teaching both geography and history, in the process of communication between the map and the student, it is the teacher who plays a key role. They are considered to teach how to interpret the map by discussing and explaining its content. However, at the high school level communication in the school–student relationship no longer requires the participation of the teacher, as the map takes on a direct dimension.

KEYWORDS: communication, education, school, geography, history, cartographic.

1. INTRODUCTION

A map is a visual representation of geographical aspects of a particular area, designed for various applications, where spatial relationships play the most important part by showing objects and their characteristics, resulting from a creative process of selection by its creator.[1] Map creators, while representing any

[1] D. Gotlib, Metodyka prezentacji kartograficznych w mobilnych systemach lokalizacyjnych i nawigacyjnych, Politechnika Warszawska, Prace Naukowe, Geodezja, z. 48, Warszawa, 2011, p. 12.

objects or phenomena, use graphic symbols which map users should be able to understand intuitively or through description. In this respect, maps are a form of visual communication and are subject to all the rules associated with it. The primary aim of every cartographic publication is to provide information about objects, phenomena and the area where they appear in a way that is legible and understandable to the user. However, the correct interpretation of the map content is possible only after gaining basic knowledge in this field, mainly at school. In other words, the map is a form of visual communication and its correctness can be judged by the effectiveness with which it is able to convey the message.[2] To prepare a correct map one must know the principles of map editing. Therefore, while preparing a map, one must firstly identify its intended use; that is, state the purpose of its preparation and characterize the traits of its user. In the case of maps used at school the user is a student who, depending on the teaching level, has different perceptive abilities related to their developmental stage. Once the purpose of the map and its target audience are defined, one can decide on the content, symbols and the methods of data presentation which are appropriate and match the student's perceptive abilities. On the one hand, maps are ubiquitous in today's social communication system – from weather maps to political preference maps to car navigation maps. On the other hand, map-reading and map-using skills are still insufficient due, among other reasons, to limited access to topographic maps. Taking all this into consideration, one can understand the particular importance of cartographic education at school. Therefore, the aim of this chapter is to address the significant aspects of the topic, namely: how maps should be used as means of communication at various teaching levels; how technological advances affect the process of modernization of maps as a tool; how this translates into the potential effectiveness of education; and how students can use their acquired skills outside school. The authors also point out that as the boundary between the humanities and the natural sciences is becoming more blurred, it is important that in the near future the concept of a "common" map as a universal tool for teaching both geography and history is introduced at all school levels. To illustrate the abovementioned issues, the authors use the example of traditional (printed) maps as well as multimedia (interactive) ones, the latter being increasingly used and compatible with modern methods of teaching through demonstration. Particular attention is given to the examples of combining historical and geographical data on maps.

[2] See e.g. Judy Olson, Experience and the improvement of cartographic communications, "Cartographic Journal" Vol. 12 (1975), No. 2, pp. 94–108. The author has devoted most of her article to this issue.

2. MAPS IN TEACHING GEOGRAPHY AND HISTORY

When the map content and the methods of cartographic presentation are subordinated to the purpose of teaching, such maps are called educational maps. These include – according to traditional terminology – wall maps, concise (quick reference) maps, and atlases. Because they are used at all teaching levels, preparing such maps requires a different approach to content selection and its graphic representation, depending on the developmental level of students. Maps prepared according to the above principles are essential teaching aids that support the educational communication at school. Therefore, teaching both geography and history requires these two disciplines in combination because of the message conveyed, and with pedagogical and psychological sciences because of the students' ability to assimilate this message. The cartographic publications belong to the system of symbolic images because they represent geographical or historical data by using the set of cartographic symbols. These publications are the most important link in the process of communication between a teacher and a student, when the former explains phenomena and processes taking place in the geographical space to the latter. However, it is worth noting that in addition to cognitive values, they also have an educational function. They are used in developing the awareness of spatial relationships, acquiring observational skills, interpreting symbolic images and understanding the evolution of spatial phenomena over time. Recognizing the importance of cartographic publications as necessary teaching aids for geography and history classes is connected with the specifics of maps, which are the key to fathoming the processes inextricably linked with space and, when it comes to history, with time.

The knowledge acquired through maps from both geography and history may become useful in learning geography as well as history. Undoubtedly, it should be easier for students to comprehend the socio–economic aspects of life in the modern world if they are given an historical background. Likewise, geographical knowledge is undoubtedly helpful for learning history. Students will master the content presented on historical maps better if during geography lessons they learn how to read and use geographical maps as aids. The knowledge about landform features and climate or hydrography will permit the understanding of, for example, the sequence of war events, the development of settlement or the validity of political decisions. There is a direct methodological correlation between geography and history. It is crucial, however, to introduce the given content during one subject where it constitutes a basis, and later make use of it in the second. By observing this sequence we obey the interdisciplinary correlation. Disturbing it (i.e. when geographical and historical facts are not presented in a proper sequence) provokes the need to introduce solutions into cartographic publications (mostly atlases), disrupting, for example, a logical content layout. For instance, at primary school level it generates the necessity to introduce the issue of preparing maps in general into the historical atlas for grade 4.[3]

The requirements related to the interdisciplinary correlation and close interrelation between geography and history also stem from principal reasons connected with the new model of perception of the world and its conditionings. The holistic approach to natural sciences and individual approach adopted in pedagogy and psychology constitutes the basis for teaching geography in today's schools. The holistic approach to teaching geography makes it possible to depart from a specified description of reality and move towards the explanation of events against more broadly understood relations. In accordance with the holistic concept, it is assumed that the Earth, together with creatures living on it, is an integral organic entity.[4] On the other hand, a modern approach to teaching history is shifting towards a more problem–oriented model rather than following the traditional chronological order. Such an approach to geography and history highlights their interdependence and the compatibility of interpretation. Since topographical objects, both modern and existing in the past, as well as past and current socio–economic events create a logical series of research objects characterizing geospace, cartography becomes the natural common ground between both, already quite similar, scientific disciplines. It depicts a geographical space, facilitates the presentation of the socio–economic issues, and furthers the analysis of both modern and historical phenomena and processes. The above mentioned parallel use of geographical and historical maps is, therefore, well–founded.

The effectiveness of teaching improves when in the educational process the same representations are used in the form of wall maps and atlases (or concise quick reference maps). It was a thesis already propagated and introduced during the interwar period (1918–39). Such an approach to teaching with the use of maps is of crucial importance in student–teacher communication, as they see the same content presented on the wall and the maps in the atlases. It facilitates not only the educational process (teacher–student relationship) but is also helpful for students in consolidating knowledge individually at home. In the Polish People's Republic (PRL) period, this attitude was abandoned and universal wall maps were designed for simultaneous primary and secondary school ues as well as in higher education. Only the maps in the atlases were prepared in accordance with the teaching programme and students' perceptive abilities. A separate preparation of wall maps and atlas maps plays a role only when paper products are in question. Multimedia or internet maps, because of the technology used, fulfill this condition in an obvious way.

[3] Atlas historyczny "Od starożytności do współczesności". Szkoła podstawowa, Nowa Era Sp. z o.o. ed. 1, Warszawa, 2012, p. 72.

[4] S. Piskorz, Introduction, Zarys dydaktyki geografii, ed. S. Piskorz, Warszawa, 1997, pp. 14–15.

2.1. FORMATION OF THE RELATION BETWEEN GEOGRAPHY AND HISTORY IN THE TEACHING METHODOLOGY

It has been assumed in the scientific literature that Collegium Nobilium, established in 1740 and administered by Stanislaw Konarski (1700–1773), was the first school in which globes and maps were systematically used in the process of teaching. The first discussions about the use of maps in methodology were associated with school reform and the work of Komisja Edukacji Narodowej (The Commission of National Education, established in 1773) at the turn of the 19th century. In the case of teaching history, the first to devote a lot of attention to the use of maps in the process of transferring knowledge was Joachim Lelewel (1786–1861). Due to him, historical maps started to be used alongside geographical maps in the Polish educational system. Before that, only geographical maps had been used during history lessons. This novelty stemmed from his opinion that historical events had to be joined with geographical conditions. It was then that such a mode of thinking emerged which modeled human activities in space, landscape and in relation to geographical areas.[5] It seems, however, that the problem of historical maps was not more broadly perceived by methodologists until the interwar period (1918–1939)[6], the indication of which was the publication of the atlas combining geography with modern history.[7] Eugeniusz Romer, its author, stated that "the more modern history approaches the contemporary, the more distanced from history it becomes and the more it becomes geography".[8]

Other events beyond the educational field also influenced the integration of geography and history, e.g. the change of the border system when Poland regained independence immediately after the Second World War, and when using both kinds of maps was recommended.[9] Therefore, in spite of a formal separation of the subjects, such situations appeared in which the linkage between geographical and historical content facilitated the process of communication.

2.2. EVOLUTION OF GEOGRAPHICAL AND HISTORICAL MAPS' CONTENT

In the evolution of school maps in connection with the scope and method of presenting content, we can differentiate a few stages. During the first, until about the end of the 19th century the majority of historical and geographical maps presented the content limited to basic elements. Historical maps were

[5] S. Bednarek, Pojmowanie kultury i jej historii we współczesnych syntezach dziejów kultury polskiej, Wrocław, 1995.

[6] H. Mościcki, Wskazówki praktyczne dla nauczycieli historii w szkołach średnich i powszechnych, Warszawa, 1925.

[7] E. Romer, Atlas geograficzny i historyczny dla IV klasy gimnazjalnej, Lwów, 1936.

[8] E. Romer, Rola mapy w nauce o Polsce współczesnej, Lwów, 1936, p. 43.

[9] C. Grot, Jakich map należy używać na lekcjach historii, "Życie Szkoły" 1946, No. 8/9, pp. 197–199.

created by juxtaposing the elements of thematic content with the geographical background consisting most often of elements such as landform features, coastlines and hydrography which – it must be mentioned – presented the contemporary state of affairs. The main components of the maps' historical layer during that period were: schematically engraved political borders, settlements (which on many maps were presented with the use of varied signatures) and terminology (connected mostly with hydrography, cities, provinces and nations). The first subjects presented in detail were warfare, expeditions and battlefields. Maps were mostly of a sectional character. By the end of the interwar period (1918–1939), economic and social issues were introduced into the teaching of geography and history. Their emergence in geographical atlases was a result of the development of knowledge in that field, as well as improvements in cartographical methods. When it comes to historical school maps, the main reason was Poland's regaining independence. A political function was imposed on many atlases and historical maps, while economic and demographic subject matter proved the undertaken efforts to be right. The period after the Second World War was a time for interdisciplinary research groups to embark on a broad spectrum of ventures. The scope of the undertaken subject matter and changes in quantity and ways of representing different elements of map content stemmed mostly from research achievements in the field of geography, history, historical geography and general cartography. However, political needs were additional reasons for presenting or omitting certain issues more willingly. Paradoxically, the political changes and economic transitions which followed after 1989 in Poland influenced all school cartography and contributed to its dynamic development. Political transformation liberated a whole set of contents, which were not presented on maps published during the time of the Polish People's Republic (PRL). Furthermore, the conditions conducive to the creation of the free market economy furthered the establishment of publishing houses, which incorporated cartographic publications into their publishing profiles. The content of maps and atlases which emerged on the market was not only in accordance with programme requirements approved by a certain minister, but was also tailored to students' perception and was compatible with the idea of interwar didactics stating that wall and atlas maps should be identical. Thematic maps emerged on different levels of teaching which enriched school cartography with a new content, *inter alia* connected with cultural heritage, financial problems or ecological issues.[10]

Parallel to the political and mental transformation was the expansion of new technologies into the Polish market, above all multimedia and the Internet,

[10] W. Ostrowski, Nowe mapy tematyczne w atlasach szkolnych PPWK, "Polski Przegląd Kartograficzny" 2001, Vol. 33, No. 3, pp. 231–234.

which broadened the ability to communicate by introducing multimedia and interactive maps into teaching. With the use of new technology, maps ordering facts and phenomena as linear in time gained a new quality of the multilayered and dynamic presentation of processes changing in time. This enhanced the power of influencing students' imagination in the communication process.

2.3. TECHNOLOGY OF MAP PREPARATION VERSUS THE EFFICIENCY OF THE COMMUNICATION PROCESS

Nowadays it is hard to imagine effective education without the use of new technologies. The representatives of Generation C (those born after 1990) do not remember the world without the Internet and computers. They are fully multimedia-oriented and cannot imagine life without mobile technologies. Getting through to them is a challenge for parents and teachers because they read, communicate and learn in an entirely different manner to the previous generations. At the same time, young people are perceived as very creative, which to a large extent is supported exactly by the common access to new technologies. Within the framework of the project "Start a Career" ("Start w karierę"), the University of Łódź conducted a survey among 259 students above the junior high school level in the voivodeship of Łódź.[11] The survey showed that almost all (91.5%) young people surveyed use social media, almost one half play computer games, and over 14% run a blog. Every third respondent admitted that he or she paints, draws or creates graphics, animations and websites. These people are referred to as "digital natives", as they use IT tools every day and are the most active Internet users. It is beyond any doubt that in the everyday life of the youth today a crucial role is played by computers, the Internet, e-mail, text messages and GPS. That fact may be asserted, and in the discussion a question may be asked of how far and in which areas young people identify with the new media or what alternative they see for further, newer technologies. However, these modern tools still seem to serve more for the purposes of entertainment than learning – research among junior high school students, who indicated that they more often use a computer for work and communication with friends than for searching information, listening to (downloading) music and learning.[12]

Therefore, one may not question the fact that new technologies offer wide communication opportunities. They are readily used, if they are accessible. Owing to the development of IT networks, it is possible to browse through geographic databases all over the world. Multimedia maps and atlases contain additional data arising from the technological possibilities offered by this form

[11] http://natablicy.pl/mlodzi-ludzie-urodzeni-po-1990-roku-wybieraja-kreatywny-styl-zycia,artykul.html

[12] A. Kamińska, Rola nowych technologii w nauczaniu – przykład fizyki, [in:] Nowe media w edukacji, ed. T. Lewowicki, B. Siemieniecki, Toruń, 2012, p. 51.

of presentation. Interactive maps are usually linked with a static (iconographic) or dynamic illustration (3D models, fragments of popular scientific films, travel films, documentaries or, less frequently, feature films) and sound. Most important processes and phenomena presented on maps are in a form ready for listening to or reading on one's own. Usually, the whole content may be printed. The majority of teaching aids of this type also contain sets of additional materials which allow some understanding of the difficult language of the map. In geography teaching, in the process of map reading, the image of geographic space created under the influence of a system of symbols used on the map is confronted with the geographical reality. In the case of history teaching it is much more difficult to refer the image created as a result of map reading to objects which no longer exist in real life. In these cases, combining iconographic databases with fragments of documentary or feature films plays an important role in making communication and learning the language of a map more efficient. In that process one cannot underestimate the role of the Internet, owing to which it is possible to visit the websites of all types of museum exhibits, or in the case of geography use the images delivered by cameras placed in different parts of the globe or by websites offering the possibility to see an object in the form of a virtual journey.

Multimedia combine many types of media, such as video, animation, text, images, narration, music and other sounds. The interactive character of multimedia programmes allows the user to consciously view and search for information with the possibility to return to the most useful pieces of information at any given moment. Each piece of information found may be rendered in various ways, augmented with a film or sound, leading to heightened interest in the penetrated topic, increasing the degree of remembering and understanding the information.

The available programmes may be divided into two groups. The first comprises encyclopedia–type programmes whose basic task is to deliver as much information as possible to the user in the form of text and sound, and static and dynamic images. The second group of programmes are packages which, apart from their encyclopedic function, may generate various problems to be solved by a student. For contemporary education, the media constitutes an irreplaceable source of information and a tool for intellectual work, both for the student and the teacher.

The possibilities offered by new technologies are taken into account in the course of map preparation, making it a dynamic and interactive visual aid. The process of communication in comparison with a static map is much more effective. Within a shorter time, in a manner more attractive for the student, it is possible to convey more content. A static map, irrespective of the medium (printed on paper or presented in a raster format on a computer screen), is not an attractive form of presentation for a young person today. Nevertheless, a paper map hanging on the wall in a geography or history classroom, unlike any other form of space, may easily be remembered.

The Internet or a combination of networks of people who use it, programmes used for obtaining information and information itself create – apart from the classic methods of teaching with the use of static presentation and visualization techniques (paper maps and atlases or foliograms) – new possibilities with the use of the computer technology. New information technologies are conducive to the concept of active teaching composed of cooperation with the remaining members of the group, active presence in the group, full control over the surrounding environment and a feeling of freedom of choice and action.[13]

The role of the Internet in the activation of students and stimulating their creativity is also created by the teachers themselves. The scope of the benefits is presented through such statements as: "While working with a multimedia programme, students not only have the opportunity for observation, but also by acting they partly create the screen reality. They are aware of their conscious participation in classes, they select fragments, choose the order of analyzed problems on their own, they cooperate. Giving them wide leeway evokes in them a feeling of responsibility, or even freedom in school which (in the students' opinion) is full of prohibitions up to the limit."[14] For contemporary education the media are an indispensable source of information, a tool for intellectual work, both for a student and a teacher.

3. MAPS AS DATA CARRIERS AND COMMUNICATION TOOLS AT DIFFERENT LEVELS OF TEACHING

3.1. COMMUNICATION AS A SOCIAL PHENOMENON

In the social aspect, communication is the process of "people sharing thoughts, ideas and feelings with each other in commonly understandable ways"[15] in different areas of activity, such as politics, economy, science and education. What is more, everyone who sends a message directly influences the other person and affects the subsequent communication process.

In this day and age it is unquestionable that the current state of globalization is connected, above all, with the development of the technical mass media transmitting knowledge, thoughts and specific solutions. Owing to new possibilities to communicate, stemming from the emergence of interactive tools (digital broadcast or dynamic interface), individual participation in communi-

[13] A. Jelonek, Rola masmediów i Internetu w dydaktyce, www.nauczyciele.mom.pl/publikacje

[14] R. Rippel, Multimedia w edukacji polonistycznej, "Forum Humanistów" 2000, Vol. 2, p. 25.

[15] Ch. Hamilton Communicating for Results: A Guide for Business and the Professions, Polish translation by A. Cybułko, ed. for Polish edition by T. Rzepko, PWN, Warszawa, 2011, p. 26.

cation circulation is accelerated. Interactive tools enable the users to give feedback concerning their expectations and freely choose the content which they wish to access or receive.[16]

3.2. COMMUNICATION IN SCHOOL CARTOGRAPHY

All mechanisms influencing the development of not only tools, but also methods of using them in the process of social communication are reflected in cartography. Communication is effective when both the sender and the receiver of information share a pre-established system of analyzing it. For people that means languages, for computers communication protocols, and for maps cartographic symbols which convey information about the geographical space. It seems that when it comes to modern technologies, graphic cartographic symbols are accompanied by additional aural symbols, raising the effectiveness of communication with the use of maps. They are easy, fast and effortless to use through new technologies, enabling teachers to discuss the map and simultaneously show images, fragments of documentaries or feature films on screen, play additional sounds, etc.

Every form of multimedia map presents us with an opportunity to stimulate attention processes by influencing different senses. A variety of forms guarantees a wide range of stimuli activating the students. However, the communication process should be structured in an easily comprehensible way for the students. Dynamic and multimedia maps allow for the presentation of a certain phenomenon as many times as the full communication process requires. This is also facilitated by the correct way of preparing point, line and area cartographic symbols. For the effect of communication to be optimum, it is necessary to adjust the kind of representation to the students' perception level. In primary education such graphic symbols are used which, through their shapes, are directly linked to the object they represent. At junior high school level and above, more symbolic signatures are used which are intuitively associated with the represented object. There is also a direct link to the narration of a textbook, which is adjusted to the receiver's perception level.

4. MAP INTERPRETATION IN THE SCHOOL COMMUNICATION PROCESS

4.1. SIGNS AND THEIR MEANINGS IN VERBAL AND SPATIAL CONTEXTS

A language is the basic means of social communication, a fundamental element of human culture and the condition for the existence of knowledge. In the linguistic context the study of signs, i.e. semiotics (semiology), apart from

[16] P. Krajewski, Postrzeganie świata jako funkcja techniki, [in:] Kultura–Nauka–Media. Jak media transformują świat? Szanse i zagrożenia. Materiały z konferencji 16 IV 2002, ed. P. Rudzki, Wrocław, 2002, p. 60.

verbal expression and paralinguistic codes, encompasses areas such as various forms of social communication (e.g. ceremonies, clothing, signboards) and esthetic codes (literature, art).[17] In the general context, semiotics concentrates on sign theory, the typology of various forms of signs, sign substance and the role it plays in society when it comes to the communication process. The meaning and changes of the meaning of words (signs) are what semantics focuses on.

Maps also have their own specific language. The effectiveness of communication with the use of maps is related to cartographic symbols together with their denoted meanings, adequate to a certain level of teaching determined by students' perceptual abilities. The catalogue of cartographic symbols is abundant; it consists of modified point symbols – related to point topographic objects and line symbols – linear in character in the field, and area symbols related to a certain area. While selecting symbols and, above all, creating new ones, it is essential to adopt a certain logic and consistency in using graphic variables as it guarantees an effective communication. Graphic variables used in cartography, introduced by J. Bertin[18] and modified by J. Puszkarska,[19] are variables creating the image (position, size and changes in color intensity) and diversifying it (through granulation, direction and shape). With the use of the natural features of graphic variables, one can specifically pinpoint relations between objects, such as: similarity, differences, order and proportion. The point of using them, however, is the presentation of the characteristics of an object or phenomenon on a two dimensional surface.

Depending on the level of teaching symbols denoting the same phenomenon, an object or event might have a different form. For primary school students graphic symbols resembling pictograms will be used, for junior high school students symbolic signs, and for high school and university students symbolic or abstract ones (see Figure 1 below).

4.2. PRAGMATICS – THE ESSENCE AND THE SCOPE OF CONTENT IN SCHOOL MAPS

Pragmatics in cartography is the choice of forms of graphic transmission which adds up to a map's content and provides effectiveness in its reception, in terms of legibility and comparability. Thus, also of vital importance is the aim of the map and the receiver to whom it is addressed. Pragmatics in school cartography must take into account different levels of teaching and should also define the essence and scope of the communicated content. The easiest way to present this issue is with the example of historical narration, whose characteristic

[17] Encyklopedia wiedzy o języku polskim, Ossolineum, Wrocław–Warszawa–Kraków–Gdańsk, 1978, p. 299.

[18] J. Bertin, Semiologie graphique. Les diagram mes, les reseaux, les cartes, 2 ed. Paris–Le Huye, Mouton, Gauthier–Villars, 1973.

[19] J. Puszkarska, Zmienne graficzne, p. 1, http://zk.gik.pw.edu.pl/Edukacja/Wyklady/Grafika1.pdf

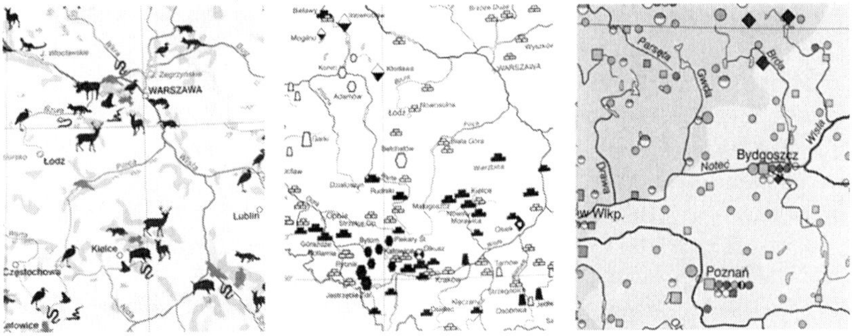

Figure 1. Fragments of maps with different signs: pictorial signs – communication at primary level, symbolic and geometric signs – communication at junior high school and high school level.

features are diachronic and synchronic structures of the elements of a historical image, with different saturation in different time and spatial periods. Embedding different phenomena in time on a historical map is done with their simultaneous marking in geographical space.[20]

Cartographic narrations create systematic knowledge.

History teaching uses the cartographic narrations created with their receivers in mind, i.e. students at different levels of the education system. They are characterized by simple structures, their accessible language, and the saturation of perceptual, imaginary and conceptual elements relevant to the intellectual and emotional level of the development. This is depicted by the following examples at primary and high school levels (see Figure 2 below).

4.3. INTERPRETATION FACILITATING UNDERSTANDING

There are significant differences between written language signs and cartographic ones – we read a text in a linear way and letters themselves are discontinuous and similarly oriented signs, and a text is not limited by space (one word does not take the space of another). Maps convey their message through visual symbols and inform us about the spatial relations of the presented content.

Lech Ratajski dealt with the linkage between systems of cartographic symbols and their analysis in the Polish literature.[21]

He represented the linguistic and semiotic approach and thus distinguished three interrelations: syntactic – defining the formal composition of a map, semantic – attributing individual symbols with meaningful content, and pragmat-

[20] A. Zielecki, Szkolna mapa historyczna jako narracja historyczno–dydaktyczna, [in:] Z dziejów kartografii, Vol. XI: Mapa w pracy historyka, ed. T. Bogacz i B. Konopska. Materiały XIX Ogólnopolskiej Konferencji Historyków Kartografii, Wrocław, 10–12 września 1998, Instytut Historii Nauki PAN, Biuro Rozwoju Wrocławia UM, Wrocław, 1999, p. 135.

[21] L. Ratajski, Pewne aspekty gramatyki języka mapy, "Polski Przegląd Kartograficzny" 1976, vol. 8, nr 2, pp. 49–61.

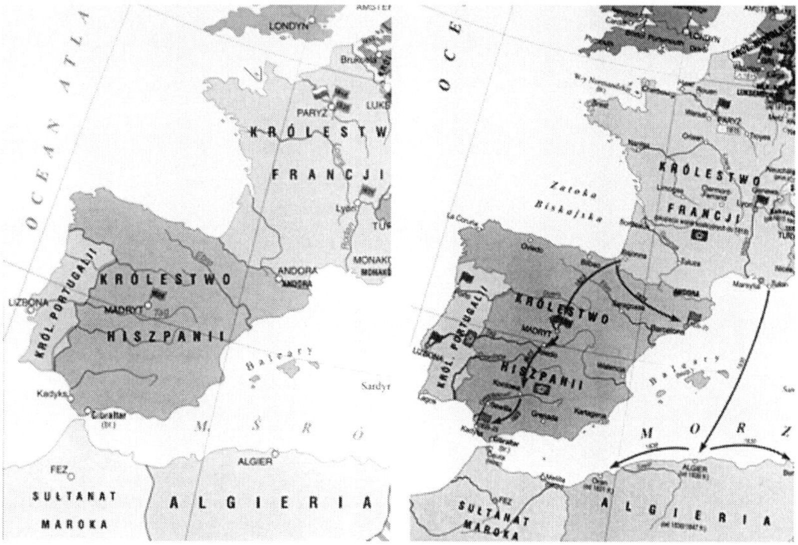

Figure 2. Fragments of historical maps with different saturations of content: a) primary level, b) high school level. Source: Atlas historyczny. Szkoła Podstawowa, Wyd. 1. PPWK, Warszawa–Wrocław, 1999, p. 28; Atlas historyczny. Liceum, Nowa Era. Ed.1, Warszawa, 2008, p. 82.

ic – dealing with the relationship between a map and its user. Ratajski acknowledged that the language of a map has its own grammar, i.e. a system of word forms, which are cartographic symbols, and a system of joining these words into sentences. The elements of geographical reality and the selected phenomena are presented by means of these symbols. On the basis of Ratajski's idea, the linguistic approach to cartographic semantics has been established which adopts a theory that a map's language is of a natural character. Owing to Ratajski, the idea of the language of a map has been connected to semiotics.

The following example shows how semantically rich a symbol on a map is in contrast to a word sign, which is often unequivocally interpreted. It also makes us aware that obeying the rules when it comes to homogeneity of symbols used, especially in school maps, is of the utmost importance (see Figure 3 below).

The school map on different levels of teaching should be characterized by a strict approach to the definition of scope of content and the ability to saturate it with cartographic symbols.

The map will become a source of knowledge for a student when he or she masters its scripture and language to the extent that they can read and comprehend it. It is established that "the ability to read maps by students should become one of the basic educational aims of teaching history."[22]

[22] A. Zielecki, op. cit., p. 137.

WRITING		MAP	
SIGN	MEANING	SIGN	MEANING
HOUSE	house		City
			River
			Railway
			The citi is at the river
			The city is at the south of the river
			The river flows at the north at the city
			Railway runs thought the city
			The railway crosses the river
			The railway runs from the north to the south
			The river flows from southern-west to the north-west
			This is a meandering river

Figure 3. Significant semantic differences between language and cartographic signs. Source: L. Ratajski, Zasady logiczno-semiotyczne uporządkowania i standaryzacji znaków kartograficznych, Polski Przegląd Kartograficzny, v. 3, 1971, no 3, p. 109.

4.4. MAPS AS TOOLS FOR PROCESS EXPLANATION (THE JUXTAPOSITION OF GEOGRAPHY AND HISTORY)

A step forward in map interpretation at the school level is its use to illustrate and facilitate students' understanding of broader political, social or economic phenomena and processes. For the interpretation to be thorough, it would be most advantageous to join historical and geographical content on both subjects and hence simultaneously use historical and geographical maps. While explaining to students, for example, the modern Polish economy, apart from using an economic map teachers should also resort to a weather map, a soil map, a topographical map with hydrographic features as well as a historical map with economic changes.

While talking about Polish relations with the Teutonic Knights, for instance, apart from a historical map presenting the border system with a territorial scope and the main events, it would be advisable to include a geographical map in the interpretation presenting *inter alia* the specifics of the terrain. The ideal solution would be for the geographical approach to consider the state of the environment for the historical period in question. In the latter case such a reconstruction depends on the state of research in the field of historical geography.

Exemplary solutions must encompass multimedia maps to a large extent, as a statistical or paper (wall or atlas) map will not fulfill the expectations.

Depth and space are very easy to present in computer graphics free from all deformations and distortions (other than those stemming from editorial development) which are present when shading the contour lines while drawing by hand or creating a model. Computer technology permits the observation of an object from any perspective and in any scale. As a result, we obtain different, optimally chosen perspective representations, mainly of landform features.

4.5. SPATIAL THINKING AS THE KEY TO UNDERSTANDING GEOGRAPHICAL AND HISTORICAL PROCESSES AND AS A LASTING VALUE

Preserving spatial phenomena in memory, which should be facilitated by school education is connected with the opportunity to return to the observed picture/map on the one hand and, on the other, with a variety of transmissions from different data carriers.

Preserving in memory is one of the vital stages leading to the perception and understanding of phenomena and processes, above all historical and geographical ones, through surface. It also involves the inclusion of spatial images into other activities, both theoretical and practical in character. Ideally, after graduation each student should forever possess not only the ability to understand and use maps, but also to think spatially, which would enrich his or her knowledge about the outside world, and in the social context bring about the so–called "cartographic culture" at a higher level.

The fulfillment of such expectations is facilitated by the individual predisposition, as the ability to gather spatial images and its preservation has its source in the human mind's specificity. It is, on the one hand, deeply rooted in the past and oriented at the inter–generational transmission of information, while on the other it is directed towards the future and stimulated by dreams, predictions and visions.[23] Globalization, as the fundamental condition of the modern world, filled with electronic communication technology, is the meaningful effect of the above.

5. CONCLUSIONS

This chapter provokes a few conclusions. On the basis of the presented material one can undoubtedly state that the map is a precious methodological tool, vital in the process of educational communication, continuously improved technically and content–wise owing to the development of information technology. It must be added that it is a tool more and more appreciated by teachers of visually and aurally impaired children and teenagers. The communication with the use of these maps is carried out in a similar way for such students,

[23] P. Krajewski, op. cit., p. 62.

but the specifics of their perception must be taken into consideration during a map preparation.[24] Maps for the blind and visually impaired are printed on a special surface with colors distinguishable by such students, or monochromatic (relief) ones using the Braille alphabet. Modern technology permits the preparation of maps presenting various object or places by connecting them with GPS or audio files.

Another conclusion is connected with the fact that in the teaching practice maps are linked almost solely with two subjects – geography and history. Classrooms have divided their cartographic resources according to this premise among themselves. This article has proved that this is unjustifiable. Maps should be seen as a universal tool reaching beyond one subject, if we seriously take into consideration the claim to perceive all phenomena and processes connected with human activity as related to space. Therefore, it seems advisable to use maps more broadly during other classes, dealing with, *inter alia*, literature (e.g. motifs in literature juxtaposed with spatial conditions), art (e.g. art motifs and their environmental sources), or the shaping of ideas and political doctrines in the modern world (differences are generated, *inter alia*, by specific space).

Referring to the main train of thought, i.e. geography and history at school, the optimum solution for the time being seems to be the parallel use of geographical and historical maps on both subjects. In a broader perspective it is a proposition for the authors of teaching aids. While taking into account new technologies in cartography and the need for a new approach to subject matters, the aim should be the creation of interactive maps which combine geographical and historical content and can become a universal tool in educational communication, also useful when depicting other issues. Such an approach would limit the trouble stemming from the lack of correlation between the subjects. It would also allow for withdrawal from the traditional division between subjects still present in Polish schools.

REFERENCES

Atlas geograficzny. Świat, Polska, Nowe Era, ed. IV, Warszawa, 2004. Atlas geograficzny. Świat, Polska, Nowe Era, ed. V, Warszawa, 2005.

Atlas historyczny. Liceum, Nowa Era. ed.1, Warszawa, 2008.

Atlas historyczny "Od starożytności do współczesności". Szkoła podstawowa, Nowa Era, ed. 1, Warszawa, 2012.

Atlas historyczny. Szkoła Podstawowa, ed. 1. PPWK, Warszawa–Wrocław, 1999.

Bednarek S., Pojmowanie kultury i jej historii we współczesnych syntezach dziejów kultury polskiej, Wyd. Uniwersytetu Wrocławskiego, Wrocław, 1995.

[24] I. Krauze–Tomczyk, Polskie mapy dla niewidomych i słabo widzących, "Polski Przegląd Kartograficzny" 2001, Vol. 33, No. 3, pp. 237–240.

Bertin J., Semiologie graphique. Les diagram mes, les reseaux, les cartes, 2 ed. Paris–Le Huye, Mouton, Gauthier–Villars, 1973.
Encyklopedia wiedzy o języku polskim, Ossolineum Wrocław–Warszawa–Kraków–Gdańsk, 1978.
Gotlib D., Metodyka prezentacji kartograficznych w mobilnych systemach lokalizacyjnych i nawigacyjnych, Politechnika Warszawska, Prace Naukowe, Geodezja, z. 48, Warszawa, 2011.
Grot Cz., Jakich map należy używać na lekcjach historii, "Życie Szkoły" 1946, nr 8/9.
Hamilton Ch., Skuteczna komunikacja w biznesie, translated A. Cybulko, ed. T. Rzepko, PWN, Warszawa, 2011.
Jelonek A., Rola masmediów i Internetu w dydaktyce, www.nauczyciele.mom.pl/publikacje
Kamińska A., Rola nowych technologii w nauczaniu – przykład fizyki, [in:] Nowe media w edukacji, ed. T. Lewowicki, B. Siemieniecki, Wydawnictwo Adam Marszałek, Toruń, 2012.
Krajewski P., Postrzeganie świata jako funkcja techniki, [in:] Kultura – Nauka – Media. Jak media transformują świat? Szanse i zagrożenia. Materiały z konferencji 16 IV 2002, ed. P. Rudzki, Wyd. DTSK Silesia, Wrocław, 2002.
Krauze–Tomczyk I., Polskie mapy dla niewidomych i słabo widzących, "Polski Przegląd Kartograficzny" 2001, vol. 33, nr 3.
Montenello D.R., Cognitive map–designe research in the twentieth century: Theoretical and empirical approaches, "Cartogr. And Geogr. Inform. Science" Vol. 29, no 3.
Mościcki H., Wskazówki praktyczne dla nauczycieli historii w szkołach średnich i powszechnych, Warszawa, 1925.
Olson J., Experience and the improvement of cartographic communications, "Cartographic Journal" Vol. 12 (1975), Number 2.
Ostrowski W., Nowe mapy tematyczne w atlasach szkolnych PPWK, "Polski Przegląd Kartograficzny" 2001, vol. 33, nr 3.
Piskorz S., Introduction, [in:] Zarys dydaktyki geografii, ed. S. Piskorz, PWN Warszawa, 1997.
Puszkarska J., Zmienne graficzne, http://zk.gik.pw.edu.pl/Edukacja/Wyklady/Grafika1.pdf
Ratajski L., Pewne aspekty gramatyki języka mapy, "Polski Przegląd Kartograficzny" 1976, vol. 8 , nr 2.
Ratajski L., Zasady logiczno–semiotyczne uporządkowania i standaryzacji znaków kartograficznych, "Polski Przegląd Kartograficzny" 1971, vol. 3, nr 3.
Rippel R., Multimedia w edukacji polonistycznej, "Forum Humanistów" 2000, z. 2.
Romer E., Atlas geograficzny i historyczny dla IV klasy gimnazjalnej, "Książnica–Atlas", Lwów, 1936.
Romer E., Rola mapy w nauce o Polsce współczesnej, "Książnica–Atlas", Lwów, 1936.
Świat wokół nas. Atlas. Przyroda. Szkoła Podstawowa, PPWK, Warszawa, 2002.
Zielecki A., Szkolna mapa historyczna jako narracja historyczno–dydaktyczna, [in:] Z dziejów kartografii, Vol. XI: Mapa w pracy historyka, ed. T. Bogacz and B. Konopska, Instytut Historii Nauki PAN, Biuro Rozwoju Wrocławia UM, Wrocław, 1999.

2. MEDIA COMMUNICATION

Mirosława Wawrzak–Chodaczek
Małgorzata Biedroń
University of Wroclaw

THE PSYCHOLOGICAL AND SOCIAL CONSEQUENCES OF PLAYING "AGGRESSIVE" COMPUTER GAMES FOR CHILDREN AND TEENAGERS

ABSTRACT

The huge popularity of computer games is a phenomenon drawing the attention of the representatives of many scientific disciplines and first of all marketing experts, as these products form a very profitable sector of trade. Currently, we can observe a great amount of computer games. Producers of suitable software or games compete in creating more and more attractive, more and more realistic (sometimes shocking) visual effects and sounds. Unfortunately, a considerable part of their products, because of their drastic content, should only be accessible for adults. Although many manufacturers place appropriate warnings on the packaging, those games get into the hands of young, immature people and have a destructive influence on their psyche and their social interpersonal relations. This chapter attempts to answer the following questions: is there any connection between sex and the level of aggression of young people and the kind of games they prefer, and is there any connection between the time spent on First Perspective Person games and the level of long term stress? 1,520 children between 7–13 years old participated in this investigation conducted in 2009. Thirty–five percent were persons with raised levels of aggression, and 32% with raised levels of stress. To answer the above questions a chi test and correlation were used with reference to question one, and a test of importance and correlation factor with reference to question two. Over 53% of boys and 18% of girls participating in the investigation, regardless of age, prefer various kinds of games including violence. The male part of the examined population began to play aggressive games in the initial classes of primary school and their fascination has not stopped even after reaching a mature age. For girls, the "adventure" with the analyzed forms of entertainment began several years later and only in some cases lasted longer than a few years. The numerical data unambiguously shows a strong connection between the time spent on games including violence or cruelty and manifested level of aggression, with an insignificant superiority in the male group. A similar correlation was observed during the investigation of stress level. Young people spending more time on computer games manifested higher levels of stress, especially long term stress, than persons playing less. The observation denies the theses promoted by users (and many persons who draw profits from the production and distribution of games) about a cathartic effect, neutralizing the negative emotions connected with playing violent games. On the contrary, it was observed that using violence to achieve desirable aims not only increases the level of aggression, frustration and stress but also enriches the spectrum of undesirable behaviors and transfers them to real life social situations.

KEYWORDS: communication, media, computer games, influence on psyche, aggression, frustration.

In classical works on cultural anthropology, sociology or psychology, games and play are perceived as one of the primary forms of human activity and the immanent element (although changeable in quality and quantity) of each biography. They also constitute an important factor of culture creation. Giving evidence of intellectual and moral values and anti–values, they contribute to their specification and development.[1] Both games and play have always been essential instruments of adopting and training the determined competences which could be transferred into real social situations. It is accepted that a game has a bigger influence because it requires strict rules and a uniform structure, limiting randomness, and the player learns self–discipline and the conscious control of his/her own actions with reference to the definite rules.

Ludic behaviors can take different forms depending on individual preferences and rules or community life. Agon will fulfill the will of fight and rivalry at different levels, mimicry will enable role–playing and impersonating various characters, "trying" diverse identities, and ilinx and alea will give an exciting feeling of uncertainty, hazard, and an additional dose of adrenalin. The constantly modernized "toys" will make the ways of satisfying desires more and more attractive.[2] The technical development and common accessibility of specialized devices have opened numerous possibilities within multidirectional development support, improving social competences and fulfilling ludic needs. It turns out that, in spite of the multiplicity of offers on the market of electronic media and the accessibility of attractive educational programmes adapted to each age, games are the most frequently purchased type of software. It can be legitimately affirmed that game players have become a part of a large number of computer users. The attractiveness of games manifests itself at different levels of pleasure. For some people games are time killers, e.g. the Windows sapper game or solitaire, while others treat them as a peculiar test of cleverness, dexterity or agility. For an addicted player they are often the whole world, and its complexity grows each year, wherein you can rule using a few keys and fulfill the need of having control over something. The participant staying "inside the game" is so absorbed that they can feel relief from the pains of real life. The game frees the player from making decisions, very often burdening them with irreversible consequences and taking on responsibility, calming them with clearly set rules of conduct, as opposed to the rules of the "exterior" world which are sometimes unpredictable. J. Boroń and T. Zyss claim that computer games attract mainly young people who are frustrated and lost in the adult world. They give a feeling of power with unlimited influence on the vicissitudes of characters and

[1] P. Bagby, Pojęcie kultury, [in:], Człowiek – wychowanie – kultura, edit. F. Adamski, WAM, Kraków, 1993, pp. 160–175; R. Caillois, Żywioł i ład, Wyd. PIW, Warszawa, 1976, p. 328.

[2] R. Caillois, Gry i ludzie (Les Jeux et les hommes: le masque et le vertige), Wyd. Volumen, Warszawa, 1997.

events, enabling the projection of dreams and desires and, most of all, they do not expose the player to rejection and solitude. Successes in the virtual world can compensate for the lack of satisfactory achievements in real life. Nowadays, thousands of games are available. All important software companies attract potential customers with more and more attractive content, graphics and recently also with the music and sound effects of their products. Unfortunately, the majority of games available on the market contains a larger or smaller (in most cases larger) dose of violence.[3] The law undoubtedly requires the special marking of these products which should not get into juvenile hands. However, it is worth realizing that such symbols often evoke the opposite, and repeatedly intended, effect.

Let us look closer at the materials used by the examined (in September 2011) children and youngsters, and at the ways their choices influence their behaviors and emotions. Out of 1,520 children aged 7–13, 35% were diagnosed as having higher levels of aggression, and 32% had higher levels of long term stress. The following questions were asked:

- Is there any interrelation between sex and the level of aggression of young people, and the type of games preferred by them?
- Is there any interrelation between the quantity of time spent playing violent games and the level of long term stress?
- What are the psychological and social effects of playing "aggressive" games?

To answer the first question a chi test and correlation factor were used, whereas to answer the second a test of the significance of the differences between the groups and a correlation factor were applied.

AGGRESSION AND GAMES

The respondents mentioned 98 games of different kinds, which proves the thesis about the great popularity of this form of entertainment. The most popular were adventure games, played by more than a half of the questioned girls and boys. Most of young people like solving the riddles and overcoming difficulties, impersonating brave characters from different worlds, using magic and supernatural powers, and when the games are accompanied by swift action and interesting scenery, the popularity in the examined group is reasonable. Also sports games, which in most cases are football or basketball matches, karate or hockey, are very popular, especially among boys. The mentioned games distinguish themselves by perfect graphics and high sound quality and offer their users realistic emotions. We can also mention such games as car, motor, air-

[3] J.B. Switchell already in 1989, so many years before the appearance of the most brutal games, eq. FPP, indicated that violence is in almost all types of games.

craft or tank simulators. Moreover, logical games that demand reason–result thinking, where the victory depends on the correctly undertaken decisions, were appreciated by non–aggressive boys and girls.

Comprising another special type are strategy warlike games, which enable the player to show cleverness in planning and leading war actions and defeating enemies. Such games were preferred by boys. Although they contain elements of violence (shooting, bombarding, fights with the use of hand weapons), the correlation rate did not show an essential relation to the level of aggression. Few male respondents chose erotic games such as strip poker or puzzles. The pictures in these games are extremely realistic, and the participant has to arrange a date with computer characters to make them ready for sexual intercourse. Such games can be addressed to boys, girls, men and women of different sexual orientations. The choice of floppy discs or CD roms of this kind is so great that, according to the researchers examining this phenomenon, we can talk about an erotic computer game industry.

Another group of the examined population are players who spend at least 20 hours a week on their hobby (approximately 3 hours a day), with 657 people in this group.[4] It seems significant that among 24 games mostly listed in the survey, 19 have high levels of aggression and violence, wherein the ability to show cruelty, lack of mercy and cunning are rewarded. The FPP (First Person Perspective) games and TPP (Third Person Perspective) games, where the main thread is hunting for the enemy/enemies, fighting using dangerous things, shooting and chases[5] were chosen by more than 80% (the rest spent their time playing Massively Multiplayer Online Role Playing Games). The research shows that there exists a statistically considerable interrelation between the level of aggression (measured with the "moods and humors" test by A.M. Busse and A. Durkee) and the kind of chosen game.[6]

[4] The norms of safe computer usage by children and teenagers are as follows; children under 12 should not use them for longer than 1 hours a day, and between 12 and 16 they can use a computer for up to 2 hours a day. During last 5 years the time spent on playing computer games has increased by 56%. I. Ulfik– Jaworska, Can computer games be dangerous, "Wychowawca" 2002, No 1.

[5] "Carmagedon" is an example of such a game mentioned by numerous players of different ages (even the youngest ones). Its producers, after releasing it, started work on the next version and advertized it in a computer games magazine as follows: "If 'Carmagedon' took your breath away with its brutality and a lot of blood, after the second part your lungs will fall apart". Aggression and violence are intensified in this game. It is a game where you kill people using a car, the "driver" hunting for pedestrians and collecting scores for hitting them or running them over. The more imaginative the method of killing, the more satisfaction the player gets.

[6] The level of aggression and type of preferred game (chi?=82,1866,df=7, p=4,88498E–15), and sex and preferred game (chi?=57,0247,df=7,p=5,91054E–10). The Buss–Durkee Inventory contains 75 questions divided into seven categories (Attack, Hostility, Negativism, Grudge, Suspiciousness, Verbal aggression), which after summing up give a general level of aggression. M. Choynowski, Skrócony podręcznik do testu "Nastroje i Humory" A.H. Bussa i A. Durkee, Wyd. MoiW, Warszawa, 1972.

A remarkable majority of aggressive individuals (526 out of 532) belonged to this group, of which girls constituted 18%. Every fourth boy declared having played aggressive games for approximately 5 years, so for some respondents their specific hobby begins before school. The longest for girls is two years, and this group comprises 10% of the probative population. The results can provoke questions of whether the increased level of aggression is the stimulus or the effect of spending a lot of time playing such games. Certainly, longitudinal biographical research would be helpful and necessary to answer this question. Regardless of the reason, the effect relation between the variables *hic et nunc* should be recognized as the self supportive mechanism. There are still many supporters (especially among the players themselves) of the hypothesis of catharsis, or the hypothesis of "replacing" reality, who ascribe compensating functions to the games – i.e., the act of violence decreases the need to use it in real life. These hypotheses come from the psychoanalytical concept of reducing the urges with imagination. To show the weakness of these theses, you have to refer to the research demonstrating non–medical reasons of emerging aggressive thoughts and behaviors. At their heart lies the frustration felt by the individual, which means unpleasant experiences connected with the appearance of obstacles preventing them from realising the anticipated aim.

A person who wants to reduce the feeling of discomfort through the actions of the agonic character, demanding violence and physical power, can lower the physiological excitation and "vent" to "bad energy". But such a strategy does not guarantee the constant elimination of the frustration source (especially as the game itself can cause it, for example in the situation when the player loses or when technical problems arise, etc.). Thus, there is a high probability of recurrence of unfavorable emotional states and a repeated need for getting over it through aggression directed at different objects. Frustration not always has to result in violence – it can also be sublimated as a fantasy. It seems that achieving positive emotions through aggressive behaviors or "just" watching its effects or imagining them should be perceived as a deviation, not a norm. It is obvious that the state of irritation or anger (which can go back to square one and take the form of an aggression motif) are inseparable elements of everybody's life. That is why the factor of social learning to control them and finding the way to canalize. Both the theory of A. Bandura arising from behaviorism and the theory of differentiated connections (difference association) of E. Sutherland[7] show that a person internalizes these behavior patterns which in a given community are dominative and intensified. In the games mostly chosen by the respondents the player is rewarded for cruel deeds against en-

[7] A. Siemaszko, Granice tolerancji: o teoriach zachowań dewiacyjnych, Wyd. PWN, Warszawa, 1993.

emies and for following the rules, "giving no quarter". Satisfaction from achieving successive levels and respect among coevals are such strong motivations that a child may learn that violent deeds are a proper reaction in a conflict situation. The aims to be achieved by the players need some effort, but are achievable. According to the rules of motivational psychology, this is an efficient way to maximally focus on the task. The commonness likes repeatability of acts of violence. According to Sutherland, this creates the consciousness, and an act of will means committing penal acts. If a young person, in a process of socialization and education, does not acquire the ability to reduce stress in another way, aggression becomes his or her intrapsychical regulation mechanism. In troublesome situations they do not make an attempt at a peaceful solution but use (physical, verbal, symbolic) violence because they treat it as the only effective way. In the world of games most often mentioned by teenagers, the law of the strongest is primary, and cooperation happens only in the perspective of one's own benefit. Kindness, compassion or voluntary help have no meaning, and the weak should be eliminated. These rules can be defined as virtual Darwinism if not for the fact that in a game hostility and being detrimental are very often not "necessary evils" but aims in themselves. Boys and girls who spend a lot of time playing aggressive games experience a surplus of such behavior, so according to the theories mentioned above there is a great probability that they will acquire these patterns and recognize them as being right.[8]

Specific stimuli can evoke negative emotions and transmit knowledge of the abilities, memories or views concerned with aggression to the brain.[9] This is proved by research that fanatic players get angry much easier , are impulsive, and have lower tolerance thresholds. In case of people having frustrating experiences, the mechanism of rising aggression becomes extended and aggressive deeds become a pleasure, and they may be exemplified by famous people as mentioned by E. Fromm, illustrating the shaping of human destructiveness.[10] Comments placed by young players on different types of Internet forums show an unhealthy fascination with acts of aggression and a specific pleasure reached after the annihilation of an enemy. Language used by the respondents can also be a subject of scientific analysis but because of the scope of the research issues we will concentrate only on the thread directly concerning it. The most characteristic features of the statements are brutality, vulgarity, extreme language poverty, a large number of emoticons and acronyms, confu-

[8] More and more common and showing an increasing tendency for acts of vandalism, aggression, cruelty and brutality, the authors of which are juveniles, proving this hypothesis.

[9] This was proved by the effects of an experiment on a group of 210 students. C.A. Anderson, K.E. Dill, Video Games and Aggressive Thoughts, Feelings, and Behavior in the Laboratory and Life, "Journal of Personality and Social Psychology" 2000, nr 4, p. 772–790.

[10] E. Fromm, Anatomia ludzkiej destrukcyjności, Wyd. Rebis, Poznań, 1999.

sion and disobedience of grammatical rules. A preliminary look at the formal side of communication shows the pessimistic vision of L. Manovich, in which 'we will communicate using the gestures, body movement and grimaces, closed in the cave without a language, just like our ancestors ...'[11] This vision, with reference to fanatic players, becomes quite probable if we consider the time spent in front of the computer screen (at least 20 hours a week) and that 78% of the respondents declare that they are home alone while playing games. Both factors drastically confine the possibilities of improving language competences, the first through putting away from other forms of spending free time, in which contact with a correct and rich language can be made, the other by impoverishment of the possessed language patterns. The next conclusion, drawn from the analysis of the statements, is also alarming. Referring to the theories of determinism of Sapir–Worf or Widgenstein, the conceptual categories used while playing games or communicating on Internet forums, assimilated to the vernacular language can deform the ways of perceiving and interpreting reality and influence the shape of interpersonal relations. The world described by the language of fighting, domination or aggression appears as hostile, full of danger, and people are rivals who, for our own good, should not be trusted. The language, as the medium, takes interpersonal hostility to the real world which is concerned with[12] 'attributing the negative features and values to the others, and treating the others as the threat to somebody or one's own group, which leads to feeling disgust, irritation or anger for the others, and to accepting using more or less veiled aggression and violence'. The shocking statements of the forum participants prove that young people not only do not feel the effect of catharsis but intensify and develop their antisocial attitudes, creating more precise aggressive associations.[13]

The interpersonal contacts of people who play brutal games with pleasure are characterized by demanding attitudes, not respecting social norms, competitive behaviors and enslaving other people, the inability to establish horizontal contacts based on cooperation, impulsiveness in action, emotional indifference and narcissism.[14] It is necessary to stress that longitudinal research

[11] L. Manovich, Język nowych mediów, Wyd. WAiP, Warszawa, 2006, p. 133.

[12] A. Frączek, Socjalizacja a intrapsychiczna regulacja agresji interpersonalnej, [in:] Socjalizacja i agresja, edit. A. Frączek, H. Zamkley, Wyd. IP PAN, WSPS, Warszawa, 1993, p. 57.

[13] The following statement made by one of the players is an example of the autotelic treatment of violence, decrease of sensitivity and at the same time fascination with violence: "all the time people ask me: 'Vlad, how are you doing this? How did you get so good at killing people? What are you hiding?' I answer them; 'I have nothing to hide. It is as easy an activity as any other. Some men like building houses, the other men like making shoes, and I kill people. You just have to practice because practice makes perfect". K.E. Dill, J.C. Dill, Video game violence: A review of the empirical literature, "Aggression and Violent Behavior" 1998, Vol. 3, pp. 407–428.

[14] R. Dąbrowska, "Agresywne" gry komputerowe a obraz siebie, [in:] Oddziaływanie "agresywnych" gier komputerowych na psychikę dzieci, edit. A. Gala, I. Ulfik, Lublin, 2000; M. Braun-Gałkowska, Mechanizmy wyjaśniające wpływ gier komputerowych na psychikę dzieci, ibidem.

indicates a very high coefficient of correlations between the early antisocial behaviors and pathological tendencies (crimes, addictions) in adult life.[15] Huesman and Eron established that aggression 'is represented by a set of aggressive scripts steering the behaviour and solving social problems. These scripts come into being in the early time of the development of the individual, and with the flow of time they become resistant to changes.'[16] The stability is also caused when an individual actively seeks and/or creates the situations that would suit their aggressive and generalized motivation. The research by C.A. Anderson and K. E. Dill also shows that the changes of personality are permanent under the influence of computer games. People who in their childhood played games containing elements of violence more often display physical and verbal aggressiveness, negativism, suspiciousness or irritability as adults. They were characterized by higher emotional tension and less sensitivity to goodness and evil, and more often infringed the law. In this context, the protests of the supporters of brutal computer games, ascribing them cathartic meaning, resemble the specific axiological categories through their negation and contrast, as described by Baudrillarad.[17]

Out of pedagogical and clearly human duty we should ask a question of whether some specific values can really be protected by the promotion of their opposites? Even if contact with the pictures of violence does not result in committing the forbidden act, it certainly means that through watching them during the game and personally committing the brutal acts, a young person gets accustomed to them and they lose their traumatic character, cause a fall of sensitivity and stop being treated as incidental. The imagination on what is permissible broadens, and as a consequence the imperative banning of committing the forbidden deeds disappears. M. McCormick defines brutal games as unambiguously negative, referring to the traditional philosophical thought and giving examples of intuitional conviction that even participation in the simulation of immoral acts is bad.[18] If we know the plausibility of this assumption, we should ask who it is that claims relaxation through shooting (even if only virtually) at others, hurting through the use of tools, and chasing characters in a car or another vehicle in order to kill them (as stated by nearly 30% of respondents). According to Fromm, taking pleasure from watching scenes of destruc-

[15] L.D. Eron et al., Aggression and its correlates over 22 years, [in:] Childhood aggression and violence, ed. D. Crowell, I. Evans, C. O'Donnell, Wyd. Plenum, New York, 1987, pp. 249–262; R. Loeber, The stability of antisocial and delinquent child behavior: a review, "Child Development" 1982 nr 53, p. 1431–1446; D. Magnusson, Individual development from an interactional perspective, Wyd. NJ: Earlbaum, Hillsdale, 1988.

[16] H. Zamkley, Stałość różnic indywidualnych w zakresie agresji, [w:] Socjalizacja i agresja…, op. cit., p. 72.

[17] J. Baudrillard, Symulakry i symulacja, Wyd. Sic!, Warszawa, 2005.

[18] M. Mac Cormick, Ethics and Information Technology, Wyd. Kluwer Academic Publishers, Hingham, 2002.

tion and violence is one of the indexes of a destructive attitude and necrophilic character, which finds a specific fondness in 'transforming alive into dead, destructing just for destruction', for which power and violence 'are the first and the last solutions of all problems', and where exploration of 'the richness of possibilities of the human individual' change into an exploration 'of the technical functions of the artifacts'.[19]

Eugene F. Provenzo Jr claims that the greatest danger of games lies in their interactivity, which in comparison to the perception of television transmissions can bring much more serious consequences in shaping negative behaviors. H.G. Gadamer's observations of game enthusiasts during their favorite interest suggest unambiguous associations with the description of the essence of the game. According to Gadamer, the game assumes using the player as a medium. It somehow absorbs the subject in the game reality. It stops existing in the consciousness of the player as something 'external' and 'pulls him into its area and fills him with its spirit'. 'The player experiences the game, as the superior reality', into which they submerge, often losing contact with the real world.[20] The characters and events (despite the obvious deformations) seem to be probable, and with the improving qualities of sound and picture they intensify the illusion of reality offered by the programme. A special kind of narration plays a significant role in this process, presenting all actions as the actual present taking place thanks to the participation of the player. The game participant understands the intentions and realization of the actions undertaken not only by themselves but also by the computer or a living enemy. Mixing with the characters and fictional events the player anticipated a reception as if they were real and behaves accordingly, engaging themselves in the game physically and psychically.[21]

Stickgold et al.'s research shows such influence. The scientists discovered that after playing the game for a long time images from it appear in an intensified way in the form of dreams. Associating these observations with the knowledge of relations between phases of a dream after the processes of learning and the later activation of the learned information for better consolidation of the memory traces, a group of researchers concluded that the plots of video games are also 're–worked' and consolidated. This means that being in contact with aggressive patterns takes place even when the player has left the computer screen. Without speculating on the influence of images and experiences

[19] E. Fromm, Anatomia ludzkiej destrukcyjności, Wyd, Rebis, Warszawa, 1999, p. 372, 379, 385.

[20] In the statements of the Barents appeared the motives proving that when a child is playing, it is difficult to get in touch with it. The child seems to have turned off itself to all 'stimuli' coming from outside of the game.

[21] A. Arkuszewski, Quake – fenomen społecznego odbioru gry komputerowej, the thesis supervised by dr A. Mikołejko, Instytut Informacji Naukowej i Studiów Bibliologicznych, Wydział Historyczny Uniwersytetu Warszawskiego, [at:] http://www.myonid.pl/search/show_url?t=http%3A%2F%2Fklaudia.ehost.pl%2Ftolo%2Fmgr.htm, resources on 15th May 2010.

stored in the subconsciousness on the human behavior, it can be surely stated that an unstable dream, disturbed by alarming visions, intensifies stress and prevents the regeneration of the physical power necessary for the developing organism.

The intensiveness of experiences can be additionally stimulated by identification with the character of a game. Numerous programmes enable choice, creating the character that best suits the player. The configured avatar is often a fulfilment of the unreachable dreams of its creator regarding superpowers, charisma or a specific appearance. Very often, the degree of identification with a created character is so profound that it becomes an alter ego of the player. The adventures of the avatar can evoke strong reactions in the player, and the feeling of identification increases the level of aggression directed at the enemies in the game. If in the mind of a young person the border between them and the created character blurs, it may be assumed that behaviors which are profitable in a game will be moved to objective reality. Girls and boys in the described group used standard equipment, which means computers with screens of different sizes and resolutions, and the players moved their characters using a keyboard or a joystick.

We should think over the effects that can be caused by using the so called simulators, which realistically present space, structures, colors, sounds and even touch sensations. It is also essential that they have real movements and gestures (so the virtual world is precisely synchronized with the real one). The popularization of such equipment is undoubtedly a question for the near future, and soon the enthusiasts of 'aggressive' games will be able to more realistically participate in fights, shooting and chases, more realistically wound the enemies and brush with death, associate with fearful characters or have cybersex. The defenders of games containing images of violence state that aggression in a game has an instrumental character, and is used to gain a specific aim, so it is only a tool, and not the aim itself. They make an analogy with real life, which is alos 'the area of fighting'. K.E. Dill and J.C. Dill noticed that an aggressive behavior escalates if it is caused by 'the justified' motifs, because the subject becomes convinced that they are acting in good faith.[22] It should be considered whether a young individual would spontaneously follow the rule of using violence only when it is inevitable, or whether they learn to find convincing explanation for their actions (as do some adults when administering corporal punishment towards their children). The vast majority of games chosen by the respondents base the justification of violence on primitive, racial, religious or sexual stereotypes which lead to treating well–educated or industrious people like suckers, and all those whose physical appearance is different

[22] K.E. Dill, J.C. Dill, *Video game violence: A review of the empirical literature*, "Aggression and Violent Behavior" 1998, Vol. 3, pp. 407–428.

from the exaggerated or grotesque superheroes as objects for immediate annihilation.

The stereotypes are to automate the action, omitting the mechanisms of rationalization, and are additionally characterized by permanence and resistance to change. Thus, a young person, left with such sources of 'knowledge of the world', can integrate harmful schemes of interpretation. Attitudes of involuntarily borrowing such features developed in childhood and adolescence and reacting with distrust or even hostility to everything that is 'different' can in a significant way disturb interpersonal relations during the whole life of an individual. Additionally, if the victims are presented as people deserving of aggression, empathy or compassion for their suffering decreases in the player and in extreme cases there appears vehemence and no mercy. In the games discussed there are no situations where the act of mercy towards the enemy would be rewarded. On the contrary, scores are given to the player who can finish off a barely alive, defenseless adversary begging for mercy. Even with the most liberal attitude to education and deep faith in the natural goodness of human beings, it is necessary to regard the matter promoting ruthlessness and cruelty as unambiguously harmful and unacceptable.

GAMES AND STRESS

Before we answer the second research question, we would like to devote some attention to stress, which is a synthesis of a few elements mingling together. The pattern of stress reaction was discovered in 1960 by Selye and he called it General Adaptation Syndrome (GAS), being the first line of defense of an organism against potential stress factors. Attention is drawn to the role of the immune system in going through stress. They can be divided into intrapersonal, which means internal, the most important being self–assessment, and the external ones, where social support has the greatest meaning, defined as the resources provided by interactions with other people. According to the model of the main effect (related to stress), Ganster and Victor noticed that group membership intensifies well–being, regardless of the stress level. In our problem it is the membership of the group of people who meet regularly on the Internet. The buffer model is worth mentioning here, referring to the interpersonal resources, protecting from the negative effects of stress through fulfilling the specific needs as the effects of stressful situations. This model focuses on functional rather than structural support. In this case it means participation in a game with other people from the Internet. Furthermore, having friends or acquaintances, who relax and have fun with one another is also a form of support. Appreciation gives us the feeling that other people appreciate and respect us. High self–esteem plays an important role in coping with stress sufficiently. It is in the system of a game, where a player is given the possibility to establish a ranking, scores and honors, which enables real respect or even admiration for the best player. The system of a game also stipulates fulfillment of a specified role in a game, which makes the player useful, and sometimes welcome. Vital psychological aspects are the sense of control of the situation and the sense of closeness. The sense of control of the situation means being aware of the responsibility for what happens and also of our influence on the final, positive outcome.

However, there is a danger of confusing the control of a game with the control of other spheres of life, which is related to magic–wishful thinking. Social support occurs at each level of stress. As far as stress management is concerned, Antonowsky mentions three main components: rationality, flexibility and farsightedness. As for people addicted to Internet games, they often lose their rationality and become less flexible, considering playing the games as a good way of coping with stress. An important issue for many people is rationalism – logical, systematic, empiric and organized thinking – by which they aim to gain control over the surrounding reality and their own lives. However, the "happiness tools" are a trap which leads to the incapability of a rational view of the situation. A person is subject to primitive emotional drives, which are related to magic–wishful thinking. This kind of thinking is common in contemporary life, providing relief in situations when one cannot overcome difficulties and creates soothing images of the situation. In the case of the strong involvement of personal needs and desires, this kind of thinking takes control over certain spheres of life, excluding warnings and creating illusory perspectives of reaching psychic comfort through addictions, such as playing Internet games.

People have always aimed at improving one's mood and relieving pain; cultural phenomena may be the reason why various experiences and individual attitudes become habitual behaviors. The Internet is now a way of spending time and making acquaintances. Scientist examined 317 children who spent little time playing games (not more than 10 hours a week), 520 children who played games for 10 to 30 hours a week, and 343 children who played a lot (more than 30 hours a week). The research showed that there is a meaningful difference in the level of long–term stress depending on the time spent in front of the computer screen. Long–term stress was examined with the use of Cohen's Stress Perception Questionnaire. To calculate the significance of the differences between the groups a nonparametric equivalent of a Student's t test for independent groups was used, namely the Mann–Whitney test. Young people who spend more time playing games tend to be more stressed than those who play less.[23] It was also noticed that there is a re-

[23] Cohen's Stress Perception Questionnaire gives the relationship Z=1,99; p=0,05

lationship between the time spent on playing games and the level of measured stress. Moreover, it was observed that there is a relationship between the hours spent on playing games and the levels of stress among the respondents. This means that people who play games are more stress–prone. This dependence is quite strong in extreme groups, and smaller in relation to the whole population. There is a tendency to advance a contrary thesis which states that the more stress people experience, the more video games they play. Again, as far as aggression is concerned, there are a number of arguments proving that this is a self–maneuverable mechanism. The first is based on the characteristics of the social situation of people who devote a lot of time to their favorite entertainment.

We refer to the results of a public opinion poll which showed that most of the respondents play alone at home. It may be said that their social lives are limited, or that they limit them only to formal and significant relations. A young person at the stage of forming their individual and social identity may not realize that missing emotional relationships and opportunities to exercise vital social competences (such as effective communication skills, self–assertion, patience, tolerance) leads to an inability of feeling comfortable in varied social situations. These situations, regular for a socially active teenager, will be considered stressful and frustrating. It is possible to indicate a direct relation of duration and "depth" of isolation and the measure of stress resulting from social relations.

The enthusiasts of violent computer games are continually exposed to stressful stimuli. This belongs to a characteristic view of the world in these games, comprising a tendency towards competition, a compulsive need for winning and maintaining a dominant position and a related emotional irritability. In the era of the so–called platform games a girl or a boy may compensate for shortage of social relations in the real world by making contact with other enthusiasts of online entertainment. One can belong to an Internet community, which – as already mentioned – provides a kind of social support, sense of security, membership, and acceptance, creating protection from stressful stimuli. Unfortunately, bonds between the players and the rules they are subject to are essentially different from traditional ones. M. Maffesolli, in his analysis of new forms of collective life, called them neotribes. Their characteristic feature is dispersion, which does not assure a direct contact, and a biding agent is an empathic community of experience (here oriented to social needs) providing a deceptive hope of reaching a sense of closeness. Yet, neotribes considered as emotional communities are unstable, open, fluid, based upon superficial fascination, and dependent on temporary preferences, which make them socially disoriented.[24]

[24] M. Maffesoli, *Czas plemion*, Warszawa: Wydawnictwo PWN, 2008, p. 32.

An individual belonging to a neotribe is not obliged to be loyal and responsible for other members of the neotribe, but one also does not expect loyalty or responsibility from other members of the neotribe. There is a possibility that the superficiality and instability of the bond are the reasons why the nominal membership to a particular group does not increase individuals' defensive resources. Being a member of a neotribe is probably the most unstable kind of social capital. That is why it is hard to find a stable and reliable source of support. The level of self–esteem is closely related to the status of an individual in a group and a problem of membership in the group. It would not be a semantic misuse if we say that for young boys and girls the position in the group of peers decides on their good physical, social and mental condition. Fans of video games have criteria of popularity in the group, such as the ability to cope with tasks in a game, gaining new titles, abilities, and avatars' abilities. An increased level of long–term stress among people who spend a lot of time playing games or those who do not play very often suggests that the reason for stress lies in a failure (among those who do not play very often) or an order of continuous improvement and a dramatic need for getting/preserving the highest position (for those who play a lot). Another reason for long–term stress may be the game itself, or more precisely the intensive emotional impulse which is the result of the inability to cope with a task in the game, technical problems, or objective obstacles (the necessity to go to school, learning, bans and other). Such situations may frustrate a passionate player and may also intensify emotional disturbances. The heightened level of long–term stress is connected to the "victim effect". Buchman and Funk (following K. E. Dill & J. C. Dill) noticed that violent games confirm the perception of the world as a dangerous place. Experiencing violence leads to forming a distorted image of the world, in which violence is recognized as a phenomenon occurring more often than it actually does, which indicates a feeling of anxiety and personal safety concerns. "Each time people play aggressive video games they repeat aggressive behaviors which teach and intensify the skills in how to draw one's attention to the enemies in a sense of changed perception. Aggressive behaviors can be learned and intensified in real life relationships as well as expectations that people would be aggressive".[25]

A state of excessive excitation does not result only from objective conditions of the environment. It depends on the mutual impact of features of the environment and those of a person living in this society. A psychological reaction for a given stressful situation activates a sympathetic system. Physiological processes start the intensive secretion of adrenaline, noradrenalin and thyroxin, which are responsible for the management of nutrients. In a stressful situation hormones raise blood pressure, sugar level and intensively nourish the

[25] K.E. Dill, C.A. Anderson, op. cit., p. 744.

muscles at the expense of nutritional deficiencies in other organs. Chronic stress is the cause of many mental and physiological disorders such as gastric problems, neuralgia, headaches, paroxysmal dyspnoea and skin diseases. Many studies have shown that physical exercise reduces anxiety, irritability and emotional hyperactivity symptoms, and increase levels of norepinephrine and serotonin, causing a reduction in stress symptoms. A similar effect is caused by the endorphins released in larger quantities during exercise. The above show that the thesis of catharsis and treating computer games as a way to relax and reduce stress is frail.

Nowadays a great number of young people have the habit of sitting in front of the computers. It has become their lifestyle resulting in an alarming decrease of form and health conditions among children and the youth. Polish nationwide research has shown that 65% of students aged 11–15 do not reach the recommended level of physical activity and with reference to both genders the physical activity drastically decreases with age. A deteriorating physical the condition corresponds to the rapid increase in the number of personal computers. According to L. Manovich, a person who wanted to learn and "conquer" the world in the past had to be in constant motion. Nowadays, that person is forced to act in the opposite way – to stay immobile. "The price of virtual mobility was a new organised immobilization of the spectators",[26] he concludes.

It appears obvious that the situation will change for the individual as well as social interest. However, any restrictions regarding the use of computers are not the solution and could exert the opposite effect. Individuals shall be provided the alternative, the same attractive modes of spending spare time. Between addiction to and fear of technology there is space for its right use. It is worth devoting time, energy and financial means to draw the attention of the youth to the entertainment which lets cybersportsmen, cyberfighters, cybercommanders, cyberbussinessmen, and cybercitizens develop their physical conditions and social skills in good ways. It is important to realize that buying a son or daughter another computer game, or simply giving them permission to go into a virtual reality for hours, are aspects of the educational indolence of parents, excused by creating rational excuses.

SOURCES

Anderson C.A. Dill K.E., Video Games and Aggressive Thoughts, Feelings, and Behavior in the Laboratory and Life, "Journal of Personality and Social Psychology" 2000, issue 4.

Boroń J., Zyss T., Komputerowy świat iluzji, "Charaktery" 1998, issue 2.

Boroń, J., Zyss, T., Świat gier komputerowych II – badania ankietowe nad ich rozpowszechnieniem wśród młodzieży, "Psychiatria Polska", issue 2 (30), 1996.

[26] L. Manowich, op. cit., p. 192.

Choynowski M., Skrócony podręcznik do testu "Nastroje i Humory", A.M. Busse i A. Durkee, 3 MOIW, Warszawa, 1972.
Łukasz S., Magia gier komputerowych, Warszawa, 1998.
Mac Cormick M., Ethics and Information Technology, Wyd. Kluwer Academic Publishers, Hingham, 2002.
Oddziaływanie "agresywnych" gier komputerowych na psychikę dzieci, (ed.) A. Gala and I. Ulfik, ARTOM, Lublin, 2000.
Seyle H., Stres okiełznany, Wydawnictwo Naukowe PWN, Warszawa, 1977.
Siemieniecki B., Komputer w diagnostyce i terapii pedagogicznej, Wydawnictwo Adam Marszałek, Toruń, 1996.
Socjalizacja i agresja, edit. A. Frączek, H. Zamkley, Wyd. IP PAN, WSPS, Warszawa, 1993.

Zhechka Georgieva
Sofia University "St. Kliment Ohridski", Bulgaria

MEDIA AND THEIR CONTRIBUTION TO THE CREATION OF GLOBAL CULTURE AND A GREAT, UNIVERSAL PUBLIC

ABSTRACT

This subordination of research is intended to address the most general characteristics of traditional and digital media and to trace their influence in the process of forming a universal audience and global culture. Pointing out its purpose, the present introduction to the scientific work defines it as a heuristic attempt to identify diachronic and synchronic interactions, theoretical interpretations and pragmatic results in media status and development. The main task of this work is the attempt to trace the media positioning, to analyze their coordination in the context of today's globalized structures and systems, and to put their symbolism in a functional relationship with other symbolic technological, economic, socio-political, humanitarian and cross-cultural systems of modern society.

KEYWORDS: mass culture, cultural industry, global culture, media, digital media, global universal audience.

The specificity of different media, spread in a particular culture, is seen as a factor for the transformation of thought, culture and society. A similar concept for media predefines the idea of media effect, shifting emphasis from the effects of mass media on the audience to their overall effect on culture. The contemporary cultural and media era is marked by a rapid development of digital communication technology. Different means of communication work in different situations and the function of each of the possible communication modalities ought to present, implement or re-contextualize social positions and relations, sharing a particular type of knowledge with a particular audience. (9) Due to mass culture, the modern situation implies a free choice from among many and differently colored alternatives. The Digital Media Alliance, Florida defines digital media as "the creative convergence of digital arts, science, technology and business for human expression, communication, social interaction and education".

This report covers issues related to the relationships and dependencies between different factors in the media specificity which contribute to the reconstruction of the information in cyberspace into global culture and the forming of a global audience.

This work aims at examining how media function and influence the creation of a great global audience, and how their impact results in cultural transformations in the world today.

The object of the research will be the theoretical and factual treatments used to analyses the functioning of modern and postmodern mass communication systems where, apart from suggesting new, rapid and much more reliable methods of spreading culture and values, media transform culture itself and create a new type of values. The object of the analysis will be universalizing of the global audience, and identifying and specifying such notions as cultural industry and mass culture.

Any industrial system, even if the demanded profit is ignored, seeks expansion while any mass production intended to be consumed has its own logic of maximum consumption.

The cultural industry does not deviate from this law. Furthermore, in its most concentrated, dynamic sectors it seeks a universal audience. Magazines, newspapers, Hollywood super productions or great cosmopolitan coproductions, and various productions offered by digital media offer a big scope of possibilities, conveniences and supply to the Internet, indeed, to everyone and to no one, to all ages, to both genders, to different social classes, i.e. to a national audience as a whole or possibly a global audience.

Looking for a diverse audience includes seeking diversity in the information or in the imagination, and the demand for a large audience includes seeking a common denominator.

A weekly paper like *Bulgaria* or *Capital*, for example, systematically tends to eclecticism: in the same issue there is spirituality and eroticism, religion, sports, humor, politics, games, movies, travel, research, art, private lives of the celebrities, etc. Standard films and soap operas also seek to present love, adventure, humor and eroticism in different doses. They mix male (aggressive) and female (sentimental, tearful) content for both adolescents and adults. Diversity in newspapers, films, radio and the Internet aims at satisfying all interests and tastes for maximum consumption.

This diversity is at the same time a systematized, homogenized variety complying with general rules. A simple, clear and direct editorial style aims at making the message transparent and giving it immediate comprehensibility. Editing gives one a homogeneous style – a universal style – and that universality covers different contents. When the author of a given material, the director of a big newspaper or a film producer, says "my audience" they bear in mind an average person, derived by the sale estimates or number of the site visitors, an idea which is homogenized itself. They attribute tastes and disgusts to this ideal person. Homogenization aims to make it easy for an ideal average person to understand various contents.

Syncretism is the most suitable word to convey the tendency towards the homogenization of diversity in contents under one common denominator. Full–length feature films also seek syncretism. The majority of films syncretize many topics in each major genre. Thus, in an adventure film there will be love and comedy, in a love film there will be adventure and comedy, and in a comedy there will be love and adventure. But at the same time, these topics are expressed by the same homogeneous language (even though an infinite number of forms are possible). The radio seeks syncretism – it changes the sequence of songs and emissions but the total is homogenized in the style of so–called radiophonic presentation. Big press and magazines seek syncretism by trying hard to satisfy the whole range of interests through a constant rhetoric. Since the dominance of cyberspace, the wide range of opportunities and facilities, supply and demand have syncretized endless forms – information, entertainment, communication, friends, and ideas – with one homogeneous language. Businesses, media, parties and institutions are also transferred there. With the appearance of Facebook and other social networks, as well as the mass use of them, the border between the real and virtual worlds blurs. The real world is more and more the world of deficits, whereas the virtual one becomes richer and richer, vivid, saturated with emotion and information. Today, if one is not on the Internet they are not present enough in the real world, either. Certainly, this trend is not considered unilaterally. Some respondents regard it as an inevitable consequence of the technological and social progress. To others it is only one of the symptoms of the global social crisis, which has made the real world cold and uninviting and has driven its residents into the virtual world. Analyzing the consequences of the technical reproduction of a work of art, Walter Benjamin, for example, indicates the imperfections of reproduction and the inability to preserve the uniqueness and originality of the being of the work of art. (3)

One thing is indisputable for all. With the increasing accessibility of the Internet combined with the great number of opportunities it brings, it has become a necessity rather than luxury; it has created the 'Attention era'. (23) This new world changes the lifestyles and hence the actors in the so–called real world. For some it is a threat, for others a new opportunity.

Syncretism seeks to unify, to some extent, both the information and adventure sectors in the industrial culture. In the information sector various facts predominate (i.e. this part of reality where the unexpected, bizarre, criminal, accidental and adventurous invade everyday life). Everything in real life that is like a novel or a dream is privileged. Moreover, the information is wrapped up in romantic elements, often invented or made up by journalists (such as love stories of stars or princesses, and gossip and intrigue related to celebrities). Mass culture is revived by this double movement of the imaginary, the immigrating real and the real taking the colors of the imaginary. The double contamination of the real and imaginary, the amazing and sublime syncretism, are added to the search for maximum consummation and give mass culture one of its major characteristics.

In the early twentieth century the barriers of social class, age and educational level determined the boundaries of cultural areas. The press of the social opinion differed greatly from the accessible information press. Popular literature was heavily structured according to the models of the melodramatic and the spicy. Children's literature was pink or green – novels for obedient kids or for travelling fictions. The nascent film was an amusement show.

These barriers have not been removed. New overlays were formed and a specific audience was created. These new overlays should not hide from us the fundamental dynamism of mass culture. Many media products are designed equally well for both cultivated and uncultivated people, for ordinary people; for both men and women; for both the young and the elderly. All of them look for universality and obtain it. They do not attract all readers but they attract those from all levels and categories. They create a new pole of attraction, a dynamic style of varieties. Meanwhile, cinema has become a show for everyone. In a competitive way, the female themes have also evolved in the press and TV programs. They have specialized mainly in female–directed content, developed or implicated in the male–female theme. Thus, the homogenization of production continues with the homogenization of consumption, which seeks to reduce the barriers between ages. Undoubtedly, this trend has not implemented all its features yet, i.e. it has not reached its limits. This homogenization of ages tends to fix on one dominant. The youth theme is one of the main elements of today's culture. Not only young people but also the elderly are consumers of different media products, which are strongly emphasized by the ubiquitously increased need of the unlimited possibilities of the Internet. The mass culture subjects are also "young" subjects. Cultural boundaries are broken down in the common market of the Internet and traditional mass media. Of course, divisions are made inside the new culture. For instance, watching different TV channels and programs depends on their specificity and the spectators' tastes and preferences. Radio listening differs depending on the choice of stations and programs. This difference of taste is also a partial social differentiation.

The information era puts the traditional media under pressure to redefine and protect their place in society. Traditional media yield ground to the online editions, where the audience is divided into blogospheres. Bloggers and other contributors to do–it–yourself journalism are free to express their own opinions, even at the price of unbalanced information. Blogs are a niche, filling the gap in publicity due to the lack of freedom of speech. Often in journalism, whole themes are absent from the editorial, investigations and especially from publicism. Blogs are a sort of publicism, where the personal opinion of the author weighs in. The public confidence is not won easily and at once. The public has a choice of what to read and the ability for personal position and opinion, and blogs provide that opportunity in its purest form, being the spotlight of public opinion on which this form of communication has an impact. Blog communication is multi–dimensional, for even though articles and news are published, the culture of communication is much more open and dynamic. In the blogosphere (an analogue of media) the majority of blogs belong to people who share their personal opinions and discuss them with others. The purpose is not to spread news but to start a discussion and share sources (photos, video, and quotes). Even though most of the media have sites on which readers/spectators can comment, their attitude towards visitors, information property and even the methods of work differ significantly from those of bloggers. Popularity is easily gained or lost on the Internet and thoroughly unknown blogs can attract huge attention within hours. Dynamism and freedom of communication help to exchange ideas, cite texts, develop concepts, coordinate civil actions, etc. without formality and legal complications. All these are things which are regulated and even stigmatized in media due to their mass character, but they underlie the blog culture. (21; 22)

If we consider that classes and social groups remain divided in labor in terms of prestige or relationship between seller and buyer, supply and demand, divided by residence in neighborhoods, we can claim that industrial culture is the only big space for communication among social classes. At the same time, the poor and the rich will have watched the same program on television or the same film, will have benefitted from the rich tools of the Internet, and they will have consumed the same digital products.

Prestige, conventions, hierarchies and demands differentiate and subdivide this mercenary class, but what unifies them is the identity of consumed values. It is these shared values that media transmit. It is that unity that characterizes mass culture.

Thus, this matches a new class in the process of homogenization and heterogenization (these two controversial trends occur on different levels) culture, which is also in a process of homogenization and heterogenization. Therefore, this industrial culture will be the culture which will develop in the medium of a new universal audience. And if this is true, we can assume that the new culture is also consistent with the dominance (or the progress) of the values of the "middle class".

In other words, the new culture fits into the sociological complex composed of the economy, democratization of consumption, and the growth of certain values. The new culture is a common place and means of communication among different layers and different classes. The leveling of social inequalities is part of the standardization of tastes and interests which mass media display and contribute to.

The homogenizing trend is at the same time a cosmopolitan trend which seeks to attenuate the national cultural inequalities in favor of a culture of big transnational spaces. The industrial culture adapts local folklore themes, transforming them into cosmopolitan ones such as western, jazz and tropical themes (bachata, tango, samba, mambo, cha-cha-cha, etc.) On the one hand this favors cultural syncretism and on the other the anthropological themes, i.e. those adapted by one dominator common for humanity. The industrial culture in its most concentrated and dynamic sector is already internationally organized.

The industrial culture is developing in the plan of the world market, hence its overwhelming tendency to syncretism – eclecticism and homogenization. It does not always completely overcome the inequalities but its imaginary, ludic, aesthetic stream breaks down local, ethnic, social, national, age, sex and education barriers. It deracinates themes from folklore and traditions which it universalizes. It invents universal themes spontaneously.

Who is that which is universally human? Is it just that which is human, i.e. common for all degrees of humanity? Yes and no. Yes, if it refers to an imaginary person who complies with all images through identification or projection. Yes, if it refers to the human-child who is in everyone, the curious one who loves games, entertainment, myths and tales. Yes, if it refers to the person who disposes of one common sense everywhere it their abilities to decipher and intelligence.

In this sense, the average person is a kind of universal anthropos. The aspiration of the mass culture for universality is based on these anthropological grounds, revealing and generating a primary universality. At the same time it creates a new universality out of those typical for the cultural elements of modern civilization. That is why a contemporary person is more than just a compilation of the average human developed by the new civilization seeking universality. Therefore, the trend to universality is based not only on the elementary anthropos but on the dominant stream in the planetary era. Indeed, the cultural production creates a mass, universal audience. But, at the same time it rediscovers what was beneath: a human pillar, common for the mass audience.

In other sense, cultural production is determined by the market itself. This feature also distinguishes it from other cultures which also use media, more and more, but which have normative characters, imposed pedagogically or autocratically as orders or bans. Compared to the Internet, which is considered the realm of freedom, traditional media – for their dependence on the state, advertisers, publishers, editors, self-censorship or those who own them –

are always suspected to serve a certain self-seeking personal or group interest. Mass culture is not imposed by social institutions, it depends on industry and trade; it is simply being offered. It tolerates taboos (imposed by religion, the state, etc.) but it does not create them; it offers models and trends, but it does not impose anything. It always passes through the mediation of the market product, which obeys the market laws of supply and demand and for that reason borrows some of those features. Its main law is the market law, where its relative flexibility comes from. Mass culture is a product of the correlation between production and consumption. *A priori* it is a kind of a dialogue between them. The production of different media offers products, expressing itself through the language. The consumer estimates and makes a choice. They listen and watch or refuse to listen or watch. They choose how to react or whether to react at all. The new media based on Web 2.0 or Google Web Lab, representing a series of interactive "web experiments", demonstrate the progress of the Internet in recent years, which literally wiped out the boundaries between information producers and consumers. They give the consumers the possibility to create and spread content on their own, thus eliminating the information monopoly of the traditional mass media. Day by day the audience ceases to be passive, takes part in the process of developing the new media content and influences the formation of the new informational agenda of the society. The ordinary consumers' opinions are becoming a mass product of the communication process.

It should also be asked whether media make audience or whether audience makes media, whether mass culture is imposed from the outside to the audience or it reflects its needs. It is obvious that the real problem is that of the dialectic between the system of cultural production and the cultural needs of users. This dialectic is too complicated because, on one hand, what we call audience is an abstract economic consequence of the laws of supply and demand (this is the "ideal average audience"), and on the other hand state pressure (censorship) and the laws of the industrial system weigh on the nature of this dialogue.

As a result, mass culture is a product of a production/consumption dialectic, which is part of the global dialectic of the society in its integrity. Media are a great social power, an interactive mediator of communication. They act as a factory, an information source, an advertising channel, a cultural industry, a critical and correcting tool, an ideological tool, even as a manipulative tool (4), as well as a means of development of information technology.

Jean Baudrillard sees media as an "external genetic code" that regulates the mutation of human situations (2). Therefore, the total of all metamorphoses in human culture, at a given stage of civilization, can be registered and described objectively only if they are included in the main contact zones between the person and the media which determine their cultural actions. Fidler, who analyzes and summarizes the latest technological changes in the human system for communication and in contemporary media practice, claims that the neologism "media–morphism", which he coined in 1990, denotes such media transformation which occurs under the influence of complex interactions between perceived needs, competitive and political pressures and social and technological innovations (7).

There is no doubt that various online communications are increasing their influence as sources of information. Generally speaking, they implement the main function of mass media, raise actual questions from political, social and other spheres of our life and focus their readers' attention on them. Their significance grows with the increasing number of users on the Internet. For example, digital printing technology provides conveniences and opportunities at lower costs for production and processing; free and easy access; text links, graphics, pictures, animations and videos; information search opportunities; easy distribution; the opportunity for feedback through the ability to communicate with the media, no limit in time and space for usage; instant news updates; the ability to post for the reader, which gives them the opportunity to develop and expand the topic via links to other web addresses (blogs, forums, other electronic media, broadcasts, publications); and choice and rejection of a prognosis what will reach the audience.

The same is valid for the other digital media, such as television and radio. The increasing specialization in the demand of media product is a current trend in digital technology development. Digitalization allows for extending software (downloads, cable and satellite channels, DVD). The interactive communication allows the users (audience) to control the communication process, interacting both with the source of communication and the content of the message.

On the Internet one can find lectures, news, reference, curious or important life literature – all kinds of information. Apart from the easy and rapid access, that most of the information is free is a huge advantage. The information out there is quickly updated and can be detected and verified in different sources. Information about what is happening in the country and in the world can be received. One can obtain better comprehension of the occurring events through comments, analyses and prognoses. With the appearance of smart phones and wireless Internet the search for information at any time is easy and accessible. With the appearance and the opportunities of Facebook, which have created interest communities, the information finds the user on its own without their spending time searching for it.

Certainly, the Internet audience is aware of the fact that not all its information is objective, reliable and trustworthy. It is familiar with information pollution (spam), and suspicious or even misleading information.

There is a tendency towards loss of interest in the blogosphere and forums. For many reasons, forums attract people who need to demonstrate their stupidity or political and economic interests with deliberately placed paid participants. Interest is preserved only in blogs which are maintained by specialists in any field or who offer concise information and interesting links which they come across during their travels in cyberspace (19). Gradually, however, a range of sources is differentiated which the audience does not trust. The network tends to form authorities and now, with more chances to prove these, institutions and individuals who carry characteristics in cyberspace earn credibility and trust in the real world information space. In the global village of the Internet, with the possibilities for verification and quick orientation, the audience easily acquires its own position.

Since its appearance the Internet has been constantly expanding its position as a medium for communication and maintenance of social contacts. On the Internet some people feel freer, more sincere and frank while communicating or debating on different topics. There is no other entertainment institution that is able to compete with the Internet in terms of potential to satisfy this colorful and diverse audience. In satisfying the needs of entertainment, most people's leisure time is transferred to the Internet space. Communication is possible between people at distance from one another in real time. All this bears more advantages to "surrogate" communication rather than face to face contact. With the ability to download movies, TV series and archive shows , the can compensate for their failure to watch them during their original broadcast or publication. This also helps real contact, be it with friends or family, personal commitments, live concerts and performances and any preferred form of events and circumstances that they cannot or do not want to delay. The power of the Internet makes entertainment possible that was previously inaccessible, as well making it easy to combine the pleasant with the useful without wasting strength, energy and time to organize it in real life. The Internet is also becoming more and more useful and convenient in other practical applications such as participation in civic initiatives and protests, banking, job searching, shopping and services (e.g. booking hotels, tour packages and tickets concerts).

Certainly traditional media, although existing on the Internet, have their audiences, but are limited in terms of the opportunities offered by the Internet. Their success is obviously among different audiences with different interests.

Digitalization has made it possible to watch many TV channels in high–quality. New technologies preserve the influence of television. What holds interest in this medium is the successful effort of some TV channels to become interactive. The fact that television is still the most powerful medium means that many people see leading television networks as powerful institutions or strong brands, factors keeping spectators in front of their TV sets.

Within the busy populations of cities, radio listening is reduced to being used while at work, while travelling by car, while visiting public places – as generally part of the background while doing something else.

The mass audience has an ecological position related to the use of paper in printed editions, which leads to the reckless cutting back of forests, along with its use of toxic chemicals in printing.

Media convergence (in the sense of mutual alignment, merger, achieving the same purpose) is the process of blurring the boundaries between different media in the digital age where the old criteria of differentiation between the individual and mass media are becoming more difficult to apply. As for "integration", it is associated with a process in the contemporary media industry which leads to the unification of different mass media.

The new generation was born in the digital world and they are both consumers and authors. They create a culture of participation (in groups), they solve problems in collaboration and make decisions, interact with other users in the network while distributing, sharing and re–publishing different types of content. According to Henry Jenkins, most people have the knowledge and ability to take media into their own hands and make the flow of ideas and images. He argues that every student should acquire basic social skills and cultural competences that reflect the requirements and opportunities of living in a "culture of participation" (8).

In modern education there is a tendency whereby not the amount of knowledge but the skills for coping in situations matter. We can say that the Internet, with its digital capabilities, is such a versatile teacher of contemporary audiences. The modern human has a connection with the whole world and even though, according to Ken Robinson (13, 14), the twenty–first century is the century of individual approaches and solutions, we need to consider the significance of the role of someone who is conscious of their importance and uniqueness, but at the same time actively involved and working on the issues and causes affecting the universal values affecting the global audience. Globality does not have personal preferences, opinions, conclusions, tastes, and identities. Globality consists of offering a colorful range of infinitely numerous opportunities and alternatives. It is an ocean of information, where everyone has the right of access and equal opportunities. While talking about the unification of a great audience, it does not mean its depersonalization but, through the possibilities which the global net offers, that the individual will find and realize their place in the world, the meaning and the importance for themselves, they will have the opportunity to know, understand and make sense of the difficult, the controversial and the misunderstood. They will build an informed, motivated position, based on tolerance, ethics and universal values. This leads us to one of the big questions about the relationship between media and culture: the ability of mass communication to universalize and popularize culture to such an extent as to attribute a planetary character to it and, essentially, make it a culture without borders.

Emphasizing the fact that the human race, for the first time in its history, can now dispose of uniform planetary culture, Edgar Morin states that mass culture integrates myths, symbols and images from real and imaginary worlds and starts to rival such cultures as the traditional, the humanistic and the religious ones (11). Looking into the genesis of mass culture we must take into consideration that its emergence is logically grounded by the needs of a mass audience which already has the will and the time to communicate with various cultural values, to identify with them and see their dreams come true, but in the conditional reality of media.

In fact, today it is impossible to find an influential culture that is isolated from media. Why are mass media to blame, then, if they are a product of progress, science and technology, designed to facilitate in everything related to information. At the level of possibilities, mass media cannot dominate the social, economic, political and cultural premises which determine them (1).

By displaying and presenting cultural products, standards and values simultaneously all over the world, media build and develop an integral cultural system where similarities prevail over discords. Gradually but persistently and consistently communities and groups of exchanged and shared values and characters are created. The united efforts and new possibilities of media create a global culture (6).

Toffler argues that the more we are unified the less we need to know about each other to predict our own and others' behaviors. As people around us become more and more individualized or demassified, we need more information signals and signs to foresee even vaguely how they will treat us (18).

Mass culture connects the civilization it has created, and for that reason it is the first universal culture in the history of mankind. (16) While examining cultural spaces on the Internet, Maria Popova notes that if, so far, the mass culture is that space where the concepts of the elite, folklore and underground culture are unified, the multiple media cybernetics of the network construct a virtual model extrinsic for all of them, yet recognizable for its contingent features (15). James Lull (10) perceives a dynamic global culture which is being transformed as a result of global communication. The media researcher argues that it is ridiculous to coddle local cultures and maintain them as museums or tombstones, because it is quite natural and normal for these cultures to change due to the influences of other cultures in the worldwide information network.

The Internet has become the hyperbolic form of the term "media" with completely new features (20). The digitalization of information, the integration of electronic communication, the segmentation and diversification of the mass audience and the larger application of the interactive networks are reasons for the appearance of a culture of real virtuality. As a result of the powerful influence of the new communication system, through the medium of social interests, government politics or business strategies, a new culture has been born – the culture of the real virtuality (5). This new culture can be conceived of as a heterogeneous, fragmented and extremely mobile form of cultural realization via computer–mediated communication, information communication technologies and the Internet.

To sum up, we can make the following conclusion: globalization does not impose cultural standardization by force. The penetration of the global in the local at the cultural level – so–called glocalization – is implemented by means of intercultural communication. The principle "I respect" is the basis of the dialogue between cultures and underlines the respect of the rights of cultural choice, self expression and originality. Supporting and protecting the variety and diversity help intercultural communication, making it fruitful and sensible. It is not a question of unification and homogenization, but of reading the cultural signs individually (12). It is good to remember the fact that respect for different cultures, tolerance and benevolence for the customs, traditions and arts of different groups, ethnicities, peoples and nations are qualities of humanity and ethically oriented cultures and societies. Mass culture does not only entertain, it also cultivates (17). In the global world there is a place for everyone and for everything. The capsulation or the isolation from the whole is neither possible nor sensible. Stagnation leads to decay. Today's dynamic world is constantly changing and that is its beauty and expression of its evolution.

Providing its global audience with that wide range of possibilities, at relativistic speed, the Internet simultaneously universalizes, unites and converges it. All these advantages can categorize the Internet as a colossal, universal, syncretic hypermedia. The presence of social communication, cultural exchange and interpersonal dialogue generally acquires a new global meaning and significance for the formation of a global audience.

REFERENCES

1. Angov C., Is Almighty TV: polls, Sofia: FJMC of Sofia University, 1992, p. 157.
2. Baudrillard J., The illusion of the end or the strike of events, Sofia: Critique and Humanism, 1995, p 132.
3. Benjamin W., Artistic thought and cultural awareness / Composition. and intervention, Atanas Natev studios, Sofia: Science and Art, 1989.
4. Bondikov V., Manipulation and Social Communication, Publisher: Siela, 2009.
5. Castells M., Information Age: Economy, Society and Culture: T. I: The rise of the network society, Sofia: LIK, 2004, p 330.
6. Derrida J., Globalization / Mondializatsiya: War or Peace?, Literary Gazette, No 42 (483), 18–24 December 2001 [cited 30 July 2008]. Available from: http://www.slovo.bg/old/litforum/142/jderida.htm.
7. Fidler R., Mediamorphosis: Understanding Media Technologies, Culture and Changes, Thousand Oaks, California: Sage Publications, 1998.
8. Jenkins H., From New Media Literacies to New Media Expertise: "Confronting the Challenges of a Participatory Culture", Revisited http://www.manifestoformediaeducation.co.uk/2011/01/henry-jenkins/.
9. Kress G.R. Literacy in the new media age, London: Routledge, and also Kress, 2003, G.R. (2009) Multimodality: A Social Semiotic Approach to Contemporary Communication.

10. Lull J., Media, Communication, Culture: A global Approach, 2. ed. New York: Columbia University Press, 2000, p. 161.
11. Morin E., Zeitgeist, Sofia: Hristo Botev Publishing, 1995, pp. 28–31.
12. Parizhkova L., Glocalization – nature and conversions / / Public communication, globalization and democracy / Composition. and learned. order. Minka Zlateva Todor Petev. Sofia: Sofia University St. Kliment Ohridski, Faculty of Journalism and Mass Communication, 2006, 216 to 217.
13. Robinson K., Out of Our Minds: Learning to be Creative, Capstone 2nd Edition, 2011; Video & UCSB's Art & Lectures series: Sir Ken Robinson | lynda.com interview: http://www.youtube.com/watch?v=PYuWRwZ37lU&feature=youtu.be 06.03.2012.
14. Robinson K., Lou A., The Element: How Finding Your Passion Changes Everything, ROI Communication, 2010.
15. Popova M., Virtual man: Social and communication features of the Internet user, Sofia: East–West, 2005, pp. 97–125.
16. Stefanov I., The Nature of Culture, Sofia: Ascoli–Publications, 1998, p. 310.
17. Stefanov I., The Nature of Culture, Sofia: Ascoli–Publications, 1998, p. 313.
18. Toffler A., The Third Wave, Sofia: Publishing PKYavorov, 1991, p. 222.
19. Teri. keep art blog / Teri. <managingEditor> teri@bglog.net. January 29, 2006, 19:34. [Cited 10 August 2008]. Available from: http://bglog.net/BGLog/3.
20. Tsvetkova M., Information Culture: The name of reading, Sofia: Gaberoff, 2001, pp. 153–160.
21. Yordanova L., Media Are blogs?: Debate / / moderator / Capital, 2 July 2010 to 20 July 2010. Available from: http://www.capital.bg/interaktiv/debati/7_medii_li_sa_blogovete/927253_medii_li_sa_blogovete/.
22. Yurukov, Boyan. Media Are blogs / / Capital, July 20, 2010. Available from: http://www.capital.bg/interaktiv/debati/7_medii_li_sa_blogovete/927253_medii_li_sa_blogovete/.
23. http://ivosiliev.com

Anna Kuzio
University of Zielona Gora

THE AMELIORATION OF STEREOTYPES IN COMPUTER–MEDIATED COMMUNICATION VERSUS VOCAL COMMUNICATION: A REPRODUCTION INVOLVING THREE THEORETICAL MODELS

ABSTRACT

Recent research (Epley & Kruger, 2005) has evaluated the effects of computer–mediated communication (CMC) and vocal communication on the perseverance of stereotypes and disputed that CMC essentially hinders their diminution. The present study confronts this assertion theoretically by proposing competitor hypotheses concerning the unequal capacity of CMC and vocal communication to ameliorate stereotypes. Methodological matters are addressed concerning the effects of restraining interactive communication during impression formation, and the operationalization of CMC as being equal to the verbiage created in speech, not taking into account vocalic cues. An original experiment acquiesces findings showing that CMC is functionally comparable with vocal communication in its ability to lessen negative stereotypes and that it can be superior in designing and/or retaining positive impressions.

KEYWORDS: computer–mediated communication, stereotypes, face–to–face communication.

INTRODUCTION

The question concerning the issue of how Internet communication influences users' impressions of other people is one of the central foci of computer–mediated communication (CMC) studies. Notwithstanding much research on the matter, comprehensions about technology's effects are separated. Within the subject of impression formation online, one of the most interesting questions has been whether the characteristics of text–based CMC overstate or ameliorate stereotyped perceptions, in comparison to multimodal (multiple cue system) interaction. Taking into account a notion that CMC sorts out nonverbal cues and the personal information that those cues normally communicate, some researchers dispute that the Internet may reduce prejudices that face–to–face (FtF) interaction often involves as CMC blocks the non–verbal cues that otherwise prompt prejudicial categorizations (cf. Sproull & Kiesler, 1991). Based on similar reasoning about CMC's lack of ability to convey information about communicators' actual characteristics, the present study disputes that when stereotypes are invoked before interaction – even false ones that do not depict the actual communicators – the deficiency of vocal cues deters communicators' capacity to dismiss such expectations (Epley & Kruger, 2005). On the other hand, different perspectives dispute that CMC users use verbal and textual cues to accomplish relatively normal interpersonal impressions, or even to create impressions more favorable than they might in face–to–face interaction (Walther, 1996). The potential effects of CMC on stereotyped perceptions maintain societal and scholarly concern (e.g., Rosenbloom, 2008; Walther, Van Der Heide, Kim, Westerman, & Tong, 2008). So far, one's understanding of impressions and biases from CMC continues to be conflicted.

A group of experiments by Epley and Kruger (2005) presented empirical demonstrations that CMC makes the persistence of pre–interaction stereotypes for intelligence possible to a greater extent than voice–based communication. A number of aspects of their study raise questions about the fundamental nature of CMC and how one comprehends it (with particular regard to the notion of interactivity), and raise concerns that methodological factors reveal unstated assumptions and may or may not occlude conflicting hypotheses.

The current research suggests a reproduction of Epley and Kruger's (2005) study to not only evaluate a single study but also to raise higher–level questions concerning the theoretical and ontological assumptions about vocal and electronic communication embedded in the aforementioned work. An experiment was created to examine the soundness of Epley and Kruger's claims but without unnaturally limiting spontaneous communication in CMC, with the purpose of seeing how interactivity furthers individuation, and whether communicators are able to employ CMC strategically to improve others' perceptions regardless of the lack of nonverbal cues in the medium. The findings propose a reversal to prior conclusions about the effects of CMC in the persistence or amelioration of stereotypes.

PREVIOUS RESEARCH

Epley and Kruger (2005) examined the differentiation between vocal communication and what they called email – in reality, real–time chat – in terms of the capability of these media during brief interviews to dispel falsely–instilled stereotyped expectations about another person. Following a review of the literature which controlled both optimistic and pessimistic proposals about CMC's utility in expressing meaning and personality, they conclude that because it has no nonverbal cues CMC is "inherently" too ambiguous for people to communicate meaning with it. They equate the capability to deduce people's intended meaning with creating an impression of who they are individually, and disputed that "gesture, inflection, pronunciation, vocal expression, fluency, and tone are each cues to a speaker's meaning – and to personality" (2005, p. 415). They further disagree that without such information it is too complicated to distinguish the falsity of a bogus, pre–existing stereotyped expectation. Epley and Kruger's experiments instilled stereotypes among inexperienced "interviewers" by offering them pre–interaction profiles featuring bogus racial and biographical cues, and a list of six standardized interview questions to solicit among interviewees. The first test concerned intelligence stereotypes. Interviewees were either portrayed as Asian, majoring in physics and philosophy, and high school valedictorians, or as Caucasian, Hotel Administration majors, and former high school football stars. In all cases the interviewees were essentially randomly assigned males, controlled on racial characteristics. They were all Caucasian, dissimilar to the information in half of the bogus profiles. Half the interviewers posed the interviewees the questions, and heard their responses via telephone. In the CMC condition, interviewers asked the questions one at a time, employing a CMC chat system. Rather than have the interviewer in reality exploit email or CMC chat with real dyadic partners, a lab assistant transcribed telephone interviewees' verbal responses into text and transmitted them to CMC interviewers. This was done in an attempt to remove variation attributable to differences in verbiage between conditions. Post–interaction ratings of intelligence indicated a medium–by–expectation interaction: CMC interviewers' ratings of their apparent partners' intelligence revealed important differences in the direction of the pre–interaction expectancy, whereas no differences were persevered in the voice condition.

Epley and Kruger's conceptual explanation of the impression formation process disputed that people usually verify the validity of preinteraction stereotypes by hypothesis–testing, i.e. looking for confirmation of information through conversation (see Snyder & Haugen, 1994). If replies are vague, stereotypes endure. The authors argued that CMC maintains stereotyping because of its inability to communicate critical personality information in the manner that voice does. Epley and Kruger's approach raises a number of issues, including questions about what their methods entail about understanding the communication process in general with regard to dynamics such as interactivity, and the differences and similarities between CMC and voice in general.

CMC AS "SPEECH MINUS VOICE"

The statements about CMC embedded in Epley and Kruger's research depend on other traditional approaches to CMC. Early research concentrating on the lack of nonverbal cues online claimed that users could not acquire individuating impressions of one another (e.g. Hiltz, Johnson, & Turoff, 1986). Many experiments in the 1980s and 1990s highlighted the psychologically impoverished nature of CMC as a result of the lack of nonverbal cues and inauthentic exchanges (Kraut et al., 1998). Epley and Kruger's research methods imitate a similar but more focused assumption about the relationship between CMC and speech. Their effort to minimize random differences between voice and CMC conditions by transcribing the voice condition's interviewee responses into text to represent CMC suggests that CMC is nothing more than speech denuded of voice. Clearly, plain–text CMC does not transmit vocalics. The essential question, however, is whether individuals who know that there is no vocal component to textual CMC simply type out the same words they would have employed in a spoken conversation, or whether they select different means to express themselves online in a manner that compensates for the nonverbal cues they do not have.

A significant body of work in CMC research and theory characterizes CMC as quite adaptive to the absence of nonverbal cues. In accordance with some views, users simplistically adapt their language to accommodate the affective and social cues online that would be expressed nonverbally in less mediated settings. For example, the social information processing theory of CMC states that when CMC users are adequately motivated, they (a) readily become accustomed with language and discourse information about themselves, their emotions, and their attitudes (Walther, 2007), and (b) draw inferences based on these linguistic cues with the intention of forming impressions and developing relationships (Ramirez, Zhang, McGraw & Lin, 2007).

Walther, Loh, and Granka (2005) placed dyads in FtF rooms or in CMC chat conditions and had them talk about a controversial issue. In each dyad, one subject was asked to perform significant levels of liking or disliking for his or her partner. Inexperienced partners rated these impromptu confederates on their level of affection after the conversations. Coders examined vocalic cues, kinesic cues, and verbal transcripts from FtF dyads, and transcripts from CMC dyads. The results revealed no differences in the general level of affection between CMC and FtF. Specific language variations in CMC explained an equivalent amount of variance, as did vocalics plus kinesics in FtF dyads. The verbal language of FtF settings was not identical and did not have the same impact, as did the kinds of verbal constructions that CMC subjects expressed in a native CMC environment.

Other works have recognized ways in which language affects communication (Węgłowska–Rzepa et al. 2008, Kowal et al. 2010a, 2010b). Extraversion is readily noticed in email (Gill & Oberlander, 2003), as is power and status (Adkins & Brashers, 1995; Selfe & Meyer, 1991) and sarcasm and irony in other CMC forms (Hancock, 2004). As Feenberg (1989, p. 272) noticed some time ago: "Users of electronic bulletin boards ... and computer conferences appear to each other only through explicit written language ... The communicating subject is profoundly modified by the generalization of such highly controlled forms of self-presentation". Given these contradicting threads of evidence, questions occur over whether different methodological strategies may have influenced the results.

Since the transcripts exploited by Epley and Kruger to conjure up CMC responses were strictly the verbal transcription of speech, whatever information that had been transmitted vocalically in the audio condition definitely failed to convey to CMC. However, had the "email" conditions in their experiment actually concerned real interviewees employing CMC, it is not inevitable that the wording choices would have rendered a set of messages as socio-emotionally barren.

INTERACTIVITY

Interactivity is another probable of CMC (or any form of dyadic communication) that was systematically barren in Epley and Kruger's CMC condition but not their voice condition. While interactivity is commonly understood to exist in face-to-face dyadic communication, its existence in new communication technology is sometimes less apparent. Interactivity via new media has been conceptualized in a range of ways, from being able to click to activate on-screen material (Sundar, Kalyanaraman, & Brown, 2003) to more conventional notions such as the extent to which source and receiver exhibit interchangeable roles and reciprocal influence (Pavlick, 1996; Stromer-Galley & Foot, 2002). To the extent that CMC may encourage interactivity, defined in this manner, the CMC condition in Epley and Kruger was methodically prevented from accomplishing it, since interviewers did not actually communicate with interviewees.

One of the most comprehensive, formal definitions of interactivity is Rafaeli's (1988) conceptualization. This approach concentrates on the accumulation of communicative utterances and how meaning appears as further messages implicitly refer back to prior messages. Beyond a simple linguistic adjacency pair (such as question-and-answer) Rafaeli's scheme offers that to attain interactivity, a series of three or more related exchanges ought to emerge, where the third or subsequent message denotes prior messages and is interpretable and meaningful only in that context. When interactivity takes place, a conversation is expected to increase in acceptance, satisfaction, performance quality, motivation, fun, learning, openness, and sociability (Rafaeli & Sudweeks, 1998).

Prominently, Rafaeli's definition of interactivity is autonomous of medium. Specifically, while face-to-face communication may sustain interactivity, it is not necessarily the case that it always does. Face–to–face partners who simply ask and answer a series of questions would not accomplish interactivity. On the other hand, CMC users whose comments extend beyond question–and–answer to include feedback and back channeling may reach interactivity. An empirical study by Rafaeli and Sudweeks (1998) noticed a good deal of interactivity in online conversations. An assessment of postings in 32 online discussion groups found that 40% of the topically–related threads of postings and follow– ups that took place constituted interactivity.

By occluding interactivity in the CMC condition but not in the voice condition, Epley and Kruger (2005) may have further falsely stilted the apparent replies and the potential for give–and–take in the CMC condition. If CMC interviewers indicated any follow–up questions or remarks to their so–called interviewees, how strange it must have appeared to have received no feedback to those comments. When it comes to stereotyped impressions of intelligence or shyness, which were the foci in Epley and Kruger, it is conceivable that an interviewer's perception that an interviewee is not very responsive – as may very well be the case when they were not in fact really communicating with each other – might lead to more extreme attributions based on previous information. In a voice condition in which actual interactive communication occurred, it is far more probable that impressions would become individuated, not on account of the abundance of cues conveyed by the voice alone but by the interactive connectedness of spontaneous questions and comments.

The Epley and Kruger (2005) studies controlled CMC in two critical ways, adding methodological concerns about the soundness of their conclusions to theoretical concerns about the ways in which users become accustomed to the expression and detection of personal characteristics of CMC. One of these methodological issues was the simulation of CMC responses employing transcriptions of speech rather than actual messages real CMC users might have composed, identifying they had only words with which to express themselves. There may be differences in the way users create written CMC messages, relative to the verbiage of spoken messages, in terms of word count, number of statements, message personalization, and other linguistic features.

Second, by precluding interactivity in the Epley and Kruger (2005) studies, interviewers could not increase conversations and could get no unprompted feedback from interviewees in CMC as they might have done through feedback and back channelling via the vocal system. The current research allowed dyads to interact freely, surrounding the question–and–answer exchanges such as those used by Epley and Kruger. It is expected that interactivity will impact the employment and proliferation of a variety of statement types, from repetitions and elaborations to off–topic statements. It will be further anticipated that these exchanges offer valuable, cumulative data for developing interviewers' impressions of their interviewees, in both voice and CMC conditions, that will encourage the amelioration deterioration of stereotyped expectancies. With the intention of predicting and testing these effects more precisely and generally, three rival hypotheses are offered, each informed by different theoretical frameworks.

HYPOTHESES

"Cues filtered out". As recommended above, early CMC research posited that the medium's lack of nonverbal cues limit its aptitude to support interpersonal communication. These "cues–filtered–out" (CFO) approaches propose that when nonverbal cues are not present, communication becomes impersonal and less relationally–oriented than in FtF communication (see Culnan & Markus, 1987; Walther, in press). Epley and Kruger's (2005) presentation follows this line of thought. If the CFO position is approved, then a reproduction involving unrestricted CMC should discover nothing different. The voice medium will offer a better exchange of individuating information than text. Thus, taking Epley and Kruger into account, pre–interaction stereotype expectancies will persist for those dyads employing CMC but will be reduced for those dyads communicating via voice.

H1: Preinteraction inductions of stereotyped expectancies for greater versus lesser intelligence generate greater post discussion diversities in intelligence perceptions in CMC than in voice communication.

Hyperpersonal model of CMC. The hyperpersonal model of CMC (Walther, 1996, 2007) presents four aspects of CMC (sender, receiver, channel, feedback) working alone and in concert to generate predominantly intense and/or intimate interpersonal relationships online. In particular, the hyperpersonal model proposes that CMC users can employ selective self–presentation by capitalizing on the capabilities of the CMC channel. CMC allows senders to craft information about themselves more effortlessly than in offline channels, giving them heightened control over their image presentation and enhancing their ability to communicate socially desirable impressions. In the current case, interviewees might make use of the characteristics of the CMC channel to optimize self–presentational (and particularly overcome false, negative expectations) to a greater degree than individuals communicating in vocal channels, absolutely affecting receivers' (interviewers') impressions.

H2: There is a channel (CMC/voice) by expectancy (intelligent/unintelligent) interaction effect such that post–discussion intelligence ratings are higher in CMC than in voice communication, although a central effect of expectancy continues in that those offer the intelligent expectancy rate of their partners as more intelligent than those presenting the unintelligent expectancy.

Social information processing (SIP) theory. Another competitor hypothesis to H1 is informed by SIP theory (Walther, 1992). SIP argues that interactants can express and detect interpersonal impressions employing language and other symbols in CMC, despite the lack of nonverbal cues. SIP also comments that in comparison to the hasty pace of multimodal communication, the exchange of personal and affective information, and their accumulation in the mental representations of the partners, take longer in CMC than in multimodal communication, which conveys more information in a comparable interval. Therefore, for CMC dyads time and message accumulation are fundamental factors in the capacity of CMC to make the exchange of individuating information that may disconfirm preinteraction stereotypes possible. Furthermore, the temporal and exchange requirements of SIP propose that, in as brief an exposure as a 6–answer interview, CMC should track voice communication in its capacity to support developed impressions or, in this case, to dismiss false expectancies.

H3: There is an interaction effect of message accumulation by media type such that as the number of messages amplifies there are smaller differences between pre–interaction stereotype inductions and post–interaction ratings of intelligence, but this effect is greater in voice than in method.

PARTICIPANTS

Fifty–seven students from a Polish university took part in the exchange. Among the male participants, 19 were consigned to answer interview questions (interviewees). Their ages ranged from 18 to 26, M = 20.3, SD = 1.89. Each of these subjects was interviewed by two interviewers, one via voice and one via CMC.

Of the 38 participants who took part as interviewers, 20 were female, 17 were male, and one participant failed to report their gender. The mean age for interviewers was 19.8 (SD = 2.05), ranging from 18 to 30 years old.

PROCEDURE

The procedures imitated Epley and Kruger's (2005) in most respects. Participants assigned to the role of interviewer were located in a small, private research room and informed that they would be conducting a brief interview. All participants had their picture taken and were given a short personal information questionnaire to complete. They were told that their picture and personal information would be swapped with the person they were interviewing. In actuality the information was never exchanged; the exercise was done to amplify the believability of the stimulus material the participants established.

Interviewers were randomly assigned to either an intelligent or unintelligent–expectancy condition. Intelligence–expectancy was manipulated in a manner that directly mirrored the stimuli from Epley and Kruger (2005). Interviewers were equipped with a brief biographical form and a photo which they were told reflected the interviewee with whom they were about to interact. The questionnaire featured the actual name of the interviewee in each session, but it also featured additional information that was bogus. Just as in Epley and Kruger's first study, the intelligent–expectancy stimulus contained a picture of a professionally dressed, Asian–American male who had excellent school achievement. The unintelligent–expectancy stimulus consisted of a picture of a European– American male wearing a Metallica T–shirt. He had average educational achievements and was recognized as the "most valuable player" of the football team.

The expectancy stimuli were first subjected to pretests to determine whether the attributes and their combinations initially discussed by Epley and Kruger (2005) would appear. The results confirmed that the combinations used by Epley and Kruger worked successfully.

Interviewers were also randomly assigned to either a voice or computer–based chat interview condition. For the voice condition, a wireless microphone system was employed. For CMC, a private online chat room was created. All participants performing the role of interviewer were instructed to ask the same list of pre–determined questions to their conversation partner, collected from questions used in previous research, such as "If you had the opportunity to meet one of the presidents, either living or dead, who would it be and why?", "What would be your favorite way to spend Spring Break?" and "If you could ask a genie to grant you any wish, what would you wish for?". Unlike Epley and Kruger's protocol, interviewers were not asked to avoid making statements other than the prohibited statements. After asking all six interview questions, interviewers were prompted to complete the questions. Such unprompted and unscripted remarks help constitute interactivity, and thus they were neither encouraged and nor did the questionnaire containing the dependent measures discourage such remarks.

The males who were accidentally assigned to the interviewee condition were led to a small, private research room. Epley and Kruger (2005) attempted to minimize extraneous variance due to individual differences between voice and CMC responses by simulating CMC messages using the verbal portion of interviewees' responses in the voice condition. In the present study, interviewees were interviewed by two different individuals sequentially, once employing a voice system and once using online chat. This technique also minimized the potential effect of random individual differences between voice and chat interviewees, by controlling them rather than by occluding actual communication, with the intention of rendering a more realistic CMC conversation environment. The ordering of the interview chats was balanced throughout the study.

MEASURES

The perceptions of interviewees' intelligence were assessed employing nine bipolar adjective items measured on 7–interval response scales, counting the three items described in Epley and Kruger (2005) and an additional six original scales measuring intelligence from McCroskey, Holdridge, and Toomb (1974). Examples contained "dumb/smart" and "uninformed/informed". Cronbach's alpha reliability for the combined scales was .92. As in Epley and Kruger's study, additional characteristics were also assessed. In the present case, the perceived extraversion of the interviewee was assessed using five 7–interval bipolar adjective scales adapted from McCroskey et al. (1974). Social attractiveness (how much one is inclined to be friendly with the target) was also assessed employing Likert–type scales from McCroskey and McCain (1974), including "this person just wouldn't fit into my circle of friends" and "we could never establish a personal friendship with each other" (a = .88), and McCroskey and McCain's 5–item measure of task attractiveness (how much one would like the target as a work partner), including "this person is a typical goof–off when assigned a job to do" and "I couldn't get anything accomplished with this person" (a = .86).

CODING

All comments exchanged by interviewers and interviewees were recorded for later analysis, either as audio recordings that were transcribed, or as native CMC transcripts. Two trained coders unitized the transcripts into thought units, i.e. independent clauses or utterances that marked a shift in topical focus, and vocalized pauses and laughs in the vocal records, and intentionally–spelled–out laughs (LOL, ha ha) or pauses (ellipses) in the CMC records. Both coders unitized 50% of the transcripts, for which reliability achieved Cohen's kappa =.89. Disagreements were determined through subsequent discussion, but given the acceptably high reliability the remaining 50% of the transcripts were unitized individually by one or the other coder.

RESULTS

Although each interviewee reacted to two interviewers, once by voice and once by CMC, no important main effects or interaction effects with other independent variables affected interviewers' ratings of interviewees' intelligence or other attributes. Therefore, medium order was excluded from further analysis.

Initial analyses were carried out mirroring the approach reported by Epley and Kruger (2005). A two–way analysis of variance (ANOVA) examined the effects of the intelligent/unintelligent expectancy stimuli and media type (voice/chat) on perceived intelligence. Whereas Epley and Kruger reported an important interaction effect, the main effect of intelligence–expectancy on perceived intelligence, $F(1, 37) = 3.1$, $p = .87$, and the interaction between intelligence–expectancy and media type, $F(1, 37) = .505$, $p = .48$, were both nonsignificant. However, following Epley and Kruger, t tests were employed within each media condition. These tests indicated that perceived intelligence was considerably greater for the intelligence–expectancy condition within the chat condition than in the unintelligent–expectancy condition, t (17) = 2.10, p = .026 (one–tailed), d = 1.02. Within the voice condition, no distinction was detected on perceived intelligence, t (17) = .651, p = .26 (one–tailed). See Table 1 below for more descriptive statistics.

Table 1. Means for Perceived Intelligence by Medium and Expectancy

Medium	CMC				Voice			
Expectancy	Smart		Dumb		Smart		Dumb	
Perceived intelligence	M	SD	M	SD	M	SD	M	SD
	5.50	.72	4.67	.93	4.88	1.53	4.52	.75
N	8		11		9		10	

The pair wise t tests propose that the intelligent/unintelligent stereotype persevered in the CMC condition, although not in the voice condition. The pair wise significance tests imply the same effect that Epley and Kruger's (2005) research produced, in the production of greater differences in CMC than in voice in the directions stimulated by the prediscussion inductions. However, the overall pattern of the means was unlike that in Epley and Kruger's results. In their study, the interviewers noticed much lower intelligence among the apparent (but unreal) CMC/unintelligent interviewees. In the current study, the CMC/unintelligent condition created relatively high intelligence scores. The nature of these differences is revealed more closely in the following analyses.

Subsequent analyses used contrast analysis with the aim of testing the nature of the relationships among means more accurately, and to propose a focused test of the hyper–personal model's hypothesis. Contrast weights were allocated to study the prediction that CMC users are able to present themselves more astutely than voice discussants, regardless of a persistent effect for the initial smart vs. dumb induction. Within each of the smart and dumb conditions, CMC users' scores were contrast weighted to reflect higher perceived intelligence: intelligent/chat (+2), intelligent/voice (+1), unintelligent/chat (–1), and unintelligent/voice (–2). The results were consistent with the hyper– personal prediction, t (34) = 2.0, p = .027 (one–tailed), d = .69.

Consequently, although CMC seems to facilitate a greater perceived dissimilarity between the smarter and dumber conditions, the rationale for this difference is in contradiction of the explanation tendered in previous work. It appears to be the case that the smart CMC interactants were mainly able to craft a positive impression. The dumb–expectancy CMC users overcame the initial stereotype to at least as great an extent as voice communicators did. It was this condition – dumb–expectancy CMC – that was singularly lower than others in

Epley and Kruger's (2005) study. The current results clearly do not reflect the notion that CMC, when employed in an interactive manner, constrains users' abilities to express personality characteristics and adjust partners' perceptions, as Epley and Kruger claimed. Rather, it points to CMC as a particularly useful way to enhance positive perceptions.

A final imitation of Epley and Kruger's analyses investigated whether any other perceptions of interviewees were affected by the combination of medium perceptions by expectancy conditions. The prior study examined perceptions of being fashionable, happy and friendly, although no rationale is offered for the use of these attributes. Friendliness is reflected in the current study employing social attractiveness or extraversion, whereas task attractiveness offers some counterpoint. Preliminary analysis discovered that social attraction revealed modest correlations with both extraversion ($p = .06$) and task attraction ($p = .03$), and therefore a multivariate analysis of variance (MANOVA) was applied to assess any further effect of the independent variables. The MANOVA indicated multivariate effects for both intelligence–expectancy, Wilk's $L = .610$, $F (3, 32) = 3.84$, $p = .008$, and for media type, Wilk's $L = .70$, $F (3, 32) = 2.55$, $p = .049$, but no significant interaction effect. The patterns of means showed no predominantly greater split within the CMC conditions attributable to the intelligence induction than in the voice condition.

A third hypothesis reflected the dynamic notion from SIP theory that as the exchange of utterances becomes greater in CMC, the more the information provided in these messages refines one's impression of a partner. In the present case, it was hypothesized that as messages are more numerous, the greater the amelioration of prediscussion stereotypes. Just as Epley and Kruger (2005) describe vocal communication, we may expect that when the intelligent stereotype is instantiated prior to discussion the more messages are exchanged, and the less intelligent the interviewee appears to be; when the unintelligent stereotype is activated, the more messages are exchanged, and the smarter the interviewee is perceived to be.

It is also probable that interviewers' expectancies, or the interactions between interviewers and interviewees influenced the message frequency of both partners. An analysis indicated that the number of messages created by interviewers correlated with those produced by interviewees, $r (65) = .36$, $p = .003$. This effect was more robust in the intelligent/unintelligent CMC conditions, $r (18) = .66$, $p = .003$, than in the parallel voice conditions, $r (15) = .30$, $p = .28$. Although Epley and Kruger (2005, p. 417) dispute that "only the words of the target could alter the first impressions of the interviewers", and their experimental design precluding interactivity made sure this was so, it seems that interviewers and interviewees may have equally influenced each other, and the interviewers' behaviors may also have had some role in their own perceptions of the targets. This would be consistent with the naïve hypothesis–testing view of impression formation mentioned in much contemporary psychology (e.g. Snyder & Haugen, 1994). Because of this, both sources of message data were distorted in further analyses.

The next hypothesis predicted that as message frequency increases, interviewees' impressions become less stereotypical. This effect implied a bidirectional change: the smart get dumber and the dumb get smarter. A single variable was formed to reflect these two trajectories. Interviewers' ratings of interviewees' intelligence in the dumb–expectancy condition were brought into the new variable as is, since higher scores on this measure reflected movement away from the dumb expectancy. Yet, before importing interviewers' ratings of their partners' intelligence in the smart induction, scores were re–coded with the intention that higher scores reflected less intelligence, i.e. movement away from the smart preinduction stereotype. As such, higher scores on this new variable indicated deviation from either respective predicussion stereotype.

This new variable was tested for its correlation with the number of messages exchanged between partners. The overall correlation concerning both CMC and voice was considerable, $r(33) = .36$, $p = .02$ (one–tailed). Within the CMC condition alone, the relationship $r(18) = .42$, $p = .04$ was also present. The relationship did not emerge in the voice condition, however, $r(15) = .33$, $p = .12$.

A final test of the hypothesis investigated the predicted interaction effect of expectancy x medium x message frequency on the variable representing movement away from the prediscussion expectancy. It had been predicted that terminal intelligence perceptions were attributable to an interaction between frequency of messages and initial expectancy in the CMC condition, but not in the voice condition. The SPSS MIXED procedure was exploited due to its generalization of interaction analysis involving categorical and continuous variables, and the analysis rendered a significant interaction effect, $F(4, 28) = 5.26$, $p = .003$. Supplementary analyses showed that, within CMC, the expectancy x comments effect retained significance, $F(2, 15) = 15.37$, $p < .001$. In the voice condition, though, the interaction effect was insignificant, $F(2, 12) = 1.72$, $p = .22$.

DISCUSSION

Following the preliminary efforts of Epley and Kruger (2005), this research explored how various media–CMC versus vocal communication–influences the perseverance or reduction of stereotypes as a consequence of interaction. The current findings imply implications for a number of theoretical frameworks. First, differences between prediscussion stereotypes and postdiscussion intelligence ratings within medium conditions were in the same direction as those reported by Epley and Kruger, tentatively signifying support for the CFO perspective (H1). However, it is significant that the overall pattern of means in the prior research was not replicated, and the present findings undermine the predictions informed by CFO. The pattern of means on intelligence assessments in the present experiment support the hyperpersonal model in that CMC users were able to improve self–presentation of intelligence more so than were voice communicators (H2). This finding appears to displace Epley and Kruger's claim that CMC is not suited for interpersonal information exchange.

Another vital difference between this study and the previous efforts lies in the relative position of the intelligence ratings of the CMC dumb–expectancy condition, which was considerably lower than all other conditions in Epley and Kruger's (2005) research, and which seems to be considerably higher in the present replication. It can be understood as a "behavioral disconfirmation" (Ickes, Paterson, Rajecki, & Tanford, 1982) in which interviewers given the dumb stereotyped impression about their interaction partners acted in an attempt to help or improve the apparently unintelligent interviewee (i.e. interviewers treated "dumb" interviewees as if they were smarter). Interviewers' behaviors, both unconscious and inconsistent with their initial impressions, may have provoked behaviors by the interviewees causing them to act against, rather than according to, type. The interviewers may have been especially attuned to these so–called changes. The behavioral disconfirmation procedure may have elicited the post–discussion stereotype reductions found in the present study and elsewhere in CMC research (Walther, 2007).

The current results also specify that Epley and Kruger's (2005) methodological decision to constrain CMC dyads created a confounded response that influenced their results. Epley and Kruger employed verbal transcripts from the voice–condition interviewees to constitute the CMC messages in their study, so as to reveal that words without voice do not affect impressions. Their method prevented the potential generation of alternative wordings by CMC users from contaminating their comparisons. By elating this restriction and exploiting live CMC interviewees, the present research indicated the significance of interactive discussion in the impression formation process. The results propose that the prevention of spontaneous message composition by actual CMC users involving the kinds of changes that CMC organically encompasses may not offer a stimulus that fairly generalizes to email or CMC. In the current study, variations in the number of messages exchanged during CMC discussion particularly impacted the amelioration of stereotypes (H3). In agreement with SIP theory, the findings disclose that as more messages were exchanged, preinteraction stereotypes were reduced – the dumb got smarter and the smart got dumber.

It seems that certain methodological choices in CMC research that are made for admirable reasons can nevertheless hide true effects. The over–control of a variety of conditions in CMC experiments is a very old problem. Early studies in CMC have indicated that they tend to be limited in their generalizability by equalizing relatively short periods of time across media conditions, even though these efforts were originally undertaken for the sake of experimental control. Because CMC use engages numerous technological, social and temporal factors, it is easy to control levels of one extraneous variable that nevertheless interacts with other, active variables in the communication process. Through replication, intricacies of this kind have been and should continue to be resolved.

Epley and Kruger's (2005) research included additional experiments. The second focused on stereotypes connoting outgoingness, and the stimuli instantiating these stereotypes consisted of fake photos of Asian or African American females with no biographies. Once again, the experiments offered interactive interviews in the voice condition, and verbal transcriptions of voice interviewees to the questions written by "email" interviewers.

The fact that some support was found for three competing theoretical models implies that while each theory has some explanatory power, they may lack the satisfactory boundary conditions that make them fully relevant to the phenomenon under investigation. On the other hand, the constraints of an experimental, 6–question interview setting may limit the power of the study to attain effects that are theoretically mutually exclusive. It may also be the case that the situation is more complex than it appears to be, and that no one theory is able to capture the uncertainty reduction and hypothesis–testing processes underlying such a complex phenomenon; there may be competing processes at work that are not attributable to a singular theory, making it hard to discern which mechanisms are operating at any given time. Future research should apply each theoretical framework to determine the unique impact of each perspective.

REFERENCES

Adkins, M., & Brashers, D. (1995). The power of language in computer–mediated groups. Management Communication Quarterly, 8, 289–322.

Epley, N., & Kruger, J. (2005). What you type isn't what they read: The perseverance of stereotypes and expectancies over email. Journal of Experimental Social Psychology, 41, 414–422.

Feenberg, A. (1989). A user's guide to the pragmatics of computer mediated communication. Semiotica, 75, 257–278.

Gill, A.J., & Oberlander, J. (2003). Perception of email personality at zero acquaintance: Extraversion takes care of itself; Neuroticism is a worry. Proceedings of the 25th Annual Conference of the Cognitive Science Society (pp. 456461). Hillsdale, NJ: Lawrence Erlbaum Associates.

Hancock, J.T. (2004). Verbal irony use in computer–mediated and face–to–face conversations. Journal of Language and Social Psychology, 23, 447–463.

Hiltz, S.R., Johnson, K., & Turoff, M. (1986). Experiments in group decision making: Communication process and outcome in face–to–face versus computerized conferences. Human Communication Research, 13, 225–252.

Ickes, W., Patterson, M.L., Rajecki, D.W., & Tanford, S. (1982). Behavioral and cognitive consequences of reciprocal versus compensatory responses to preinteraction expectancies. Social Cognition, 1, 160–190.

Kowal, J. K. Węgłowska–Rzepa (2010a). Social communication in management and its psychological and marketing aspects. In: Proceedings of the 6th European Conference on Management, Leadership and Governance: The College of Management "Edukacja" and the Professional Development Center Edukacja Wroclaw, ed. by Ewa Panka and Aleksandra Kwiatkowska. Reading, UK: Academic Publishing Limited.

Kowal, J.A. Kwiatkowska, I. Patro (2010b). The prospects of graduates' career development in Poland: the example of the competence survey in Lower Silesian Region 2006–2010. In: Proceedings of the 6th European Conference on Management, Leadership and Governance: The College of Management "Edukacja" and the Professional Development Center Edukacja Wroclaw. Reading, UK: Academic Publishing Limited.

Kraut, R., Patterson, M., Lundmark, V., Kiesler, S., Mukophadhyay, T., & Scherlis, W. (1998). Internet paradox: A social technology that reduces social involvement and psychological well-being? American Psychologist, 53, 1017–1031

McCroskey, J.C., Holdridge, W., & Toomb, J.K. (1974). An instrument for measuring the source credibility of basic speech communication instructors. The Speech Teacher, 23, 26–33.

McCroskey, J.C., & McCain, T.A. (1974). The measurement of interpersonal attraction. Speech Monographs, 41, 261–266.

Pavlick, J. (1996). New media technology: Cultural and commercial perspectives. Boston: Allyn & Bacon.

Postmes, T., & Spears, R. (1998). Deindividuation and antinormative behavior: A meta-analysis. Psychological Bulletin, 123, 238–259.

Rafaeli, S. (1988). Interactivity: From new media to communication. In R. P. Hawkins, J. M. Wiemann, & S. Pingree (Eds.), Advancing communication science: Merging mass and interpersonal processes (pp. 110–134). Newbury Park, CA: Sage.

Rafaeli, S., & Sudweeks, F. (1998). Interactivity on the nets. In F. Sudweeks, M. McLaughlin, & S. Rafaeli (Eds.), Network & netplay: Virtual groups on the Internet (pp. 173–189). Menlo Park, CA: AAAI Press.

Ramirez, A. Jr., Zhang, S., McGraw, C., & Lin, S. (2007). Relational communication in computer–mediated interaction revisited: A comparison of participant–observer perspectives. Communication Monographs, 74, 492–516.

Rosenbloom, S. (2008, January 3). Putting your best cyberface. The New York Times. Retrieved January 8, 2008, from http://www.nytimes.com

Selfe, C.L., & Meyer, P.R. (1991). Testing claims for on–line conferences. Written Communication, 8, 163–192.

Sproull, L., & Kiesler, S. (1991). Connections: New ways of working in the networked organization. Cambridge, MA: MIT.

Snyder, M., & Haugen, J.A. (1994). Why does behavioral confirmation occur? A functional perspective on the role of the perceiver. Journal of Experimental Social Psychology, 30, 218–246.

Stromer–Galley, J., & Foot, K.A. (2002). Citizen perceptions of online interactivity and implications for political campaign communication. Journal of Computer–Mediated Communication, 8 (1). Retrieved January 15, 2004, from http://www.ascusc.org/jcmc/vol8/issue1/stromerandfoot.html

Sundar, S.S., Kalyanaraman, S., & Brown, J. (2003). Explicating Web site interactivity: Impression formation effects in political campaign sites. Communication Research, 30, 30–59.

Walther, J.B. (in press). Computer–mediated communication. In C. R. Berger, M.E. Roloff, & D. Roskos–Ewoldsen (Eds.), Handbook of communication science (2nded.). Newbury Park, CA: Sage.

Walther, J.B. (1992). Interpersonal effects in computer–mediated interaction: A relational perspective. Communication Research, 19, 52–90.

Walther, J.B. (2007). Selective self–presentation in computer–mediated communication: Hyperpersonal dimensions of technology, language, and cognition. Computers in Human Behavior, 23, 2538–2557.

Walther, J.B., & Carr, C.T. (in press). Internet interaction and intergroup dynamics: Problems and solutions in computer–mediated communication. In H. Giles, S. Reid, & J. Harwood (Eds.), The dynamics of intergroup communication. New York: Peter Lang Publishers.

Walther, J.B., Gay, G., & Hancock, J.T. (2005). How do communication and technology researchers study the Internet? Journal of Communication, 55, 632–657.

Walther, J. B., Loh, T., & Granka, L. (2005). Let me count the ways: The interchange of verbal and nonverbal cues in computer–mediated and face–to–face affinity. Journal of Language and Social Psychology, 24, 36–65.

Walther, J.B., Van Der Heide, B., Kim, S., Westerman, D., & Tong, S.T. (2008). The role of friends' behavior on evaluations of individuals' Facebook profiles: Are we known by the company we keep? Human Communication Research, 34, 28–49.

Węglowska–Rzepa, K., J. Kowal, H. Lee Park, K. Haeng Lee (2008) The presence of spiritual archetypes among representatives of eastern and western cultures. Jung Journal. Vol. 2: 3, pp. 58–72.

Magdalena Sirecka–Wołodko
College of Management "Edukacja" in Wroclaw

THE USE OF ICTS FOR TERRORIST PURPOSES

ABSTRACT

Information and communication technologies which accelerate economic and social growth in developing countries also constitute a very useful tool in the hands of terrorists . At the turn of the 21st century the operations of terrorist groups underwent significant qualitative changes, largely as a result of the implementation of ICT in developing countries, from which these groups often come. The widespread promotion of computers, mobile phones and the Internet has allowed terrorists to streamline the communication process within their organizations, expand their sources of funding and create a network–based, transnational structure with a global range. ICTs, especially the Internet, have also impacted the manner with which terrorist groups communicate with their auditoriums, making it more direct and tailored to the needs of potential recipients. Yet another result of the application of ICTs by terrorists refers to the increase of their operational capabilities to plan and coordinate attacks, and at the same time use new technologies as a means to attract and destruct (so–called "cyber terrorism"). The extensive application of ICT in terrorist activities undoubtedly makes them more dangerous and unpredictable. It poses a major challenge both for developed countries which are dependent on the smooth operation of information and communication systems and developing countries which have increasingly based their development on investment in ICT and at the same time do not have resources for their effective protection and sufficient experience in this field.

KEYWORDS: terrorism, cyber–terrorism, techno–terrorism, the Internet.

INTRODUCTION

Information and communication technologies (ICTs), like all other technological achievements, though invented to serve humanity, can also be used against it by various criminal groups and organizations. Thus, though ICTs have undoubtedly accelerated economic and social progress, it cannot be ignored that they also constitute a very useful tool in terrorist activities, which are considered to be one of the biggest threats of modern world. Leaders and members of terrorist organizations have very quickly appreciated the benefits of highly advanced technologies in the fields of communication, information acquisition and its processing. Therefore they make use of a wide range of possibilities offered by the technological achievements of the modern world. Two basic methods of making use of ICT in terrorist activities can be indicated at this point (Madej, 2007):

1. ICTs are used as an auxiliary means and so–called force multiplier – an instrument which strengthens the effects of terrorist attacks. In this sense, ICTs are used as propaganda tools, a means of internal communication between members of terrorist groups or a source of information on targets of these attacks, new types of weapons, improved fighting techniques, etc.
2. ICTs constitute targets of terrorist attacks; they are also used as a new kind of weapon.

The extensive interest of terrorist groups in modern information and communication technologies comes mainly from the fact that they are a very convenient tool in combat led by unconventional methods. It must be emphasized that terrorism itself, often called "a weapon of the weak", is a special mode of action applied by groups of people coming out against governments, countries and nations who are unable to achieve their objectives in the combat conducted with conventional methods. Terrorist groups are not equipped with the capabilities of regular armies, their own budgets or fixed legal systems, and thus are forced to search for methods and means which would allow them to achieve their assumed objectives in spite of huge differences in potentials between them and state entities. In this seemingly unequal fight, terrorists make use of such factors as: action by surprise, drama and psychological effects of terrorist attacks (panic, fear), and innovative approaches in the selection of methods and means of action. ICTs perfectly fit into this type of unconventional methods of operation because:

1. Modern tele–communication technologies enable terrorists to efficiently communicate and coordinate actions simultaneously in many parts of the world. They allow for the intensification of the effect of surprise but also increase the drama of terrorist attacks.
2. Accomplished and potential attacks on the telecommunication and information technology infrastructure allow the more intense effects of panic and fear much desired by terrorists. In this manner, terrorists exploit the growing concerns of nations and societies (being more and more dependent on the smooth flow of information) against possible communication and information paralysis.
3. Modern tele–communication and information technologies raise innovative approaches within terrorist activities which are now planned by means of modern computer software and conducted with the use of IT and tele–communication equipment (for example, mobile phones as detonators of explosives, and the Internet as a target).

The application of ICT in terrorist activities undoubtedly makes them even more dangerous and unpredictable. This poses a major challenge for both developed countries which are dependent on the smooth operation of information and communication systems, as well as for developing countries which have increasingly based their development on investment in ICT and but do not have resources for their effective protection and sufficient experience in this field.

IMPACT OF THE DEVELOPMENT OF ICT ON THE PHENOMENON OF TERRORISM

Modern terrorism, known in the literature as "post–modern terrorism" or "modernistic terrorism", is characterized by its rapid adaptation to the processes of globalization and technology. The very fact that we are now talking about terrorism as a phenomenon with an international scope is undoubtedly the result of factors such as increased global relations between and among nations, countries and their economies, faster means of transport (for example, air travel) or emerging ICTs. The latter have contributed significantly to the phenomenon of terrorism together with the introduction of such technical achievements like computers and software, mobile phones, the Internet and services offered for general civil use. Observing the changes in the manner of organization and operation of terrorist groups within the past 20 years, it can be concluded that ICTs have changed the face of modern terrorism at least in some of the following aspects. New technologies have significantly influenced the organizational model and manner of communication within terrorist groups. Traditional terrorist organizations used to be based on their centralized structures, strong leadership and limited members. Communication within groups was limited to contact with their decision centers and – for safety reasons – exchanging information within these organizations was limited (Baylis, Smith, 2008). The territorial scope of operations was also limited as their activities were usually within one country. The processes of globalization and the emergence of new communication technologies have changed the method of communication for terrorist groups, enabling the creation of network–based, trans–national structures of terrorist organizations. A network structure of a particular organization stands for (to put it simply) flattening and centralizing its structure, which means reducing the degree of its hierarchy and distributing its components around the world. Contemporary terrorist organizations, usually devoid of central decision–making centers, are based on the operation of distributed, autonomous units and local decision–making centers which, if needed, co–operate with each other, co–ordinate their activities, and share their resources and knowledge. Communication within organizations most often takes the form of a so–called all–channel network in which all units communicate with each other by means of the Internet, mobile phones or satellite links. It should be noted that such a process of communication within organizations is better and well protected as terrorists use modern encryption programs, anonymous proxy servers, public access internet points, pre–paid mobile telephones or other tools which hinder their identification (tracing) and information decryption.

The network structure of terrorist organizations is undoubtedly an expression of the adaptation of terrorist groups to the process of globalization and technological progress. It enables more flexible and efficient operations and simultaneously hinders the penetration of terrorist organizations and the identification (tracing) of their members by state security services. As R. Nye writes: "Moving from their physical hiding places of the 90s to the virtual ones of today, terrorists have reduced their chances of detection" (Nye, 2012).

Secondly, new technologies, especially the Internet, have significantly impacted the manner of terrorists' communication with their surroundings. The terrorism itself is a kind of communication based on violence, intimidation and extortion. In order to achieve the desired psychological effect and thus their objectives, terrorists must get their message across to the wider public, and therefore the mass media – the press, television and the Internet – are vital. The phenomenon of a peculiar symbiosis between terrorists and mass media has been fairly well described in the literature on the subject and does not require any broader explanations at this point. It is worth mentioning that the press and television, though still useful for terrorists groups, have recently started losing their appeal in the Internet's favor.

It may be boldly said that nowadays the Internet has revolutionized the manner of communication of terrorists with the world as it has allowed the direct flow of information to their audiences. The advantage of the Internet over official media refers above all to the independent and unrestricted construction of the content of their message which bypasses so–called "editorial processing" without risking being ignored, censored or altered by editors, journalists or owners of media companies (Aleksandrowicz, 2008). Thanks to the Internet, terrorists have also impacted on the time and manner of reaching the public with their message as well as significantly expanding the group of potential recipients. Interestingly, the Internet has become a new channel of communication between traditional media and terrorists. One example refers to Al–Qaeda communication consisting of sending an e–mail to editors with warnings of their planned attacks, justifications of their motives, recordings of executions etc. Gabriel Weimann suggests that in this way – via the Internet – a two–stage flow of information is formed: terrorists communicate directly with journalists and indirectly with the public (Weimann 2006).

Another advantage of the Internet refers to its interactivity and extensive range of capabilities in the scope of selection of forms of propaganda content ranging from films, video–clips through comics, animations to computer games. Thanks to these varied forms of media, terrorists can tailor their messages to various groups of recipients, for example young people, children, women, and people in higher education, and make them more understandable and attractive. Such practices are applied, among others, by Hamas which created a website designed in the form of a comic with the content aimed at children and young people. In turn, Hezbollah in 2003 released a computer game "Special Force" in several languages, simulating a terrorist attack on Israel, also aimed at younger Internet users.

Thirdly, ICT has changed the manner of conducting terrorist attacks. Highly advanced technologies in the field of communication significantly raised the operational capabilities of terrorist groups, giving them the ability to trace targets precisely, exchange information and coordinate actions rapidly. It is well known today that popular and easily accessible mobile phones with prepaid cards played a major role in the preparation and precise co–ordination of the USA attacks of 11 September 2001. Mobile phones are also used by terrorists as detonators of explosives (as evidenced, among others, by the attacks accomplished on commuter trains in Madrid in 2004). It should be noted that in recent years terrorists have used mobile phones more cautiously or stopped using them at all due to the high risks of being tracked and tapped by anti–terrorist services. For these reasons, Osama Bin Laden, when hiding from American services, stopped mobile phone communication which, according to M. Sagemann, significantly reduced his effectiveness as leader of Al–Qaeda (Sagemann, 2008).

In turn, computers, portable storage devices, modern software and the Internet play an increasing role in planning attacks. Specialized software programs are used by terrorists to perform and stimulate terrorist attacks. The Internet is a means of communication and also a source of information about potential targets of attack. Terrorists make use of publicly available satellite maps, plans of public buildings, power plants, water supply systems, etc., as well as attempt to access classified, strategic information from the point of view of national security.

Fourthly, information and communication technologies have become new tools and targets of terrorist attacks. The modern world's dependence on technologies and information flows has caused forms of technical terrorism and cyber–terrorism to appear.

Technical terrorism (or techno–terrorism) consists in the physical destruction (by means of conventional methods) of elements of technical infrastructure such as transmitting and relay stations, servers, components of energy, and water and telecommunication networks. Such attacks are mainly aimed at disorganizing work or paralyzing public institutions and infrastructures, evoking chaos and panic. Techno–terrorism is not a new phenomenon, becoming a popular method of terrorist activity as early as the 1970s and 1980s. Currently, such destruction of technical infrastructure is usually treated by terrorists not as an end in itself but as a supporting activity of more extensive terrorist attacks. Attention is also drawn to the fact that such acts of terrorism may cause adverse effects, usually at the local level. Therefore they do not threaten the global structure of communication (Adamski, 2007). However, that they can seriously disrupt the functioning of states and endanger the life and health of citizens should not be underestimated.

Cyber–terrorism is a relatively new phenomenon, and has become an effective tool in the hands of terrorists together with the spread of the Internet. It should be noted here that the concept of cyber–terrorism has raised some controversy and in the literature on the subject there is even confusion over its definition. This largely stems from the fact that the mere phenomenon of terrorism has not been clearly defined as yet. In addition, terrorists make use of the same methods and approaches as other entities conducting criminal activities on the Net, resulting in a tendency to identify cyber–terrorism as cyber–crime and treating it very broadly as any criminal and hacking activity on the Internet. The controversies over the concept of cyber–terrorism have consequences not only at the level of academic discourse but also make it difficult to combat it through state services, which are not always able to determine whether a particular attack in cyberspace is a terrorist attack or just an act by ordinary hackers. Without going further into a definitional dispute, it is worth discussing what distinguishes cyber terrorism from other forms of IT use for criminal purposes.

While ordinary hackers and criminals conducting attacks on the Net are guided by a desire to achieve material (financial) gains, cyber terrorists are driven primarily by political and ideological motivations and their attacks are mainly against state structures. IT attacks are aimed at provoking panic and fear, causing damage to state–owned entities and impelling them to take the actions which terrorists wish them to. Thus, there is a clear parallel between political motivation and objectives of terrorists using conventional methods and cyberterrorists. It should be noted that cyber terrorism is typically conducted by the same organizations and individuals using "traditional" terrorist attacks, and in this sense is just another method of their operation.

Attacks on IT systems (for example, computers and their related facilities, the Internet, networks, data and information processed and stored by them) also conducted with the use of IT tools are the gist of cyber terrorism. IT systems are then treated by cyber terrorists as a means of destruction and as the goal of their attacks. The intended aim of these attacks is to destroy or paralyze IT systems which are vital for national security and the proper operation of numerous spheres of public life. The following types of attacks can be distinguished: cyber–attacks with their direct effects limited to virtual space (for example, blocking e–mail accounts through so–called e–mail bombing) and cyber–attacks performed in virtual space but with direct implications for the "real" world as well (Madej, 2007). The latter appear to be particularly dangerous in their consequences, as they can directly threaten the safety and security of a particular state and its citizens. The widely publicized issue refers to intrusions attempts by cyber terrorists into Distributed Data Control (DDC) and Supervisory Control and Data Acquisition (SCADA) systems which supervise the course of technological or production processes. The seizure of these systems by terrorists could have catastrophic consequences in the form of blocking the supply of energy, water, gas, paralyzing life–saving devices, securing against air or rail disasters, etc.

While conducting attacks in cyberspace, terrorists basically make use of the same methods and techniques which Internet hackers and criminals do. It even happens that terrorist organizations employ experienced hackers to conduct complex operations on the Net. It is stressed that – as terrorists usually do not have highly advanced technological equipment and specialized skills – the cyberattacks conducted so far have been based on relatively simple hacking methods and techniques. The most common techniques used by cyber terrorists include: e–mail bombing, taking over websites and replacing them (hijacking), overloading IT equipment and Internet connections (flooding), breaking into computers and interfering with their information resources, distribution of so–called viruses, worms, Trojan horses, logic bombs, etc.

All attacks conducted using the above techniques have not caused considerable damage to the Net and ICT systems or significantly threatened public safety. Therefore, some researchers see cyber–terrorism as not a real threat but a phenomenon created and demonized by the media and terrorists themselves to "heat up" the atmosphere of fear and panic (Szubrycht, 2005). Terrorists are also seen as not interested in paralyzing the Internet or telecommunication networks as they constitute valuable for them. However, the majority of countries and international organizations (e.g. the UN, NATO, the EU) do not minimize the risk of cyber terrorism and treat it as a real hazard. It should be remembered that even simple methods of hacking used at the right time and place (target) can threaten elements of the so–called critical infrastructure of countries. It is also expected that terrorists will continue to develop and improve their hacking skills and perhaps in the future will be equipped with more advanced devices, making their attacks more sophisticated and dangerous.

It is also worth noting that, although it is recognized that developed countries are mostly exposed to cyber–attacks, the problem has increasingly been affecting developing countries which are more and more dependent on the smooth flow of information and the efficient operation of telecommunication systems. This is evidenced by India, which in 1998 became a victim of hackers who had broken into computers administered by the Bhabha Atomic Research Centre and accessed information on nuclear weapon tests. For a number of years the coalition of pro–Pakistan hacker groups linked with Al–Qaeda attacked the Indian government servers and websites of large companies and published on–line training materials for novice hackers on the methods of cyber–attacks on the Indian ICT infrastructure (Bógdał–Brzezinska, Gawrycki, 2003). In recent years, Estonia and Georgia have become victims of cyber terrorism. In this case, these attacks were probably inspired by Russian authorities, and thus conceive a new form of terrorism – state terrorism.

THE INTERNET – A NEW TOOL IN THE HANNDS OF TERRORISTS

Undoubtedly, the Internet has been a particularly useful and willingly used tool by terrorist organizations in recent times. Virtual space is characterized by certain features which make it particularly attractive to terrorist organizations.

Trans–nationality and a–territoriality are relevant attributes of the Internet which allow users to cross geographical, economic and cultural borders without physically moving. The Internet is also "mono–cultural", which stands for far–reaching standardization in the scope of software, offered services and procedures. Together, all these features allow terrorist organizations to communicate directly with people on the other end of the globe, 24 hours a day, and basically with no restrictions.

The Internet also provides anonymity and allows for minimizing the risk of being tracked by state anti–terrorist services. A large number of users, high–volumetric flows of data and information, and the use of wireless Internet access in public areas are key factors hindering the identification (tracking) of terrorists in cyberspace. In addition, to increase their security terrorists use coded methods of online communication. Extensive encoding and decoding software, which is easily available, cheap (or even for free) and above all effective, is at their disposal. Methods of encoding, particularly willingly used by terrorists, are based on steganographic techniques which enable them to hide messages in graphic or music files (Choudhary, 2012).

The Internet also the potential for extensive propaganda. In order to achieve these purposes, terrorists make use of a wide range of online services: they create magazines and web sites, and make use of e–mails, online TV or discussion forums. The presence of terrorists on popular social networking sites such as Twitter and Facebook is a relatively new trend. However, due to the fact that these forums are strictly regulated and their accounts may have been closed by administrators, they are forced to hide their identities. Hence, they often imitate organizations with rather innocuous–sounding names and do not express their radical slogans. An account set up on Facebook by members of Hamas claiming to be a non–profit organization under the name "Palestinian Information Centre" is an example of this. Frankly speaking, the account owner does not include any content which incites acts of terror focusing on the publication of information and links to articles with anti–Israeli and anti–American aspects.

As previously mentioned, the features of web services are as follows: the possibility of profiling propaganda campaigns for various social, age, cultural and ethnic groups and the possibility to respond to the individual needs and preferences of Internet users. The specificity of Internet communication encourages extremists to use populist slogans and simplistic pictures of the world. It enables terrorists to radicalize the moods and emotions of both Internet users who are characterized by already–formed radical views and among people who are ideologically vague. A group which is particularly vulnerable to web propaganda is the young people familiar with modern technologies who spend more and more time in cyberspace and at the same time look for their own identity and group membership. Islamic extremist organizations very effectively make use of radicalizing moods among young people, deprived of perspectives, from the underdeveloped countries and of a sense of discrimination and eradication felt among descendants of Muslim immigrants living in highly developed countries. M. Sagemann notes that Islamic terrorist groups primarily turn their attention to alienated and isolated individuals, giving them a sense of community with the idealized "virtual mythical umma of the Salafists" (Sagemann, 2008)

Another characteristic of the Internet which is favored by terrorists refers to the fact that this is a relatively difficult to regulate area and is not controlled by state authorities. The technical possibilities of tracking terrorists on the Net are very limited and not always effective, especially in situations where terrorists operate beyond the jurisdiction of a state against which their actions are directed. Any attempts to suppress websites run by terrorists are not very effective because of the possibility of moving them to other servers located within countries which favor terrorism or places where legal regulations do not prohibit the publication of radical content. Countries with their democratic systems also pay the price for their observance of freedom of speech and civil liberties. The governments of these countries must take into account public protesting against the limitation of freedom of speech and surveillance of its users. Yet another problem is the fact that both international regulations and national jurisdiction systems have not kept pace with the rapid development of ICT technologies and have loopholes for business on the Internet. Problems with a clear definition of what actions on the Net are criminal in character result in making it difficult to combat terrorism effectively both by enforcement authorities and justice institutions.

All the listed features of the Internet make it a very convenient tool in the fight against their greatest enemies – the states and their governments. It should be emphasized once again that terrorists – to achieve their objectives – are forced to search and use unconventional methods which allow them to compensate for the potential gap between them and state entities. In cyberspace, traditional components of force lose their significance and impact. The capabilities the countries have in the real world do not give them any predominance in the virtual world (or their significance is very limited). This in turn enables terrorists to achieve the so–called potential balancing (force equalizer) effect and act effectively against state structures The application of the Internet in terrorist activities is very broad. According to the report published in 2012 by the United Nations Office on Drugs and Crime entitled "The Use of the Internet for Terrorist Purposes", the Internet is used by terrorists to achieve the following goals:

1. running propaganda activities (including recruitment of new members, radicalization of moods and emotions, incitement to attacks);
2. fundraising;
3. training of members and supporters of terrorist groups;
4. planning of terrorist attacks;
5. data mining;
6. performance of terrorist and cyber–terrorist attacks.

The problem of using the Internet as a means of communication and propaganda tool has already been covered, but it is worth paying attention to dealings related to recruitment and training activities by terrorist organizations on the net. The acquisition of new members and supporters of terrorist organizations via the Internet has been a relatively new phenomenon and is usually conducted via websites, e–mails, chat rooms and social networking. Above all, extremist Islamic organizations have become more and more effective in these actions. They refer to the idea of global jihad and build a virtual umma of fighters on the Net. According to Marc Sagemann, although the Internet is not yet a source of direct recruitment for this type of organization, as it still requires face–to–face contact with potential candidates to assess their physical and mental capabilities, the net can be used to shape their socialization in the ideology of global Salafi jihad (Sagemann, 2008). The danger of this phenomenon was reported in 2010 by the Secretary General of Interpol, Richard Noble, who indicated that recruitment of members of Al–Qaeda via the Internet is now run on a large scale among youths (from the lowest social layers and the middle class) who are the main recipients of such actions (see wiadomosci.gazeta.pl). It is difficult to thoroughly assess the effectiveness of recruitment conducted by terrorists on the Internet, but given the large number of network users it may be suspected that it allows them to acquire a considerable number of supporters. More and more often the Internet has also become a place of first contact of young people with the ideologies of extremist terrorist organizations.

The Internet has been also a place for the extensive training of terrorists. There are websites of terrorist groups and their supporters which contain instructions and training videos on the construction and use of various types of weapons or plans for suicide attacks. For example, in 2005 training materials on constructing bio–weapons were published at the website of Mustafa Setmariam, one of the most influential members of Al–Qaeda (Aaron, 2008). In 2010, Al–Qaeda published its online magazine (*Inspire*) which contained training materials on constructing bombs in home conditions. The legendary "Mini manual on urban guerrilla" by Carlos Marighelli was published in its electronic version (this is a veritable mine of information on methods of organizing terrorist attacks). It is worth mentioning that one of the effects of propaganda, recruitment and training activities conducted by terrorists on the Net refers to the emergence of a new generation of terrorists – so–called "lonely wolves" who are not members of terrorist groups but who draw their ideological inspiration and knowledge from the Internet and perform attacks on their own. The attack in Boston, USA in April 2013 by Dżhokhar and Tamerlan Tsarnaev, who were probably motivated by the already–mentioned *Inspire* magazine, are a good example.

The Internet has become a very convenient tool for acquiring funds for terrorist groups. These funds are derived mainly through appeals for financial support published on websites and the online sales of books and gadgets. There is also evidence that terrorists have attempted to extort money from financial institutions by conducting attacks on their IT systems. The Russian financial system has become a victim of such attacks probably conducted by Chechen terrorists (as a result of which it suffered losses estimated at $300 million). The scale of this phenomenon has not been examined well, as most financial institutions do not disclose information on the subject, afraid of losing their image, reputation and customer trust (Adamski, 2007).

All up–to–date observations on the activities of terrorists indicate that they make use of the Internet mainly for propaganda purposes and to facilitate communication within their organizations. Its role has also increased in the recruitment and training of terrorists, in the process of operational identification and preparation of attacks and in the acquisition of funds for terrorist goals. So far the Internet has relatively rarely been used as a direct target or a tool of terrorist attacks. However, it may be assumed that a new generation of terrorists better educated and acquainted with modern technologies will more often use hacking techniques as a tool to support conventional terrorist attacks, or as a new method of fighting in cyberspace.

CONCLUSION – THE NEW CHALLENGES FOR DEVELOPING COUNTRIES

The extensive application of ICTs by terrorist organizations proves that terrorism is a phenomenon which has been adapting well to the realities of the modern world (which is increasingly dependent on the seamless flow of information and continuous technological progress). Today's terrorists have almost mastered the art of using relatively simple and widely available information and communication tools, making their activities even more effective, unpredictable and dangerous. Of course it has serious consequences for countries which need to adapt their security policies to new challenges and threats. Increasingly, the issue has also concerned the group of developing countries for a number of reasons.

Firstly, some of these countries (for example Russia, Egypt, India, the Philippines, Indonesia and Colombia) are areas of activities conducted by terrorist organizations and potential targets for their attacks. Also, countries which have not been directly threatened by terrorist attacks must reckon with the fact that the transnational terrorist network will cover their territories with their terrorist activities. Indeed, through the use of ICT today's terrorists can easily cross borders, recruit and train their members abroad, establish contacts with local criminal organizations (for example, drug cartels) and create their organizational units over much of the world.

Secondly, these countries – implementing ICT in private and public sectors to accelerate their development – must take into account the increased risks of potential attacks on their telecommunications and information technology infrastructure. It should be noted that in the case of developing countries, their infrastructure is relatively poorly protected due to the lack of adequate funding and experience of counter–terrorism services in this area.

Thirdly, developing countries and their legal systems often do not keep pace with the development of modern technologies, which creates favorable conditions for the unhindered activities of terrorist groups. Nowadays, terrorists are keen on placing their web sites on servers in developing countries due to the existing legal loopholes and lower risks of detection. On the other hand, there are legitimate concerns that some of these countries wish to use anti–terrorism regulations to restrict the freedom of speech on the Internet or surveillance of their citizens. The SORM program implemented in Russia can be considered as an example of this, on the grounds of which the Federal Security Services have conducted investigative actions by monitoring e–mails or phone calls. The program was introduced under the pretext of combating terrorism and crime online; however, its critics argue that it provides space to interfere with the e–mails of ordinary citizens and without legal sanctions (Rogoża, 2012, www.osw.waw.pl).

Fourthly, in these countries both political elites and individual users are not aware of hazards derived from the use of ICTs by terrorists. For a long time the issue was and has been underestimated by most countries in Asia or Latin America, resulting in serious failures in the area of information security. Risks arising from online terrorist activities have become the subject of interest of some institutions for the regional cooperation of developing countries. In 2004, the Organization of American States General Assembly adopted a resolution entitled "The Inter–American Integral Strategy to Combat Threats to Cyber Security", in which all the states' members agreed to deepen their co–operation to prevent cyber–crime and cyber–terrorism (oas.org). Also, in 2011 the APEC countries adopted a document entitled "APEC Consolidated Counter–Terrorism and Secure Trade Strategy", in which they declare their joint efforts to secure their so–called critical infrastructure, including telecommunications infrastructure and cyberspace.

The assertion that together with the implementation of ICT in the public and private sectors, developing countries should ensure the provision of appropriate solutions to secure them against the use of new technologies by terrorist organizations, seems to be obvious today. At the national level the issue requires, first of all, the development of relevant legal regulations, the establishment of procedures and institutions responsible for the safety and security of the ICT infrastructure, the conduct of information campaigns in their societies and the setting up of a public–private partnership to develop the principles of information security. Developing countries should also be fully involved in the mechanisms of international cooperation to combat terrorist activities online and acts of cyber–terrorism. The proper course of action seems to refer to the co–operation (launched, among others, at the APEC Forum) of developing countries with developed countries which usually have more experience and resources to combat terrorism.

REFERENCES

Aaron D. (2008), In Their Own Words. Voices of Jihad: compilation and commentary, Santa Monica: RAND Corporation.

Adamski J. (2007), Nowe technologie w służbie terrorystów, Warszawa: Wydawnictwo Trio.

Aleksandrowicz T. (2008), Terroryzm międzynarodowy, Warszawa: Wydawnictwo Akademickie i Profesjonalne.

Baylis J., Smith S., (eds) (2008), Globalizacja polityki światowej. Wprowadzenie do stosunków międzynarodowych, Kraków Wydawnictwo UJ.

Bolechów, B. (2010), Baza w sieci. Wykorzystanie internetu przez Al–Kaidę i jej zwolenników, [in:] Liedel K., Mock, (eds), Terroryzm w medialnym obrazie świata. Terroryści, dziennikarze, administracje w epoce walki informacyjnej, Warszawa: Wydawnictwo TRIO.

Bógdał–Brzezińska B., Gawrycki M.F. (2003), Cyberterroryzm i problemy bezpieczeństwa informacyjnego we współczesnym świecie, Warszawa: Oficyna Wydawnicza ASPRA–JR.

Brown C. (2007), The New Terrorism Debate: Alternatives "Turkish Journal of International Relations", Vol. 6, No. 3 &4, Fall & Winter 2007, [2013, 28th June].

Choudhary K. (2012), Image Steganography and Global Terrorism, [online], Global Security Studies, Fall 2012, Volume 3, Issue, http://globalsecuritystudies.com/Image%20Steganography.pdf, [2013, 5th July].

Madej M. (2007), Zagrożenia asymetryczne państw obszaru transatlantyckiego, Warszawa: Polski Instytut Spraw Międzynarodowych.

Musiał M. (2005), Cyberterrorism. A Virtual Threat or a Real One?, [in:] Wallas T., Wojciechowski S., (edt.), The power of terrorism, Poznań: Adam Mickiewicz University.

Nye J.S. Jr. (2009), Konflikty międzynarodowe. Wprowadzenie do teorii i historii, Warszawa: Wydawnictwa Naukowe i Profesjonalne.

Nye J.S. Jr. (2012), Przyszłość siły, Warszawa: Wydawnictwo Naukowe PWN.

Piotrowska D. (2007), The latest war in Iraq and Hacktivism and Cyberterrorism – a real Threat?, [in:] S. Wojciechowski (ed.), The Modern Terrorism and its Forms, Poznań: Institute of Political Science and Journalism Adam Mickiewicz University.

Rogoża J., Internet w Rosji: kolebka społeczeństwa informacyjnego, [online], Ośrodek Studiów Wschodnich im. Marka Karpia, http://www.osw.waw.pl/pl/publikacje/komentarze-osw/2012–03–21/internet-w-rosji-kolebka-spoleczenstwa-obywatelskiego, [2013, 1st July].

Sagemann M. (2008), Sieci terroru, Kraków: Wydawnictwo UJ.

Skrzypczak J. (2013), Europejska architektura bezpieczeństwa teleinformacyjnego jako fundament rozwoju społeczeństwa informacyjnego, [in:] Wojciechowski S., Wejkszner A. (eds), Kluczowe determinanty bezpieczeństwa Polski na początku XXI wieku, Warszawa: Wydawnictwo Difin.

Szubrycht T., Cyberterroryzm jako nowa forma zagrożenia terrorystycznego, [online] Zeszyty Naukowe Akademii Marynarki Wojennej, Rok XLVI Nr 1 (160) 2005, http://www.amw.gdynia.pl/library/File/ZeszytyNaukowe/2005/Szubrycht_T.pdf [2013, 26th June].

Weimann G. (2006), Terror on the Internet. The New arena, the new challenges, Washington: United States Institute of Peace Press. http://www.oas.org/cyber/documents/resolution.pdf, [2013, 7th July]. http://www.apec.org/Home/Groups/SOM–Steering–Committee–on–Economic–and–Technical–

Cooperation/Task–Groups/Counter–Terrorism–Task–Force, [2013, 7th July]. http://dziennikzbrojny.pl/aktualnosci/news,3,4343,aktualnosci-ze-swiata,al-kaida-opublikowala-11-numer-magazynu-inspire [2013, 5th July].

Rozmowa Tomasza Stawiszyńskiego z dr Krzysztofem Liedlem, [online], Krytyka Polityczna z dnia 26.04.2013: http://www.krytykapolityczna.pl/artykuly/swiat/20130426/liedel-rodzi-sie-nowa-forma-terroryzmu [2013, 3th July]. http://wiadomosci.gazeta.pl/wiadomosci/1,114873,8409904,Interpol_Al_Kaida_rekrutuje_w_sieci_Na_wielka_skale.html, [2013, 7th July].

UNDOC, The use of the Internet for terrorist purposes, New York 2012, [online], http://www.unodc. org/ documents/frontpage/Use_of_Internet_for_Terrorist_Purposes.pdf [2013, 5th July].

Łukasz Kłuskiewicz
University of Social Sciences and Humanities in Warsaw

THE PHENOMENON OF SCRIPTED REALITY PROGRAMS BASED ON PAMIĘTNIKI Z WAKACJI ("HOLIDAY DIARIES") SERIES AS AN EXAMPLE

ABSTRACT

This chapter includes an extensive analysis of the revolution in Polish television in 2011 through Polsat TV, which managed to question every single basic programming dogma and eventually confirm the changing audience's preferences. The said dogmas implied that the audience is conservative about its behavior and choices, used to the particular programs in the schedule and not really looking for alternatives. Polsat TV successively introduced the Pamiętniki z wakacji ("Holiday diaries") series in October, gaining huge popularity in a short time and taking the leading position among the 16–49-year-old audience group, which is a problematic group for broadcasters as they require more encouragement to watch TV.

KEYWORDS: communication, media. television, reality programs.

WHY IS PAMIĘTNIKI Z WAKACJI A PHENOMENON?

The autumn schedule for Polish television in 2011 brought about a revolution. Polsat TV questioned every single basic programming dogma and eventually confirmed a change in their audience's preferences. The said dogmas implied that the audience is conservative about its behavior and choices, used to particular programs always present in the schedule and not really looking for alternatives, meaning that competing with and an established and popular program would require time and be extremely difficult or even impossible. A spectacular failure of several programs that tried to conquer TV giants proved as an example of this argument and eventually led to acknowledging the giants' inviolability. The most memorable is the attempt to confront the newly started Fakty ("Facts", TVN) with the emission of Wiadomości ("News", TVP1). The ambition of direct competition to get the audience's attention at 7:30 PM had to quickly give way in the face of awareness that watching Wiadomości was almost a ritual for Polish people. Those responsible for creating schedules, learning from this and similar experiences, started to confront the program giants of the competition with their new creations. Not so long ago competing with Teleexpres (TVP1), M jak miłość ("L like love", TVP2) and also Fakty ("Facts", TVN), broadcast at 7 PM for many years, seemed futile.

At the same time, Polsat successively introduced the Pamiętniki z wakacji ("Holiday diaries") series in October, and it gained huge popularity in a short time, going for the leading position among the 16–49-years-old audience group, which is a problematic group for broadcasters since it is less attracted to watching TV. The TV station wasn't scared of competing with the giant Polish TV providers for this timeslot. Pamiętniki z wakacji won the competition against quiz show Jaka to melodia ("What's this tune?") and a series Ojciec Mateusz ("Father Matthew", TVP1), the main edition of Panorama along with the weather broadcast and sport news (TVP2), and popular quasi-culinary shows such as Kuchenne rewolucje ("Kitchen revolutions") and Ugotowani ("Cooked", TVN). Every episode of the series was watched by approximately 2.3 million of people.

Table 1. Audience of main TV stations during the first season of Pamiętniki z wakacji (Nielsen Poland telemetric panel)

Station	Everyone 4+		16–49
	AMR	SHR %	SHR %
TVP 1 Father Matthew, What's this tune?	2,443,215	18.77%	13.84%
Polsat Pamiętniki z wakacji	**2,276,347**	**17.56%**	**20.17%**
TVP 2 Panorama, Sport, Weather broadcast	1,813,667	13.94%	8.93%
TVN Kitchen revolutions, Cooked	1,810,463	13.91%	18.34%

This achievement could shrugged off and summarized with "they were lucky", but we have to think about the fact that Polsat encouraged a very particular group of viewers to watch Pamiętniki. An analysis of the audience profile proves the democratization of the program – women watch it with the same interest as men. In terms of location, people watching Polsat's scripted reality represent a group with a profile close to that characterizing the entire population of Polish viewers (the AFF marker under 80 or over 120 points to under-representation or over-representation). Still, the most interesting thing is the fact that Pamiętniki managed to gain interest of young audience, meaning children aged 10 to 15. This is a very specific age group, always proving a challenge for every TV station – especially for the general-themed ones.

Table 2. The profile of Pamiętniki z wakacji's first season audience (Nielsen Polska telemetric panel)

		ADH %	AFF
Gender	Men	43.28%	90
	Women	56.72%	109
Age	4–9	4.06%	68
	10–15	8.01%	118
	16–19	4.50%	80
	20–24	5.11%	65
	25–29	6.84%	77
	30–34	8.30%	100
	35–39	7.47%	101
	40–44	5.62%	88
	45–49	7.92%	115
	50–54	10.10%	126
	55–59	9.14%	118
	60	22.93%	114
City size	Wieś	47.55%	121
	< 50 tys.	23.92%	99
	50–100 tys.	6.14%	71
	100–200 tys.	7.83%	97
	> 200 tys.	14.56%	72
Occupation	Top management	4.03%	46
	Mid-level employees	10.53%	70
	Manual workers and farmers	24.77%	124
	Pensioners	30.99%	121
	Others	29.68%	97
Education	Primary	61.23%	136
	Secondary	21.60%	73
	Higher	5.11%	41
	Other	12.07%	95

It seems fully justified to form basic questions regarding both the TV program as a cultural text (the text structure, narration, construction of the presented universe, aesthetics, distinguishing elements, main storyline themes, characters, constructed image of the universe and existence in said universe) and the questions regarding the audience spending time watching Pamiętniki from a choice of about 180 Polish TV stations. If Polish people – including the young – felt convinced enough to watch a semi–documentary series showing different situations and dilemmas of their fellow country people on holiday, it's safe to assume that they found the content they were looking for in this particular series. The program reacts to some needs and is somehow useful to the audience. It compensates for something or is convergent with some aspirations. Still, the attempt to see Pamiętniki as a modern morality, which educates (has a chance to socially educate?) young people, seems to be most interesting. Such a research perspective does not *a priori* ennoble Polsat's scripted reality, but lets us rather look at it without prejudice, free from a stereotypical way of seeing such productions and rejecting aversion and the temptation to mock it, which can bloom within a more reflective viewer (who has media competences and can read TV texts as code opposition) after seeing not more than a single episode of the series.

To justify the subject and topic of research it has to be said that Pamiętniki z wakacji became a phenomenon, the vitality of which extends much further than the TV screen. Right now it's basically an example of a fan culture object. Individual episodes available on YouTube get hundreds of thousands of views and hundreds of comments – both affirmative and negative. Friends send the best scenes to each other via e–mail – mostly those thought to be the most curious, showing most coarse stereotypes or the least intellectually sophisticated. Viewers also create their own videos parodying the series, and make so–called "demotivators" (photos signed with a funny comment and satirical drawings), published on popular entertainment sites or their Facebook profiles. The series is being discussed both on the Internet and in real life, proving to be a very good topic for different discussions – sometimes funny, other times serious, but almost always vivid and provoking emotional responses (even if just for amusement). The number of requests for new episodes is so great that after broadcasting the first season of Pamiętniki (in Autumn 2011) many comments appeared on Polsat's pages regarding disapproval of the break in broadcasting during winter. The station reacted to those comments (after calculating the profitability, of course) and, starting March 2012, the second series began.

2. WHERE DID PAMIĘTNIKI Z WAKACJI COME FROM?

Pamiętniki z wakacji is a type of program called scripted reality. Their genesis is a natural evolution of popular reality TV programs. The new genre form is most likely an answer to a great demand of such content and at the same time a remedy to production limits, which up until now prejudged the fact that the realization of reality programs was both time– and money–consuming.

The essence of a classic reality show was supposed to be the reality itself and observing it, close to the assumptions of documentary art trends like Cinema Verite or Direct Cinema. The first productions of this kind implied realistic documentation and were very typical, which means that they were showing the life of representatives of typical social classes in the most typical situations, including the realization of reality most standard for a given story part. Such basis was also taken into consideration with *An American Family* – considered to be the beginning of the genre – which was broadcasted in 1973 by an American station called PBS.[1] The impulses for the improvement of such TV forms were rapid technological advances, which democratized the access to means of recording images and sound, making the camera a ubiquitous device capable of almost pornographic observation. It gave the directors an opportunity to explore life areas unavailable until now because of problems with realization. A documentary series called *Cops* (Fox, 1989), recreating the reality of American law officers, became a visible sign of change. The audience got an opportunity to accompany the police during their interventions, night patrols in the most dangerous districts or crazy chases after escaping criminals.

The same technological advancements also caused millions of more or less accidental records to function in the culture. In TV the availability of real footage led to the creation of programs based on thrilling (accidents, chases, moments of horror) or amusing video material (home video compilations).

With time, the formula of so–called reality television required a change and adaptation to the linear way of narration preferred by the audience. It forced the creator to create drama structures and thicken the narration, made possible by the advancement of non–linear montage, which made the quick viewing of great amounts of material and its efficient assembly easier. The changes within reality TV were reduced to realizing the programs, the basic concept of which was limited to staging situations and creating suitable conditions featuring people taking part in a specific experiment

The most successful realization of this trend was a show called *Big Brother* (Veronica TV, 1999). Simply put, the format was about giving the viewers the

[1] A movie produced by HBO, called *Cinema Verite* (2011), tells us about the backstage and influence of production and realization of the program on the Loud family, the characters of *An American Family*.

opportunity to carefully observe the life of a group of contestants living in a house. The experimental aspect of their functionality was reduced to limiting almost everything – the space they were living in, their freedoms by censoring discussion topics, their access to articles and products, and finally their privacy and intimacy by constantly exposing them to cameras and microphones. The show participants were encouraged towards direct rivalry during the strangest of competitions. The ability to anonymously punish fellow participants with a system of discreet nominations to expel them from the program became a special attraction. Still, the most important limitation was the partial sensory deprivation of the house inhabitants by preventing them from contacting the outside world and not letting them keep devices and instruments which would help them orientate to the flow of time.

Yet, at the same time were people trying to restore the value of documentary observation. This meant some broadcasters, mainly British ones, making documentary soap operas in which – unlike in programs like Big brother – people could see the positive influence on the society. These were mainly series showing the everyman in hard life situations, typical enough to trigger the mechanism of projection and identification in the audience. The characters fought with everyday hardships by working, learning, looking for jobs, trying to fight their addictions or coping with the feeling of being different in the worlds they lived in. Through their eyes the audience could see the life of someone else, usually in worse situations than themselves. Documentary soap operas also became a medium touching taboos, portraying social phenomena and groups which up until then couldn't be seen in mainstream broadcasts. Said to be dazzling people with sensations and human dramas, they could actually have taught viewers about social sensitivity and to become more aware of the situations of others, focusing attention on life areas thought to be of minor importance. For Polish TV trends, productions such as Kawaleria powietrzna ("Air Cavalry", 2000, director: Jacek Bławut), Nieparzyści ("Odd", 2001, director: Ewa Straburzyńska), Serce z węgla ("Coal heart", 2001, directors: Irena and Jerzy Morawscy), Prawdziwe psy ("Real dogs", 2001, directors: Krzysztof Lang, Marcin Koszałka, Patryk Vega), Przedszkolandia ("Kindergarten", 2002, director: Barbara Pawłowska) and Ballada o zabarwieniu erotycznym ("A slightly erotic ballad", 2003, director: Irena and Jerzy Morawscy) should be included in this group.

Documentary soap operas and other, sometimes very different reality TV productions made the audience used to an almost pornographic insight into reality. They also upped the appetite for the alleged truth of the broadcasts.

However, production conditions – a long time in realization and with unpredictable results – couldn't allow the producers to meet the demands. The reasons for this were most likely linked to the genesis of scripted reality productions, which kept up the appearance of reality TV, guaranteed appropriate dramatic density and were much more efficient when it comes to production. Realizing a standard episode requires not more than two shooting days. However, the simplicity of production could not play any part if the continuing series didn't interest the audience or gain great popularity and weren't willingly watched on TV, so that they couldn't extend further than the TV screen. The fact that scripted reality series dominated huge television markets and were able to provoke a significant change in the audience's preferences – as the example of Polsat's Pamiętniki z wakacji shows – can't be a coincidence.

3. WHO WATCHES PAMIĘTNIKI Z WAKACJI AND WHY?

For a cultural expert and a media researcher, a cultural text like Pamiętniki z wakacji, so enthusiastically applauded by the audience, has to provide some kind of a challenge. This series almost provokes academic analysis and investigation from various perspectives, especially since there's a great possibility of an important cultural change behind the success of scripted reality and its audience results indicate a very specific way of treating the TV medium by the viewers,[2] because I assume that we're entering a stage of development in audio–visual culture indicating the extreme polarization of the audience's tastes, but also competence in taking part in the circulation of a cultural text. The results of such polarization are going to be visible in the production of TV series. The series produced and constructed for a mass audience are going to lose their rationale, because the diversification of the TV audience based on competence, expectations towards the media and their goal of consumption is going to be too great. On the one hand, polarization means that the phenomenon we can see now – producing television content meant for a sophisticated audience (i.e. competent, familiar with audio–visual cultural texts, recognizing conventions and able to move between them freely, following the narration without regarding its complexity) is going to intensify, creating a so–called quality television product prepared for reception. For them the text of a series is, above all, entertainment, an innovative performance of a well–known story, a myth demanding deconstruction, a story being read with the fascination of a fan, and yet reservedly, from a distance.

Viewers not used to such advanced partaking in audio–visual culture are going to remain on the opposite pole. Their reception of television texts, mainly those of different series, would be much more simplified. They wouldn't be able to catch the subtlety of the narration of story–scenario complications.

[2] Research questions stated in this part of the article are to be the subject of empirical research planned for the thesis. It's also the reason why I'm going to limit the content to pointing out a few of the most important hypotheses, showing the possible reasons behind scripted reality programs' success.

Simple reception would require an equally simple medium, operating with the simplest storyline setups, serving a basic set of characters and relations between them.

An interesting academic trail is being introduced in this context of evolutionary psychology achievements, whose representatives, mainly David Nettle, point to the rules determining the storyline of narrative productions and judge them using specific structures and dramaturgic elements.[3] Those rules would also determine the popularity of particular stories and their eye-catching potential. Even though Nettle debated the creations of Shakespeare during his research, the results can still be generalized. What catches the audience's attention seems to be the fight for status and male–female relations. Nettle connects those elements with conditions of living in groups of the past. A fight for status determines a place in a hierarchy, which in turn decides about the chances for reproductive success. On the other hand, male–female relations are interesting to people because – using evolutionistic nomenclature – both the male and female need to know how to communicate with each other and what strategies to use against each other. Based on this data, Nettle created a catalogue of rules, determining the audience's interest in a particular story. Firstly, the storyline should be focused on the adventures and mishaps of a small group of people, because this is a situation most similar to that which mankind has been evolutionally programmed to experience in the natural environment of a hunter–gatherer group. This is enhanced when the group divides into sub–groups, between which rivalry ensues. Secondly, the individuals have to take actions bringing them closer to realizing their own reproductive success. At the same time, while trying to transmit their genotypes the individuals work in a way that shows their social status and diversify hierarchy in a group. Thirdly, it's necessary for the relations between characters to have a sexual dimension. In a situation like this, rivalry based on a sexual aspect should be the center of conflict (a race for the male/female, attempts to steal a partner or disavow a rival). This conflict will in turn result in the characters' emotions taking a desired temperature and the dramatic events are going to be elevated to the highest level.

How does Pamiętniki z wakacji look in such a context? Characters of different episodes are presented to the audience as representatives of a specific group – friends, family, classmates. However, in no episode does the number of characters exceed a few persons. This way, the audience can easily understand the relations between them or define the eventual divisions in the group. What's more, the characters of Pamiętniki z wakacji function as members of a hunter–gatherer group. They show up in a new territory where they some-

[3] See: T. Szlendak, T. Kozłowski, Naga małpa przed telewizorem. Popkultura w świetle psychologii ewolucyjnej, Warszawa, 2008, p. 202–206.

how test their rules and norms of social life anew. They are aware of the fact that their new situation is not permanent, which in turn pushes them to take up activities they would normally never think of doing in their everyday existence. The portrayed holidaymakers have predispositions to expansive behavior towards people and places, not really considering the consequences of their actions. They feel somewhat abstracted from their normal life conditions. So the first condition, regarding narration fitting with genre expectations, has been fulfilled. The second condition formed by Nettle regards the characters' pursuance of an individual reproductive success and is connected with the third condition, which would be the sexual aspect of their actions. To say that it's happening in Pamiętniki would be euphemistic. Almost every single one of the characters comes to a foreign resort with a strong motivation to be successful, which is more or less connected with their reproductive categories. Three friends hope to have a very nice holiday and make a bet regarding which one is going to flirt with the most girls. A high school student wants to use the romantic aura of the beach and the sea to seduce her P. E. teacher. A neglected wife hopes that a long desired holiday is going to ignite passion in her husband. An unaccepted girl wants to convince her boyfriend's parents that she's not a bad person. However, there is sometimes a sexual motivation with an opposite vector. An overprotective father wants to limit his teenage daughter's contact with boys of the same age, being worried of their intentions. An older sister tries to quickly sexually educate a sixteen–year–old, raising her awareness of the consequences of a holiday romance. A twenty–year–old can't cope with the way his friend treats his girlfriend and eventually falls in love with her himself.

The individual interests of the characters are almost always opposites, obviously leading to frequent conflicts and pushing Pamiętniki higher and higher in terms of dramaturgy and the absurd. The conflicts don't always touch the "point" of a situation, but sometimes concern a strategy the characters adapt in life, their opinions or attitudes. Pamiętniki often uses an element of simplified psychology to confront straightforwardness with cynicism. This often results in, for example, competition between two friends. One of them believes in true love – the kind of love that connects people for life and compensates them with a surplus of whatever they had to resign from on the way. During the holiday the girl looks for a soul mate, a proverbial second half. Her friend, however, mocks her every action. She was once betrayed by a man she was madly in love with and yet she takes revenge on every single man who tries to get close to her. She plays with them, objectifies them and uses them to achieve her own goals – for fun or competing with other girls.

The magnetism of scripted reality programs can also be explained by research conducted by several other psychologists. They introduce the term sensation–seeking,[4] which is supposed to illustrate a spreading personality lineament, to the literature. This regards a tendency in behavior leading to searching for experiences which are changing, new and complex, and the readiness to accept the psychological and social risks connected with it. In accordance with this theory a man has a need to constantly sustain a specific, individually diversified level of inner activity (theory of optimal stimulation). Next to a general tendency to search for constant stimulus, scientists mark out more detailed categories:

- thrill and adventure seeking, which is basically the need to experience extreme situations, for example, parachuting or scuba diving,
- experience seeking, which is a tendency to search for varieties of an unconventional lifestyle, for example, travel, artistic activities, experiments with drugs and toxic relationships,
- disinhibition seeking, which is simply "getting loose", releasing oneself from social conventions, opposing applicable customs and moral standards,
- boredom susceptibility, which is an aversion towards boredom and a tendency to feel anxious if a situation is static for a long period of time.

Taking the presented stories and the way the characters behave into consideration, the audience of Pamiętniki receives clear stimulating impulses, which fit into the category of unusual experience and "getting loose". The experience is reduced to testing social norms, ethical principles, relationships etc. while on vacation. What's more, those impulses appear one after another because of the high density of storyline events and the exaggerated reactions of the characters. The viewer is confronted with melodramatic events and the nervous or teary comments of characters. They can't, however, feel bored for a single moment, especially since all conflicts in Pamiętniki are programmatically solved on a basis of direct confrontation of attitudes, which in an obvious way leads to high dramaturgical saturation of some scenes and bears fruit in endless on–screen screaming.

The aesthetic side of scripted reality programs is very specific. It should provide recognition as wide as possible and make sure that the audience understands what kind of production they're dealing with after seeing just a few scenes. This results in visible oversimplifications in the aesthetic aspect, juxtaposition of contrasting colors and elements associated mainly with kitsch. Keeping this in mind, Pamiętniki z wakacji is a perfect example of such a strategy based on building the recognition of a television product by very characteristic, flashy elements of visual identification.

Media psychologists bring our attention to the fact that a human mind during childhood is in a stadium of preoperative image thinking, not gifted with

[4] See: P. Winterhoff–Spurk, Psychologia mediów, Kraków, 2007, p. 76.

any unusual competences and very sensitive to any aesthetic vividness such as intensiveness, contrast, movement, unusualness, surprise and inconsistency. All the things that differ from aesthetic norms attract particular attention and interest. Approaching the question, Pamiętniki z wakacji was designed to impose itself onto the audience's perception in every tiniest detail.

Even the above examples, stated randomly and not comprehending the richness of Pamiętniki z wakacji, prove that the series is a perfect answer to all postulates necessary to create a story that a human, seen as an evolutionary object, wouldn't be able to get away from. Nettle's and other psychologists' reflections regarding the driving force and charm of stories are all the more interesting when we realize that this particular field of psychology acknowledges the dogma of extreme rationality and economics of behavior between individuals. Humans only perform actions that could lead them to evolutionary success. There's only a place for those activities allowing them to strengthen their genes and up the chances of gene transmission in their area of interests. Based on this fact, indulging in the magic of fiction and losing oneself in imagined realities is an unproductive, unnecessary and redundant action for evolutionary psychologists. A mind absorbed in an analysis of dramaturgical events and following the development of interpersonal relations between made up characters doesn't necessarily commit to actions necessary for securing survival. Mankind has to benefit from the common experience of fictional stories somehow, and the benefit has to be great enough to surpass biological needs. What could prove to be of such benefit?: "Some people think that common admiration of a storyline increases solidarity in a group, as far as transmitting important norms and values shared by a group goes".[5] So, in a context of experiencing a story by people, even if the story is fictional, we can see a confirmation and consolidation of a rudimentary human bond, thanks to which it's possible to create groups and, later, – societies. Evolutionary psychology – a scientific orientation of the above reasons somewhat unfavorable towards popular culture texts – suggests a hypothesis based on which TV productions seen *en masse*, in our case Pamiętniki z wakacji, create an image of the life realities of a particular group, communicating norms and rules of existence to its members in a very suggestive way. It's nothing more than education in a social sense, preparation for living as part of a society, a transmission of knowledge which can be used practically in social life. Watching TV could prove to be equal to a process of creating opinions, which is about the acquisition of opinions and attitudes – primary cognitive processes – on the receiver's side. With such an assumption a TV program becomes a socializing instance for the audience.

Albert Badura's theory of social learning supports this hypothesis. The author of this conception notices that among a social structure people undertake

[5] T. Szlendak, T. Kozłowski, op. cit., p. 203.

certain actions, realizing and controlling them, and reflecting on themselves and changing the world, which reflects back on their thoughts, emotions and behavior. Usually, the source of a feedback reflection shaping attitudes and behaviors is the inter–individual experience. However, there is no way to personally, in direct contact and observation, gather experiences rich enough during our life for them to guarantee us access to the knowledge of everything necessary for social life. We have to learn a lot indirectly, based on our replacement experience. That's why in the course of evolution, humanity has formed an ability to enclose reality symbolically and process information, which in turn makes assigning structure, continuity and actual meaning to individual experience possible. This regularity also applies to mass media. Therefore, the claim – in accordance to terminology used by Bandura – that for some viewers television text, especially of a series standard, functions based on replacement experience, which satisfies the deficit of direct knowledge and learning, is fully justified. The expansion of television media has led to a rapid increase of experience that imprints on the human mind and which we interiorize in a process of transmission consumption. Bandura gives them a status almost equal to direct experience. Research conducted by the author clearly shows that relating to media texts influences the behavior of the audience even if it's not connected with repeated exercise or expecting a prize. What we experience is a process of social learning through media. Bandura recognizes the main mechanism of learning as modeling, known not as true and thoughtless imitation of behaviors by an observer, but as creating a symbolic representation of an observed model's activity, which proves to be a hint for suitable execution. "People can benefit not only from their own experience, but also from the successes and mistakes of others. In everyday situations there are many opportunities to observe the actions of others when they're being rewarded, punished, or when their actions don't provoke any after–effects. Considering the observed consequences of other people's behavior holds grave importance for understanding how exactly exaltation works. Firstly, observed after–effects can change behavior in a way very similar to directly experienced after–effects. Usually, observing behavior providing success for others strengthens the tendency to act in a similar way, while watching the behavior of someone who is being punished weakens this tendency".[6]

Even based on the information we already have, the hypothesis that Pamiętniki z wakacji holds an unimaginable educational potential can be justified, especially since the audience can easily relate to their characters, as they were created in a way that would trigger a possibly wide projection/identification mechanism. Therefore, this affects almost always young people, usually teenagers or people in their early twenties. The producers took good care to

[6] A. Bandura, Teoria społecznego uczenia się, Warszawa, 2007, p. 117–118.

represent the population, drawing people from everywhere in Poland, both minor and major cities in capital or distant provinces. They are students, pupils or sometimes workers. Sometimes unemployed people appear too (such as a family member invited by their daughter to Spain, where she lives and works). They represent a diversified level of education and seem to belong to different cultural–social circles. However, all of them treat the trip to a foreign country as an event similar to an initiation of starting adult life, and on many levels, such as social, psychological, sexual, intellectual, life maturity etc. The presented stories, although different, can be reduced to a basic dramaturgical structure, actually close to a construction of medieval morality. Considered to be a society's representative, the main character experiences situations which should prepare them for making the ultimate choice and choosing the side of virtue or sin, good or evil, purity or corruption, salvation or damnation. Psychomachia, which is a symbolic confrontation of personalized virtues and sins – good, evil, envy, faith, hate, love etc. – was supposed to be an important part of continuing lessons taken by the moral protagonist. This structure is present in the case of Pamiętniki z wakacji. The main characters of specific episodes find themselves facing a choice between rights, which in their opinions, at least at the beginning, are equivalent, or they experience a cognitive dissonance. However, every time they have to realize their own situation, looking at it from a critical distance and making a decision, which basically means deciding on taking one of the sides presented during the story. They have to decide if, despite many temptations, they want to nurse their belief in mutual honesty and loyalty between two people in love. They have to assertively defend their own beliefs, even if this attracts criticism from their friends. They have to realize the consequences of their own behavior and decisions. They have to understand that their actions also influence the situations of others . In such an approach we can talk about a character's social maturation, because they start to see their own behavior in a wider social context, considering interests other than particular and casual.

The way to initiate an axial conflict in every episode remains the same. This is usually caused by a character who, from the very beginning, seems to be out of the picture, not fitting in with the rest. An "other" differs in terms of behavior positively when their personal culture level and intelligence are different than their friends' or negatively when they initiate scandals, provoke others and bring criticism upon themselves. At the same time the audience is momentarily confronted with the necessity to choose to root for the character, or not.

This is going to sound extremely positivist, but in the majority of cases the protagonist in Pamiętniki eventually chooses the right side. They undergo a journey from ignorance of their own behavior and lack of reflection to a level which allows us to credit them with attributes such as responsibility, empathy, sensitivity to others and – most importantly – distance from their actions and reflexivity. Furthermore, if any vision of the world is evaluated positively in Pamiętniki, it would be the one associated with conservative views. Ultimately, straightforwardness, common sense, attachment to traditional values, respect for others, diligence and a serious approach to male–female relations are what's being praised, while those who pick the easy way out in their choices, think only about themselves, don't respect others, think only about their own pleasures, don't regard tradition, don't value relations to others, and represent cynicism in love affairs are considered to be losers.

Such content, perhaps surprisingly. clearly appears in an analysis of Polsat's scripted reality. There is, however, one condition – while reflecting on the program one has to go beyond what might at first be repulsive and provokes laughter rather than serious musing. One has to assume (to be confirmed or questioned by the planned empirical research) that some part of those questions remains coded in the audience as a model of reaction to a particular situation. This is not only an optimistic observation, but at this point of my research fully proper. The surprise regarding the potential educational and pro–social charge of scripted reality programs has to give way to academic curiosity and the desire to verify this argument regarding Pamiętniki, referring to the results of an analysis of content conducted by Barbara Lee between 1985 and 1986.[7] She thoroughly checked the content of 253 American entertainment programs and found that almost every one of them (97%) contained a presentation of at least one pro–social behavior. Those auditions actively promoted sympathy and empathy in particular showing (57%), altruistic behavior (help, sharing) (21%) and suppressing aggression and the desire of revenge (22%). Further studies proved that the pro–social results of watching TV are precisely two times higher than the anti–social ones. Putting the mass popularity of scripted reality programs to reasonable use could provide a chance to execute a wide–ranging educational project, which would operate on a language understandable to the audience and be fully accepted.

The maximal simplification of a dramaturgical structure and intentional resignation from screenplay complexity results in the fact that content typical for morality is received by Pamiętniki's audience many times. Every episode recalls and sustains an emotional charge recognized from past episodes. At the same time, another effective social learning condition mentioned by Albert Bandura is fulfilled – repetition. Furthermore, the construction of a single episode itself helps with remembering the content, preserving and grounding it, because the narration of scripted reality is based on multiple tautologies. A particular scene is firstly announced by a narrator who explains what's going to happen next. They usually add information about where the character's reactions come from, why they behave the way they do and what emotions they

[7] See: P. Winterhoff–Spurk, op. cit., p. 153.

feel at the moment. After that a particular scene is introduced in the form of a quasi–documental registration of an event. The scene is actively commented on by its participants, summarizing the course of action. They express their emotions once again and share their thoughts with the audience. Additionally, the most important information is delivered to the audience once again in the form of subtitles of the "ID's" of the currently speaking characters. The use of narrative tautologies (narrator, images, commentary, subtitles) could be seen as an aspiration to make the program as easily consumable as possible. Scripted reality is a typical representative of so–called snack TV, which can be watched carelessly, with one eye, at any moment, for as long as desired, but which is still understandable. At the same time tautologies have their own consequences in terms a TV text reception. In 1980 Laurene Meringoff proved in a series of tests that narration conducted via an audial canal better stimulates a viewer's brain.[8] Children asked to join the experiment were divided into two groups. One was learning history in the form of a narrative story, the other in the form of an animation. The reception of the listening group was more active – they were more affected by the story, commented more and drew more conclusions. Yet, the group of viewers stopped at the visual information from the movie. Using an audial canal on the same terms as a visual canal in communication with the audience could prove to be another stimulator for them, making Pamiętniki even more attractive and more effective in creating attitudes (activating the audience to enter a discourse).

Through the eyes of audience credibility, a broadcast is also built according to a genre formula, which describes the convention of a story very precisely. Scripted reality is based on an impression of a documentary recording, possibly objectified. It places the audience in a spot of an almost visual observer of events. The authors keep the impression of such an observation, even though scripted reality series are realized as feature film productions – at first a scenario is created, which is later carried out by actors. In the case of programs such as Pamiętniki the actors are not professionals, but laypeople. The deceit of this convention causes everything that would normally be considered actor's mistakes, such as linguistic errors, repetitions, hesitations or the artificiality of a creation, to gain the value of genuineness. The same rule applies to the strict recording elements. A poorly cropped shot, the presence of a camera or microphone in a frame, additional shadows on a wall – every detail such as these proves to the audience that they're dealing with material realized almost on the spot, at the very moment of an actual event.

Research conducted by media psychologists suggests that it's the quasi–documentary convention that becomes the main lure for the audience. Researchers of the sensation–seeking personality trait tested many television

[8] See: P. Winterhoff–Spurk, op. cit., p. 97.

forms in terms of inducing an excited state in the audience.[9] It turns out that nature movies induce the lowest level of excitement. Action movies, comedies and quiz shows could be considered as sources of medium–level excitement. The highest level of excitement was – not surprisingly – induced by horror movies, but they're not even close to the levels of excitement that watching pornography and non–fictional materials (e.g. reports, documentaries, news or sport transmissions) induce. So, a production disguised as a direct recording of events finds its place at a higher level of absorbing the audience's attention and stimulating their reactions thanks to this convention.

A curious thing is that scripted reality programs decline the exposition used in feature film productions, which allows us to get to know a character in terms of their job and private and intimate life, which also translates to understanding the character's motivations, thinking and behavior categories by the audience. In Pamiętniki z wakacji the audience is immediately pushed into the action. We only get to know the characters as vacationers. The information we get is rather scarce. We know where they come from, we know more or less what they do, but not much more than that. Abstracting them from the detail that would describe their personality – everyday activities, professional relations etc. – makes their characters more associated with the every person. It also defines in a very specific way the framing of the presented world, which is reduced to a seaside resort, hotel rooms, a beach and a pool.

In accordance with Albert Bandura's indications, mechanisms leading to successive modeling could be arranged into a sequence – noticing and paying attention, remembered as a symbolic representation of a specific action, transformation of abstractive models into a specific action and inducing motivation. The last stage has the most potential, and cannot be subjected to simple verification. However, the first three steps are connected to the content of a received replacement experience. In our case they're reduced to the content of the program, what is indicated by the examples mentioned above.

4. WHAT TO DO WITH IT LATER?

The preliminary analysis presented above proves that Pamiętniki z wakacji and other scripted reality productions fully deserve the title of a cultural and television phenomenon. They deserve to be seen through various academic perspectives and to be subjected to thorough analysis, because they have high educational potentials and meet the conditions that guarantee them a high level of persuasiveness and suggestiveness, which in turn makes them a cultural text that could be part of social learning. I will try to find out, based on an on–going

[9] See: P. Winterhoff–Spurk., op. cit, p. 78.

academic project, if this assumption is justified and finds confirmation in the relations and experience of the audience. This chapter provides answers to some questions and the rest is going to be appointed as a goal of my academic research. Thus:

- who watches Pamiętniki z wakacji, and other scripted reality programs?
- to whom did the message appeal – how did the audience's profile change during this broadcast?
- what kind of audience preferences can such a program indicate?
- where does such great interest in Pamiętniki z wakacji come from?
- what cultural factors determine the success of the program?
- what mechanisms are being triggered during reading – identification, sense of superiority, surprise/indignation, nostalgic memories regarding holiday, escapism (youth, nudity, landscapes)?
- why and for what does the audience want to watch what seems to be a coarse production – to gain information, strengthen a sense of identity, integration and social interaction, to be entertained (based on D. McQuail's categorization of benefits)?
- what does it provide them with – social learning and patterns of adaptive behavior, satisfaction, relation patterns, the nadve belief in simple solutions, consolidating conservative values, confirming their own ideas about intentions and the motivations of others?
- to what needs does it answer and what needs does it fulfill?
- based on what key does the decoding of such text take place?
- are the viewers aware of the ideological content of this broadcast?
- how is the broadcast constructed?
- based on what stereotypes does it operate and what stereotypes does it amplify?
- to what narrations does it refer, but also what kind of narrations does it create?
- what beliefs does it consolidate and with which does it fight?
- who are the characters of the program and what attitudes do they represent?
- what value system is being introduced in Pamiętniki?
- to what extent does the series shape an image of the world and the audience in this world?
- how can it influence the opinion of relationships?
- what conflict situations does it introduce and what ways out does it suggest?

A phenomenon of scripted reality programs requires the researcher to take a mostly innovatory and unconventional approach. It also forces an interdisciplinary character of analysis, which should connect strict cultural elements with psychological or sociological ones. In my opinion, only by being open to other academic domains and reaching for resulting methodologies will allow the phenomenon of scripted reality genres to be seen in the broadest perspective possible and in many aspects.

The main theoretic orientation – Bandura's social learning theory – should be completed with achievements of theories of use and benefit. The main representatives of such an approach are Jay Blumler, Michael Gurevitch, Elihu Katz, Denis McQuail, Alan M. Rubin and Sven Windahl, while from the Polish perspective they are Tomasz Goban–Klas and Maciej Mrozowski. In a classical approach to the concept of uses and gratification, behaviors of media consumers are considered as pragmatic and oriented to a feeling of satisfaction, characterized as conscious, intentional and selective. This basically means that the audience is looking for transmissions appropriate for themselves and expecting very specific benefits, and when they find them they make use of them. The content of notifications considered to be useful is applied to the social, psychological and cultural aspects of the audience's life. The rapid success of Pamiętniki z wakacji means that it's a text which has found its recipients, who in turn found in it what they were looking for and are probably going to use it, applying selected content to their lives. The concept of usage and benefits seems appropriate in this case, because it doesn't create a mirage of one gigantic theory explaining all aspects of media communication, but simply implies an existence of many converging theories explaining different phenomena in the contact between people and media transmissions and their usage. That way, it should be evaluated as useful and inspiring – open to other perspectives than limiting a researcher's regard towards itself and enclosing them in one theoretical school.

A logical supplement to reflections regarding the scripted reality genre mentioned above could be introducing elements ensuing from cultivation theory. According to George Gerbner's observations, television proves to be a source of images and stories, according to which particular groups of people live. That way, it becomes – as also noticed by evolution psychologists and followers of Bandura's social learning theory – a basic socialization instance. Its influence is not only based on transmitting specific attitudes and opinions, but more on creating fundamental beliefs and opinions regarding social reality.

A television transmission is relatively homogeneous, because it uses tested, multiple themes and ways of presenting them. Therefore, it aims to create a common trend of mainstream thought. Thanks to the influence of television, the audience, even though comprising individuals from different demographic backgrounds, represents similar positions and opinions more often than those more demographically similar but not watching the same programs. The cultivation theory considers both the analysis of a text itself (including its structure and content) and research regarding its influence on the audience by diagnosing its beliefs regarding a selected area of social reality.

Questions of decoding based on the theoretical foundations of Stuart Hall shouldn't be omitted in this attempt to describe the reasons for scripted reality programs. In the case of a television text as a radical form we have to take the fact that a significant number of viewers is going to see it in an extremely different way for granted, rejecting the suggested aesthetical and ideological structure, and is going to deconstruct the transmission rather than negotiating/accepting its meaning.

As a media practitioner I would like to see the phenomenon of scripted reality programs in a technical determinism perspective and changes in the method of media consumption resulting from it, because we cannot rule out the possibility that thanks to their simplification productions, programs like these are perfect examples of so-called snack media in terms of the ease of consumption, and getting used to careless reception and the contained tautologies, which allow people to understand a text without the need to read its entirety.

In the above approach, the scripted reality series (as an example of a simplified and easily consumed text, drawing the attention of the audience and with the potential to persuasively transmit attitudes and opinions) would be treated as a modern morality *biblia pauperum* and adaptation textbook by most viewers. Their influence on creating human behaviors, confirming or overthrowing opinions on the world, seeing interpersonal reactions and establishing a system of values would have to be considered as too important to overlook.

5. BIBLIOGRAPHY

Aronson E., Człowiek – istota społeczna, Wydawnictwo PWN, Warszawa, 2000. Bandura A., Teoria społecznego uczenia się, PWN, Warszawa, 2007.

Bielak T., Filiciak M., Ptaszek G. [ed.], Zmierzch telewizji? Przemiany medium. Antologia, Wydawnictwo Naukowe Scholar, Warszawa, 2011.

Blumler J.G., Gurevitch M., Katz E., Przyszłość badań użytkowania i korzyści, "Przekazy i Opinie" 1987, no. 3–4.

Dobek-Ostrowska B. [ed.], Nauka o komunikowaniu. Podstawowe orientacje teoretyczne, Wydawnictwo Uniwersytety Wrocławskiego, Wrocław, 2001.

Fiske J., Zrozumieć kulturę popularną, transl. K. Sawicka, Wydawnictwo Uniwersytetu Jagiellońskiego, Kraków, 2010.

Francuz P. [ed.], Psychologiczne aspekty odbioru telewizji, Towarzystwo Naukowe KUL, Lublin, 2004.

Hall S., Kodowanie i dekodowanie, "Przekazy i Opinie" 1987, no. 2.

Kubicka D., Kołodziejczyk A., Psychologia wpływu mediów, Oficyna Wydawnicza Impuls, Kraków, 2007.

Mrozowski M., Podejście użytkowania i korzyści w badaniach komunikowania masowego, "Przekazy i Opinie" 1987, no. 3–4.

Mrozowski M., Media masowe – władza, rozrywka i biznes, Oficyna Wydawnicza Aspra-JR, Warszawa, 2001.

Winterhoff-Spurk P., Psychologia mediów, transl. P. Włodyga, Wydawnictwo WAM, Kraków, 2007.